The Broadcasters of
BBC Wales

1 9 6 4 - 1 9 9 0

The Broadcasters of
BBC Wales

1964 – 1990

GARETH PRICE

Cover photographs: BBC Archive
Cover design: Y Lolfa

ISBN: 978 1 78461 464 5

Published and printed in Wales
on paper from well-maintained forests by
Y Lolfa Cyf., Talybont, Ceredigion SY24 5HE
website www.ylolfa.com
e-mail ylolfa@ylolfa.com
tel 01970 832 304
fax 832 782

Contents

Dead Man's Shoes

THIS IS A memoir and not an autobiography. Any thought of the latter was scotched for ever when I received a letter from a viewer in Llanfaethlu, Anglesey, who had seen me defending BBC Wales on television in January 1990, just six months before my retirement as Controller. It read:

> Dear Price
> We were disappointed with your smug inadequate appearance on TV on Monday night. You came across as a real smart-arse 'what a good boy am I' indeed.
> BBC Wales is overfunded at the cost of £39 million. Close down, keep local radio, and transmit programmes directly from London. That will get the cost of the licence fee down. You are obviously also overstaffed (who needs a Controller, Wales?); too much regard is given to a largely dead language. Everybody in Wales speaks English – very few Welsh. What is the purpose of pursuing such a course?
> Aye
> Name provided
> P.S. You should do something about your idiotic shoes.

The shoes and the job title have long since gone but the memories remain, particularly of an eclectic group of people who were attracted to an institution which, in the words of Head of Programmes Hywel Davies in 1962, 'must be a debating chamber, an exhibition centre, a publishing house, a theatre, a concert hall, a centre which, if near to its audience, can develop the national identity in English and in Welsh.'

The men and women who made BBC Wales a truly public broadcaster during my 26 years as producer and manager from 1964 until 1990 included people who were appointed as long ago as 1935 and others who are still broadcasting as this memoir is being written in 2016. Many were and are well-known voices and faces to the large audiences they have served in a collective memory span of 80 years. Many were an extraordinary mix of creative and often eccentric people making music and writing drama; celebrities in the world of sport and entertainment; or inquisitive journalists reporting on daily events and producing in-depth documentaries.

I spent ten years at 'the face' as a producer and the last 16 years appointing, enabling and leading production teams in all their varied activities. In doing so I came to understand their great strengths and inevitable weaknesses in what was a unique community dedicated to serving the Welsh public.

I do not subscribe to the extravagant view of my old departed friend John Davies, the official historian of BBC Wales, when he wrote 'Wales is an artefact created by broadcasting'. Our nation is far more than that. There will always be seminal events, however, which bring the nation together through broadcasting. In 1966 it was the anguish of Aberfan; in the 1970s a surge of national pride created by great Welsh rugby teams; in the 1980s the sadness and suffering as King Coal died a slow death during and after the last great strike of 1984–5.

John's history was about BBC Wales as an institution from its earliest days in 1923 until, effectively, 1981. Mine is a human story of people who worked through the most exciting period of growth in the history of Welsh broadcasting. In just six years, between January 1977 and November 1982, two national radio stations and S4C were launched, leading to the simultaneous relaunch of a BBC Wales TV service devoid of the Welsh language. We had no time to stand and stare.

As producers we just made programmes we hoped would attract our own people. Only when in senior management were we challenged to define what was blindingly obvious to us. I saw my country and my audience as a colourful mosaic with the Welsh language at its core, surrounded by a rich history and unique culture, its small land mass embracing a vibrant society evolving with the passage of time. It was only necessary to have a ready answer for the critics who could never understand why, as one English colleague told me, 'lorry loads of cash were always rolling across the Severn Bridge'. It is true that when I left Llandaff in June 1990, BBC Wales had a turnover of nearly £40 million and a staff of about 1,500 people. It was the largest BBC enterprise outside London. I have always thought it was a small price to pay for the end of divisive political debate and public protest, particularly when S4C was launched.

Mine is a social history of a specific era and the personalities who enlarged and revolutionised the broadcasting landscape of Wales. Our successors will regard my generation as dinosaurs given the march of modern technology during the past quarter of a century. In the end, however, only high-quality content can be the determining factor in measuring the success of public broadcasting.

I make no apologies for dwelling on the lives of those high-profile and creative colleagues who died far too young. Hywel Davies, Ryan Davies and Ronnie Williams, Carwyn James and Ray Gravell, Gwenlyn Parry and Rhydderch Jones, Derek Boote, Dyfed Glyn Jones, Lowri Gwilym, Sian Pari Huws and many more appear in these pages several times because their talents knew few boundaries. Each chapter is meant to stand alone and the whole seen from different perspectives. I have tried to check the facts against some of the leading publications from the past but the most important thanks go to those innumerable former colleagues and friends who meet in diminishing numbers at reunions or funerals and exchange stories from the past.

I am particularly grateful to several former colleagues for their help in completing this memoir. My close friend Meirion Edwards cast his critical eye over an early draft of the script and made many changes and valuable suggestions. I was asked to read relevant parts of the unpublished autobiography of my closest colleague, the late Geraint Stanley Jones. Gwyn Hughes Jones helped me on events in the drama department which were beyond my ken. Sight of a draft Ph.D. thesis by John Geraint of Green Bay enlightened me on some critical points. The pearls of wisdom from my friend Huw Tregelles Williams come from the excellent book celebrating the BBC National Orchestra and Chorus of Wales compiled by Peter Reynolds. I have also benefited from the company and reminiscences of all the following friends and colleagues who were my primary sources: Teleri Bevan, John Stuart Roberts, John Hefin, Meredydd Evans, Ruth Price, Menna Richards, Barry Lynch, John Watkin, Onllwyn Brace, Dewi Griffiths, Thomas Davies, Peter Walker, Avril Price, Rosemary Edwards, Lyn T. Jones, Lenna Pritchard-Jones and Bethan 'Port' Williams – to name but a few. Sadly, many have since passed away; none of the conversations were recorded.

I am also grateful to BBC Wales for allowing me to raid its rich photographic archive, not to speak of the time and trouble given to this exercise by its head of department Edith Hughes, as well as her colleague Lis Collins. More photographs and background material were also provided by ex-colleagues who went out of their way to search attics and computers, particularly from Mari Griffith, David Morris Jones, Gareth Rowlands and Margaret Price.

I only realised how many factual mistakes and repetitive sentences I was capable of writing when I came to work with Eirian Jones, my meticulous and knowledgable editor at Y Lolfa. She cracked the whip and shook me out of thinking that a memoir merely involved writing from memory. I shall always be grateful to both Eirian and the generous commissioning editor, Lefi Gruffudd, who allocated double the agreed original number of pages for photographs.

I wish also to thank Huw Edwards for taking the time to read the final draft and comment on the ethos of his father's generation of broadcasters.

My final thanks are due to my wife Mari and family for their support and suggestions, and in particular to my son Aled for helping a dinosaur on the use of computers, and his own perspective on the broadcasting scene.

I apologise to the hundreds of Welsh broadcasters who are not mentioned in this chronicle. I blame the receding memory of old age for all my omissions and errors and can only hope it gives the reader a taste of a unique cast of characters it was my privilege to know, all of whom did their best to please some of the listeners and viewers some of the time.

Gareth Price
September 2017

1964 – A Vintage Year for Wales

THE YEAR 1964 marked the beginning of devolution and a new chapter in the history of Welsh broadcasting. Labour Prime Minister Harold Wilson announced the establishment of the Welsh Office under its first Secretary of State, James Griffiths, which automatically added a new dimension to the coverage of news and current affairs in the Welsh media. It coincided with the launch of the BBC Wales TV service, involving an expansion of programmes in both English and Welsh to a total of some 12 hours a week. It allowed for the growth of sporting and cultural programmes in addition to journalism, and in 1964 there was much to savour.

A new Welsh sporting legend was born. Lynn 'the Leap' Davies won the long jump at the Tokyo Olympics and immediately became a regular presence on our screens. That individual achievement was followed by the brilliance of Glamorgan's 'spin twins', Don Shepherd and Jim Pressdee, who took a total of 19 wickets to bowl Australia out of a game for the first time ever. In that same August week the National Eisteddfod was being held at the Singleton Park campus of University College, Swansea, less than a mile away from the St Helen's cricket ground. BBC Wales used its new outside broadcast equipment to fill the whole Saturday afternoon schedule, also for the first time, alternating between the cricket and the final of the Welsh male voice choir competition. The cultural scene in Welsh TV light entertainment was boosted by the appointment of an academic who returned from the USA to develop the genre. Dr Meredydd Evans was charged with creating a new seam of comedy and popular music from scratch on TV.

It was also the year 'Shirl the Girl' from Tiger Bay sang her way to the top of the UK charts – and a year later the US charts – with her first Bond hit, 'Goldfinger', while an unknown 24 year old from Pontypridd, called Tommy Woodward, was recording a single in the hope of stardom one day. 'It's Not Unusual' launched the career of 'Tom the Voice' in early 1965. Wales had produced its two most famous international singing celebrities within a year and they would keep the Welsh flag flying around the world for the next half-century and more.

In the field of high culture it was the turn of Gwyneth Jones to thrill the operatic audience at Covent Garden when she first appeared as Leonora in Verdi's *Il trovatore*. In doing so she joined two other great emerging Welsh voices of the 1960s, Stuart Burrows and Margaret Price.

The cinema highlight of the year was the huge success of Stanley Baker's classic *Zulu*, complete with Ivor Emmanuel inspiring his Welsh comrades to sing 'Men of Harlech' as they went to their death and glory.

All these events coincided with my returning to Wales as a radio current affairs producer, a starter for the next 26 years. That quarter of a century would see dramatic events and changes in Welsh society. Before 1964 Wales had few national institutions. The University of Wales, the National Library and National Museum, the Wales Rugby Union, Welsh Football Association and the National Eisteddfod were all that existed before the First World War, so different from the situation in Scotland. Wales did not even have a capital until 1955, the year of the very first TV broadcast from Wales.

In 1964 I was but one of many who moved to live and work in Cardiff from all over the country, including London. New opportunities opened up in the Welsh Office, the BBC and the

13

commercial TV company Television West and Wales (TWW), the Welsh Arts Council, as well as the growing number of Welsh schools and other allied organisations which took root in the surrounding area. It all added up to what veteran journalist David Cole called 'A New Wales'.

Broadcasters spoke and sang to the nation in different ways at different times in different languages. They would embrace the whole gamut of the Welsh experience even if they would not always sing from the same hymn sheet.

Head of Programmes Hywel Davies had already defined the role of the BBC as an institution. His challenge to us as individual broadcasters was equally comprehensive:

> Broadcasting must be many things to many men. By all means let it entertain; but let it inform and educate as well. By all means let it be frivolous; but let it be challenging and serious too. Let it make men and women laugh and forget their troubles; but for heaven's sake make them worry and cry, let it make them angry, let it make them think. And I don't see why all this should spell the word 'egghead', why all this can't be, as often as not, lighthearted and exciting and attractive.

Hywel's philosophy became the mantra for my generation of public broadcasters.

1

Coffee with Pioneers

I KNEW NOTHING about broadcasting when I joined BBC Wales in 1964. Stuck in a research rut while lecturing at Queen's University, Belfast, I spotted an advertisement for a radio producer in Cardiff, applied for it and contacted two BBC friends to assess my chances. They both told me it would be pointless. I flew to Cardiff for an interview, returning the same day in case my professor had noted my absence. In order to disguise my failings in academia, I pleaded that years wasted as an undergraduate were spent on student journalism and organising the first Aberystwyth arts festival. The interviewing board was so impressed by my mode of travel that they gave me the job.

I duly presented myself to Assistant Head of Programmes Aneirin Talfan Davies, a kindly man but whose thoughts seemed to be elsewhere. He was obviously wondering what to do with me. He bought me my first cup of BBC coffee and dispatched me to the Alexandra Road studios in Swansea for a month. Aneirin had reason to know Swansea well. His pharmacy in the town had been bombed during the Blitz and he spent the rest of the war translating and reading the BBC news in Welsh from London. In 1946 he returned to Swansea as the BBC's west Wales representative, recording a host of radio features and nurturing the radio careers of the young Dylan Thomas and friends.

The Kardomah Café in Swansea was the meeting place for a unique cultural circle in the 1930s. The only, rather faded, photograph still in existence of that group in the Swansea

Alexandra Road studios features Dylan, the composer Daniel Jones, the painter Alfred Janes and poet Vernon Watkins. Behind them stands producer John Griffiths. In earlier days both John and Aneirin were at the heart of a broadcasting gold mine, even if it was difficult to harness the wayward tendencies of a famous and mainly bohemian quartet.

John Griffiths was one of the first eight programme people appointed to serve the fledgling BBC Welsh Region in 1935. At first he was the only staff announcer. A quietly-spoken, charming and mild-mannered man sporting huge white bushy eyebrows, it was difficult to believe that the BBC held a dark secret on his personal file. It was an image of a Christmas tree. John was classified by the BBC as a Communist. It was rumoured that – because one of the infamous Cambridge spies, Guy Burgess, had worked for the BBC in the late 1930s – the Corporation had decided to take no more chances. How the BBC came to know about John's political affiliation remained a mystery to me but the Christmas tree system would carry on for years, as I would discover in management.

John took me under his wing. He had been on the staff for nearly 30 years and in his early days as an announcer had often filled airtime with music recorded on eminently breakable hard discs. The Cardiff canteen gossips swore that he once played a cracked record, apologised and said, 'I am sorry about the crack in this record. Let me play you the other side.'

He was also caught out live on air chastising an actor with the words, 'If you do that again I shall kick your arse from here to Llanstephan.'

Such a delightful personality didn't seem to fit with any revolutionary activity. His programmes were strictly for entertainment. They included the first Welsh-language 'soap' on radio, *Teulu Tŷ Coch* [The Red House Family]. There were also scores of features which included an annual pilgrimage to the National Eisteddfod, complete with tent and the company of his close friend, the popular presenter and Unitarian minister, D. Jacob Davies.

16

John did talk a little about his early experiences working for the National Library of Congress in Washington DC, but his political affiliations remained a mystery.

During the war John had produced one of the earliest entertainment programmes in Welsh, *Sut Hwyl?* [How are Things?]. The Welsh Region's radio service, embarked in 1935, went into virtual shutdown in 1939. Only a limited schedule of Welsh news and religious services was allowed initially, as noted in the Appendix.

The BBC then realised the need for entertainment, offering a little relief to the British public in troubled times. Bangor benefited from the move of the BBC's variety department from London, including Tommy Handley's radio programme, *It's That Man Again* (*ITMA*), to its main wartime studio, Penrhyn Hall. Four hundred and thirty-seven people were moved to Bangor and housed in several villages around Caernarfonshire. It was said to have made Bangor one of the happiest places to live in Britain.

Thankfully, war service did not harm the lives or careers of the two greatest natural broadcasters with whom so many of us were fortunate to know and work. Ex-naval officer Alun Williams and former war correspondent Wynford Vaughan-Thomas were the doyens of their generation of radio broadcasters and arguably have never been matched as the greatest all-rounders at the microphone.

The Cardiff canteen was full of strangers when I returned from the start of my apprenticeship in Swansea.

'Who are you then? My name is Alun Williams.'

He was known throughout Wales as Mr BBC: a presenter, sports commentator, comedian and gifted broadcaster equally at home on radio and TV in both languages. He had joined the BBC in 1946 as an outside broadcast producer. Life there allowed him the freedom to travel on duty wherever he wished. Alun was the voice and face of BBC Wales, the life and soul of every party, but in the canteen or in the bar of the Overseas League, conveniently located in 37 Park Place next door to the office, he was quiet until he had an audience of at least three people. Alun went into overdrive the moment the mic was switched on. He was constantly on the move, following Lions tours, Welsh football teams, athletics and swimming at several Olympic and Commonwealth Games for decades. During these trips he would interview Welsh people wherever he could find them in the world. At a time when overseas travel was regarded as exotic, these were ground-breaking programmes. On one occasion I asked Alun to present a live pre-international radio talk show from Dublin. On the flight over he warned me, 'I expect my friend Sean MacReamonn will meet us at the airport, so I don't plan to work today.'

In the event Sean, a former Vatican correspondent of RTÉ Dublin, took us on a conducted tour of every pub on the way to a hotel which I have no memory of reaching. I do recall being in the company of two erudite soulmates, both of them highly intelligent and wicked *bons viveurs* who lived life to the limit. Broadcasting to Wales from Dublin's studios in the early 1960s meant living with the certainty that the line would be lost at some point during the programme. Alun, particularly with Welsh-speaking Sean to egg him on in the studio, would use such incidents to his advantage, taking disruptions in his stride, switching to hilarious stories of Sean's problems in sending reports from the Vatican to Dublin. Broadcasting seemed so easy when you were with Alun.

The murder of several Israeli athletes at the Munich Olympics in 1972 was the stage for his finest but saddest hour on air. He was commentating live on network radio when the news came through. Alun changed gear effortlessly and gave an immediate response, demonstrating great sensitivity and humanity steeped in a religious background. It was a situation which would have thrown lesser men. Cliff Morgan said that such was Alun's vocabulary, he never used the same phrase twice if he could avoid it. Frank Hennessy remembers working with him on *On The Road* for Radio Wales and was amazed at the people who came up to him to give impromptu interviews, his distinctive laugh signalling approachability. He was as happy cracking jokes as he was being compère of a variety show or jazzing up 'Sospan Fach' on the piano at the Grand Theatre, Swansea, when touring with Ryan and Ronnie, or entertaining a Lions squad in South Africa in the company of Dewi Griffiths and Cliff Morgan. Alun, traveller to the last, died while entertaining on a cruise ship in 1992. Some years earlier, we had sat together at the funeral of Dafydd Gruffydd, BBC Wales's first radio drama producer. Dafydd had determined that there should be no ceremony at all, just silence. Alun turned to me at the end and said, 'When I go, I want the works.'

He did get them.

Alun was younger than his uniquely gifted contemporary Wynford Vaughan-Thomas, who had made his name as the bravest of war correspondents. He had joined the BBC as the first radio outside broadcast assistant in Swansea in 1936. Both Wynford and Alun were basically serious people with a passion for words and music, as well as a rounded education and a worldly knowledge giving them the flexibility to cope with any situation on air. Wynford's iconic commentary from a Lancaster bomber flying through the flak over Berlin was the most memorable live broadcast of the entire war. He also covered the battle for Anzio; was the first journalist into Belsen; and witnessed massacres and other unspeakable horrors during the division of Pakistan and India.

Yet Wynford will always be remembered for his wicked sense of humour. He was a wordsmith, a serial storyteller, as unstoppable as a waterfall. He had a huge memory for daring limericks which Cliff Morgan (head of TV outside broadcasts in London) and Teleri Bevan (editor of Radio Wales) recorded at his Fishguard home, much to the hilarity of those of us fortunate enough to be present. In the 1980s they were too *risqué* to broadcast and remain in the BBC archive to this day. The best-known limerick sounds tame enough today, but Wynford's delivery and timing always raised a laugh however much the retelling.

In cold, damp Blaenau Ffestiniog
Girls made love for a ceiniog [Welsh for penny]
I know this for a fact
I was caught in the act.

By Lord Hailsham, then Mr Quintinogg (Quintin Hogg).

(Mr Quintin Hogg became Lord Hailsham and was the official censor as Lord Chamberlain.)

By 1964 Wynford was Director of Programmes at HTV Wales but still returned to work in radio with Teleri Bevan to complete a strenuous tour on foot over the 'Roof of Wales' – when approaching his 70th birthday – to celebrate the launch of Radio Wales in 1978. He repeated it on horseback three years later. These treks made for great storytelling each morning on Radio 4 following overnight editing.

I always recall the programme he presented for me from the White Wheat pub (from the original Welsh of the song 'Gwenith Gwyn') about the ongoing Welsh midwinter tradition of the 'Mari Lwyd' in Llangynwyd near Maesteg. I was astonished, not merely at his meticulous knowledge of Welsh history but also at his memory for the detail of local folk customs. I still cherish his handwritten links which included traditional verses dedicated to coal owner Crawshay Bailey:

Crawshay Bailey's sister Dina
Was a missionary in China
She taught coolies by the million
How to sing the Welsh Penillion.

At this point I stopped him from reciting all 53 verses of this infamous parody from his prodigious memory which were sung in the Llynfi Valley on Saturday nights after rugby matches.

Wynford always welcomed visitors to his home overlooking Lower Fishguard harbour where a seagull pecked on the

French window at 4 p.m. for its daily treat. Wynford's wife Lotte would relate how, as a secretary at BBC Cardiff working for the Head of Programmes in the 1930s, she opened a very late but interesting application for the post of radio outside broadcast producer and persuaded her boss, a Mr Hughes Jones, to interview Wynford, who was duly appointed. Hughes Jones, by all accounts an unpopular Head of Programmes, suddenly asked Lotte to go to America and live with him. She refused and resigned at once. Hughes Jones, however, was dismissed in March 1937 for incompetence. Thanks to Lotte, Wynford found a distinguished career and a wife. Lotte lost her job and found a husband. The world of broadcasting became all the richer for her powers of persuasion.

One character who didn't go to war, but certainly liked his coffee breaks while conducting the BBC Welsh Orchestra, was Rae Jenkins who had already had a very colourful career. When *ITMA* settled in Bangor during the war to avoid the London bombing, Rae Jenkins became famous for Tommy Handley's cry of 'Play, Rae!' as the show's bandleader. Rae was certainly a jolly character in private but had a reputation as a bully by players in the BBC Variety and BBC Midland Light orchestras which he had conducted before settling down as resident 'maestro' of the BBC Welsh Orchestra. Henry Horatio Jenkins was born in Ammanford but he changed his name to Rae Jenkins when he left school to work in the Betws pit for a few years. His ability as a violinist took him to the Royal Academy of Music in London where his mentor was Sir Henry Wood. Rae made a living by joining the bands which accompanied the silent movies and enjoyed playing and collecting gypsy music. His huge range of musical interests made him a 'jack of all trades'.

Rae was a broadcaster first, an entertainer second, and a classical musician third. He hated contemporary music. He told producer Alun John he was not sure it was 'real' music. Rae was well known for his strict keeping to BBC time and would speed up the orchestral piece he was conducting in order to meet the programme junction. In 1964 he was in his last year as an integral part of the music department which featured Head of Music Mansel Thomas and producer Arwel Hughes, both famous throughout Wales for composing hymn tunes, choral music and oratorios, even competing in creating the stirring sounds of the greatest 'Amens' in Welsh hymnology. It was features producer T. Rowland Hughes who wrote the words for Arwel's rousing series of Amens in his composition 'Tydi a Roddaist' [Thou Gavest] while waiting for a train at Shrewsbury station. In one broadcast from the 1,000 Voices Festival at London's Albert Hall, Alun Williams once called Arwel 'The Daddy of the Amens'.

Both Mansel and Arwel were totally in tune with the religious and choral traditions of Welsh Nonconformity. They were both critical to the launch of two new TV series which hold their own in the schedules to this day. *Dechrau Canu, Dechrau Canmol* [Start Singing, Start Praising] was so popular from its first programme from Trinity Chapel, Swansea, in 1961 that the BBC in London commissioned its English equivalent *Songs of Praise* later that year. Arwel Hughes played the organ and Mansel Thomas conducted the early programmes in the great chapels and churches of Wales. They became household names at a time when a nation, losing its religious commitment, continued to love the great hymns of William Williams, Pantycelyn, and Ann Griffiths. Arwel became Head of Music when Mansel and Rae retired in 1965. I often sat listening to him in the canteen talking about his upbringing as the youngest of ten children in the mining village of Rhosllanerchrugog, near Wrexham, a community rich in choral singing. With the help of his grandparents he made it to grammar school and studied the organ at London's Royal School of Music. On one occasion he was given money by Ralph Vaughan Williams, who thought he needed a square meal, so tight was his budget. Arwel spent his entire working life at BBC Wales and was another of the original recruits of 1935. Of all his compositions his oratorio, *Dewi Sant*, is my personal favourite, sung more than once at St

David's Hall, Cardiff, and conducted by his son Owain Arwel Hughes, the best known of all Welsh conductors. When Arwel died, Owain asked me to speak at his father's funeral in that same Tabernacle Chapel in Cardiff which had launched *Songs of Praise* on its continuing TV journey a quarter of a century previously.

If John Griffiths was the first announcer in 1935, the Head of Presentation nearly 30 years later was Morfydd Mason Lewis, her distinctive voice set in the lower registers which made one believe it was the cigarettes she smoked by the packet in the canteen which contributed to such a depth of tone. Morfydd was a delightful person, very popular with Welsh audiences when co-presenting, with Emrys Cleaver, the musical radio variety show *Aelwyd y Gân* [Hearth of Song], aided by the BBC Welsh Orchestra and live on Friday nights from halls around Wales. She was much loved by her staff of announcers which also included the classy reading voice of Nest Williams as well as a young Siân Phillips before she made a big name for herself as an actress and the wife of Peter O'Toole. Ronnie Williams was another on Morfydd's staff who would go on to star in Wales's best comedy double act, Ryan and Ronnie. He never forgot that awful night in October 1966 when he read the latest updated bulletins on the Aberfan disaster as the numbers of the dead steadily increased.

Morfydd may have needed the canteen to smoke but Goronwy Wyn Rowlands just wanted a break from his job in radio planning. He was a tiny man, pale-faced with drooping eyebrows and a slight humped back, giving the impression of somebody who had been asleep for a century and had just woken up. In fact, he was an alert and intelligent man who claimed to be he first member of Urdd Gobaith Cymru [The Welsh League of Youth]. His ageing looks resulted from being another of the early pioneers of the mid 1930s. Later, as the Head of Contracts, he was responsible for determining the scale of a freelancer's fees. Everybody called him Mr Rowlands because he always wore a bowler hat to work and referred to his wife as Mrs Rowlands, but behind the unusual formality was a wicked sense of humour. When confronted by one rising star on TV asking for a pay rise his answer was, 'What would your grandfather think?' The young star retreated, totally non-plussed. Mr Rowlands may have looked older than everybody else, but so was his Austin A40. I bought it from him for £20, even though the tax remaining on it was worth £11. He washed it thoroughly before handing it over and, as I drove away, I swear there were tears in his eyes. I called the vehicle 'Hannibal', as Mr Rowlands had driven it over the Alps a dozen times but it was still good enough for the school run. It died one year later when the body came away from the chassis.

It was always fascinating to have the company of Morfydd Mason Lewis and Mr Rowlands at the same coffee table. They had both started their BBC careers in Bangor in the 1930s working for Sam Jones, the first Head at BBC Bangor who dominated broadcasting from north Wales for 29 years from 1935 until his retirement in 1964. His charismatic status when he retired contrasted sharply with his earlier days in Cardiff when he was turned down for the Director of Programmes post because of his perceived 'instability', and he was reported to be 'angry' when first offered the post to head up the new operation in Bangor. The Cardiff establishment obviously wanted him out from under their feet. Morfydd had been appointed Sam's secretary in 1937, while Mr Rowlands had already established himself as an all-round sound engineer in the days when everything was broadcast live. They exchanged tales of Sam's pioneering genius for improvisation with the most basic of resources, cajoling all of his tiny staff to take part in the first schools programmes; harnessing the emerging talents of Charles Williams to launch the light entertainment variety series *Noson Lawen*; locking local student Meredydd (Merêd) Evans in an office until he fulfilled his promise to produce the words for a particular tune; nurturing talent, such as Merêd's popular singing trio 'Triawd y Coleg,' wherever he could find it; bullying the likes of musician Maime Noel Jones into an extra rehearsal minutes before transmission time; applauding all their efforts in a thin voice with a marked south Walian accent which led to innumerable and hilarious misunderstandings between him and the locals. Sam's stewardship of Bangor, nevertheless, launched dozens of highly successful broadcasting careers, as I would soon discover.

Evelyn Williams was the Head of the Children's Department and visited the Park Place canteen often. She was mature in years, always expensively dressed and had a splendid collection of large and colourful hats. Evelyn was totally dedicated to her job but oversensitive to jokes about her puppets Willy and Wally Panda. She cried when she overheard cameramen debating whether they were homosexuals. For a whole generation of children, however, Evelyn brought them their first TV programmes in Welsh, including the long-running series *Ar 'Lin Mam* [On Mother's Knee] with the evergreen Sassie Rees and Sheila Huws Jones performing their own compositions. Then there was Twm Taten [Tom the Potato] which the wags in the studio dubbed 'the spud that laid the golden chips' in relation to its writers. Evelyn was saved from that piece of gentle banter.

BBC canteens were more than places merely to exchange the latest gossip. They were essential as meeting places to let off steam about the shortcomings of BBC management. Above all, risking a canteen visit the day after the transmission of one's own programme could be a litmus test, a professional response to the success or weakness of the production. A stony silence on the subject might well reinforce one's own feelings as to the quality of the work. More often than not, coffee in the canteen led to inconclusive debate and gossip, but never about programme budgets which in radio only included contributors' fees and their travel costs. Producers never discussed money with contributors. Nobody gave a moment's thought as to the real costs of radio. That was the responsibility of management on the third floor of 38–40 Park Place.

25

2

The Lost Leader

IN 1964 ONE broadcaster stood out above all others in Wales. Hywel Davies was Head of Programmes, a charismatic leader energetically launching the first TV channel for Wales with a largely inexperienced team of producers. Hywel had the challenging task of selecting people new to TV in departments as varied as drama, light entertainment, children's, as well as features and documentaries. Soon after he was appointed to the post, he launched *Heddiw* [Today] in 1961 under the editorship of Nan Davies, and the late night weekly *Sports Parade* edited by rugby legend Cliff Morgan. In 1962 *Wales Today* came on stream and rapidly became the most watched programme in the schedule. In 1964 Hywel was given the opportunity to expand services in both languages – seven hours in Welsh and five in English – opening up opportunities beyond factual programmes and sport. He was a skilled executive producer as well as a highly personable presenter. Hywel's lengthy and relaxed interviews 'at home' with prominent people in their own environment were visually attractive to an ever-growing TV audience. A documentary he presented from a nunnery, *Out of this World* with D.J. Thomas, Wales's first TV producer, was a major prizewinner.

Hywel had escaped from being a shirt salesman to writing and reading radio news bulletins in London during the war. By 1964 he was already Controller-designate, with incumbent Alun Oldfield-Davies set to retire within two years. In the evenings Hywel often held court at home in what became known as the 'Radyr Set' in order to review programmes.

The 'Set' included three other formidable broadcasters – all women.

His wife Lorraine Davies had been forced to retire from her production post as she was the spouse of the Head of Programmes. She had a very strong personality, with a fiercely critical nature and an exceptional track record producing children's programmes such as *SOS Galw Gari Tryfan* – the Welsh 'Dick Barton' – and the iconic *Children's Hour* in the days when there was no TV.

The second woman was the more easygoing chief announcer, Morfydd Mason Lewis, whom I had already met for coffee and whose distinctively measured tones somehow defined a standard BBC Welsh accent.

The third was Nan Davies, the powerful Head of Welsh-Language TV. As noted, she was editor of the daily programme *Heddiw* and had been in the business since starting as a secretary to Sam Jones, the Head at BBC Bangor, in 1937. Nan was devoted to Hywel but gave as good as she got in debating professional matters.

Within two years however, in November 1965, Hywel Davies died from a heart condition at the age of only 46. BBC Wales was pitched into mourning, its leader lost at a critical time in its development.

Hywel and his deputy Aneirin Talfan Davies had monitored my first year in radio and marked me down for a transfer to TV, despite the misgivings of Nan Davies who preferred to choose her own staff. Hywel had given me regular constructive criticism and I was fortunate to have learnt so much from him in the short time left to him. There were times when I detected echoes of Lorraine's comments in his criticism, certainly the day after one programme which had had an all-male cast. Hywel was stimulating and always open to discussion but could be difficult and even devastating after a liquid lunch. Once, he and Aneirin called me in to review a new radio series I had launched at lunchtime the previous day. 'A bad programme,' Hywel said, repeating it with great emphasis several times.

I was shaking when I left. The following day I asked Aneirin whether to continue or cancel the series. Aneirin's answer was short. 'Yesterday did not happen.'

As Hywel's deputy, Aneirin had saved him on many such occasions. They had known each other since working together as wartime broadcasters based in London. When Hywel died, Aneirin was the obvious replacement as Head of Programmes. He had wider cultural interests than Hywel, had edited several literary compendia and the monthly print magazine *Barn* [Opinion]. He was well known on the literary scene, with friends as varied as Dylan Thomas and Saunders Lewis, with whom he once recorded a rare and revealing TV interview. Aneirin had also pioneered with two very early films, both religious in character. One was on the famous 'silent' monastery of Taizé in central France; the other on the Welsh religious Revival of 1904 and its leader, the young Evan Roberts. Hywel, on the other hand, focused entirely on the development of TV in Wales. Nevertheless, Aneirin was a calming influence and steadied the ship in the most difficult of times. They were an ideal professional partnership. Aneirin was thoughtful, sensitive and wise in his decision-taking. His serious nature sometimes reflected a private sadness. He had lost his eldest son, Owen, in a car crash while working as a highly promising member of the *Tonight* team in London. Unbeknown to me, Aneirin returned to work on the very day of my interview and tried to bury his grief in his work. His absent-mindedness was legendary. He would call you in to see him, sound off on something which was preoccupying him, and then ask you why you had come. When travelling to London, which was often, he was known to phone his secretary from Paddington station to find out who he was meeting, when and where. However, he was more than capable of standing up for Wales in the corridors of power in London. When one channel Controller sent him a memo berating him 'for messing around with my channel', he responded immediately with, 'I am paid to mess around with your channel'. Aneirin was a generous man. On one occasion he bumped into me and my wife on a day trip to London and insisted on buying us lunch. When he finally retired, Aneirin sold his house to us. One of my abiding memories of a gentle man was of agreeing the sale in his book-lined study with a bottle of red wine prominently placed between us. The bottle was left untouched. Only when we took our leave did he realise his forgetfulness and ran after us clutching the wine intended to celebrate the deal.

At the top of management's 'golden staircase' on the third floor of 39 Park Place – 'golden' because the steps were reinforced with shining brass tips – Alun Oldfield-Davies had reigned supreme for nearly 20 years as Controller. A very tall, old-school patrician figure, he looked down physically on his staff, wearing heavy-rimmed spectacles, speaking so slowly and deliberately I worried whether the sentence was going to end well or badly for me. Such was his age and seniority everybody called him Mr Davies. It was still more friendly than the acronym for his job, CW – Controller, Wales. The BBC's love of acronyms was due to an early need to recognise function rather than named individuals who may have moved on. Later, as life in the BBC became more relaxed, it remained appropriate to call Hywel Davies 'HPW' – Head of Programmes, Wales – in a formal committee rather than be seen as too friendly in front of others. Oldfield-Davies earned respect for his longevity in office and his old-fashioned paternalism towards the staff. His wife Lilian took charge of the children's Christmas party in the Park Place canteen and could be seen bravely rescuing three year olds from clambering on the grand piano in the large music studio. There was a feeling among us 'Young Turks', nearly 40 years his junior, that Oldfield-Davies reflected a distant pre-war age; he was a radio schools' producer before the Controllership thrust him into resuscitating the Welsh Region's radio service in 1946 after the war. In his official history of BBC Wales, historian John Davies concluded that Alun Oldfield-Davies was the 'real' creator of BBC Wales because he had fought doggedly down the years for a better broadcasting service in Wales in the teeth of constant opposition from management in London. That sense of arrogance never left HQ's management at certain levels, as we all discovered to our cost in later years. Oldfield-Davies certainly remained stoical in that fight during his 22 years in post, the longest period of any Controllership in Wales to date.

A contemporary of his, Director-General Sir William Haley, had once told his senior staff 'too much TV is not good for them', the word 'them' signifying the audience. One felt that Oldfield-Davies echoed the sentiment, living as he did mainly through an era in the BBC when TV was regarded as a somewhat frivolous 'add-on'. However, he had made sure that in Hywel and Aneirin he had appointed two people who advanced the future of the new medium in Wales.

Hywel's death in 1965 hit everybody hard. Oldfield-Davies called a staff meeting to announce his passing. The frail-looking Controller sat in front of us, his normally sallow and gloomy countenance taking on a deathly pallor. He was without Aneirin Talfan Davies, who was suffering from a bout of angina. Would Aneirin be fit enough to take over from Hywel? What did the future hold for the fledgling BBC Wales? It was a dreadful and depressing meeting.

In the event, the ageing Oldfield-Davies performed a valuable holding operation for two more years. His last major appointment was that of D.J. Thomas as Deputy Head to Aneirin. 'D.J.' goes down in history as a very underrated pioneer. A former French master at a Swansea secondary school, David John Thomas was a quietly-spoken man, always smartly dressed in a suit and tie. He had started his BBC career at the Swansea radio studios but made his name with his drama productions on the only BBC TV channel of its time in the early 1950s. These included a first commission for the young Elaine Morgan, *A Matter of Degree*, and the first live TV production of *Under Milk Wood* which, lacking any recording facility, broke down for more than 20 minutes while on air. It was par for the course at the time. D.J. was meticulous in the planning of every shot on set and gave me my first TV tutorial. He instructed me to stick to the rules of camera direction.

'You have three choices – a wide shot, a medium shot and a close-up. That is enough. On no account use the zoom lens. No need for it. Always avoid reverse angles.'

Would that modern sports directors learn the last bit.

D.J. had no studio when he made those first pioneering TV programmes in 1953. He used the Temple of Peace in Cathays Park when he could get use of the outside broadcast unit shared with the West of England. There were no recordings and no sets. His production assistant (PA) Margaret Price would borrow a table and be given flowers from local shopkeepers who were only too pleased to help with the new miracle in the corner of the living room.

Aneirin as HPW and D.J. as Assistant HPW managed the programmes until Alun Oldfield-Davies finally retired in 1967. Aneirin should have been the obvious choice to succeed him but was ignored by London's Welsh 'kingmaker' Huw Wheldon. The two men had nothing in common. Aneirin understood Wales. Wheldon merely thought he did. There was a very real danger that 'they' would appoint a Welsh-born producer of the iconic *Tonight* programme, Donald Baverstock. That might have suited those in Head Office who were tired of his aggressive attitude, but he fouled it up by behaving like a bull in the proverbial china shop even at a preliminary stage. Suddenly, a Welsh speaker brought up in Llanfyllin, John Rowley, appeared out of the back offices of HQ. He had been a District Commissioner in India before becoming the BBC's Controller (Staff Administration) in London. It is thought that Huw Wheldon appointed him as a stopgap until Owen Edwards was trained for the job. Rowley's appearance in Cardiff was totally unexpected since nobody had heard of him. His first interview for the Welsh-language weekly newspaper *Y Cymro* [The Welshman] raised a few eyebrows when he said that coping with two and a half million Welsh people was nothing compared with dealing with seven and a half million

Indians. In the event, he turned out to be a friendly, even jolly person who mixed easily in the canteen and faced a difficult five years at a time of increasing public protests about BBC Wales's bilingual TV channel. The passion of those fighting for more Welsh TV, on the one hand, was matched by the irritation felt by non-Welsh speakers who complained that the disruptive scheduling of Welsh programmes limited choice when they only had three channels. The Welsh Language Society was eliciting more and more support from academics and religious bodies, while the Labour Party was agitating to settle the problem on behalf of the English speakers. At one point Aneirin Talfan Davies was forced to wonder whether he had heard correctly when both Leo Abse and George Thomas backed the idea of a Welsh-language channel. Rowley was fortunate to have two important allies during this growing social disharmony – a strong-minded Chairman in Dr Glyn Tegai Hughes who first persuaded the Broadcasting Council for Wales that a Welsh Fourth Channel was a good idea and an Irish-born rugby referee and BBC Director-General Charles Curran, who empathised with the Welsh dilemma. At the time, however, nobody could think of a pragmatic solution.

Controller Rowley could be both eccentric and enigmatic. He sometimes talked in riddles which left people wondering what he meant. In annual interviews he was prone to confuse even fun-loving individuals on the staff who came expecting a written annual report and a serious chat. Script editor Gwenlyn Parry was once greeted by a smiling John Rowley telling him that if he, Rowley, left the room, Gwenlyn would immediately read his own personal file which was closed on the table in front of him. With that, Rowley disappeared. Gwenlyn took this as a bizarre signal to open the file. The moment he did so Rowley suddenly returned through a different door and shouted 'You rascal!' [In Welsh 'Gwalch']. 'I knew you would do that!' When he asked sports producer Dewi Griffiths where he thought he would be in five years' time, Dewi immediately answered '55!' Rowley was said to be a member of the Magic

Circle and known to entertain friends of all ages by pulling rabbits out of hats. By the time he retired he had proved to be a decent and honourable man who had his own humorous ways of trying to enjoy a stressful job. He is best remembered for saving the BBC Welsh Orchestra from the axe. The BBC in general had too many radio orchestras and 'The Welsh' was one of several on the target list. Rowley not only fought a long rearguard action, he won the day by increasing its numbers in association with the help of funding from the Welsh Arts Council. Overnight, the orchestral rank and file rose from 44 to 66 players, which not only assured its future but also opened up opportunities to play a greater range of symphonic works and attract better leaders and conductors.

Throughout the years between 1964 and 1972, the strong man holding BBC Wales together behind the scenes was the remarkably astute and highly intelligent chief assistant in charge of programme planning. Owen Thomas was certainly not strong physically but was responsible for TV schedules, programme budgets and the allocation of cameras and editing time. He had learnt his trade working in London for Joanna Spicer, one of those senior female planners who terrified the male executives of the time. Hywel Davies invited Owen Thomas to return to Wales and build a structure for an expanding service. Were it not for a chronic heart condition, Owen might well have been more confident of holding down more senior jobs, but he contented himself with organising the output and dealing with the demands of some difficult producers who were always pleading for more resources.

Ten years later, in 1974, I would be thankful that Owen Thomas was still *in situ*, allowing me to benefit from his wisdom, experience and stimulating company as a manager myself. But in 1964 I only had one thought – to learn the basics of radio production.

CHAPTER 3

The Radio Apprentice, 1964–66

I WAS LET loose on the radio audience very gently. Administrative assistant Heulwen Thomas ruled the roost in Swansea in 1964. She lent me the station stopwatch and sent me to 'produce' my first programme, timing the rehearsal of a live radio *Morning Story* for the network. The equally experienced studio manager, Nimrod Pugh, ensured nothing went amiss. John Darren was due to read his own story. His experience of reading news bulletins on the daily TV programme *Wales Today* had made him a household name. He accepted my presence courteously and I ventured to say his script was, according to my stopwatch, timed to perfection. I did not dare patronise him by referring to his brilliant reading, complete with an occasional burst of dialogue. A voice from London came 'down the line' giving instructions. Nimrod said 'Don't worry', switched on a red light outside the studio door and then a green light on the table in front of John. He was 'live' on air and relaxed. I was a bag of nerves despite having nothing to do. He read the script with the ease of the freelance professional actor he had been for many years. Then, to my surprise, he got up and walked from the chair with a limp. He never showed his artificial leg on TV. John returned to his work as a solicitor before going on to read the news later the same day. He set a standard for reading bulletins on radio and TV, emulated in Wales only by chief announcer Morfydd Mason Lewis.

Emboldened by this early triumph, I took over *Barn y Bobol*. It was *Any Questions?* in Welsh, one of the longest lasting of the live broadcasting formats. The object of the exercise is to search for that chemistry between panellists which will stimulate genuine debate and fire up the audience. Selecting the panel is easier said than done. The ideal panellists for a particular venue are often unavailable or pull out for various reasons at the last minute. Political parties expect to be treated fairly over the course of several programmes. In addition, it is always beneficial to have one well-known local voice.

Fortunately, I inherited the ideal chairman. At the time Gwyn Erfyl was one of several Nonconformist ministers wondering whether to make that full-time jump into broadcasting, such were their meagre stipends. Gwyn was already in demand.

Dozens of producers have worked on English and Welsh variations of *Any Questions?* over the years. Many moons later I did several warm-up talks for the Radio 4 version when it was broadcast from Wales. At the time the smooth David Jacobs was in the chair but I thought Gwyn was immeasurably better for his more direct and rougher supplementary questioning of the cognoscenti on the panel, turning softer with an audience unused to the microphone. I always remember a question from the audience pitched at Dr Gareth Evans, a brilliant mathematics lecturer at University College, Swansea.

'What does it feel like,' asked the questioner, 'to be an intellectual?' Back came Gareth's answer, 'Jesus Christ was a carpenter.'

Gwyn Erfyl was a born interviewer, a trained philosopher, always pondering the 'Why?' of the world. Unfortunately, he was already working part-time for HTV Wales and signed for them full-time long before I was in a position to entice him back to the BBC. I tried many times thereafter but it was too late. He was earning too much money and had much more influence at HTV than was ever possible at the BBC. He became one of Wales's most thoughtful, challenging and successful documentary producers.

At first my contact list was thin and I sometimes turned to people I had known at university in Aberystwyth, both the best lecturers and the most successful student debaters. The most embarrassing incident occurred over a documentary on Welsh emigration to America. I had invited the distinguished Professor of Geography, E.G. Bowen, to present the programme. He had lectured on the subject many times, enthralling audiences while developing his theme, jumping up and down on his soles, his face grinning like a monkey and his false teeth clacking continuously. The programme went well but I then received a letter from his colleague, senior lecturer in American History Alan Conway, who pointed out that Bowen had plagiarised his book on the subject and what was I going to do about it? I pleaded with Conway not to diminish Bowen's reputation with an apology on air and was fortunate to get away with grovelling on paper for my mistake! Plagiarism was obviously present before the age of the internet.

The scope for making historical programmes on Welsh history opened up at a time when considerable research was being done in the subject. Two erudite lecturers at Swansea were Dr Prys Morgan, who had an encyclopaedic mind on all things Welsh, and Dr Kenneth O. Morgan, author of an important publication on politics in Wales from 1868 to 1922. It was a pleasure to learn through recording documentaries with them, tapping the rich seam of Welsh history which was emerging as a critical contribution to our national identity – 'Heb gof, heb genedl' [No memory, no nation].

In those days the post of researcher had not yet been invented and, with a heavy weekly output in both languages, I had to take short-cuts. I hired the best man at my wedding, Wyre Thomas, as a scriptwriter for a new lunchtime weekly magazine, *Os Ac Oni Bai*, a phrase which translates roughly as 'Doubting'. It was a tangential look at the news from the personal viewpoint of interesting individuals. As the engineering hierarchy didn't allow the use of telephone interviews until much later, every contributor had to travel to the studios located near the old university towns and cities. There were plenty of good talkers but, other than the recording and editing of vox pops, there was very limited interactivity with the audience. Several regular contributors lived overseas. The Los Angeles-based Reverend I.D.E. Thomas was a splendid broadcaster. He made no secret of his Republican views which reflected the political leanings of the majority of Welsh-Americans, a somewhat ironic situation given that the Welsh exodus of the nineteenth century was made up mainly of people escaping Tory industrialists and landlords in search of freedom and better opportunities in life. On the other side of the world Leo Goodstadt was an editor on the highly reputable *Far East Economic Review* based in Hong Kong who had married into a Chinese family. In Cardiff, Dr Harri Pritchard-Jones stood out as a Catholic who could explain both the complexities of the Vatican as well as comment on the growing problems in Northern Ireland given many years studying medicine in Dublin. He was supported by a number of Irish intellectuals who had learnt Welsh perfectly, principally Professor Proinsias Mac Cana whose accent alone was worth a listen. In Bangor, lecturers Gwyn Thomas, Bedwyr Lewis Jones, Frank Price Jones and medical doctor Emyr Wyn Jones were four who would always enlighten the audience with their distinctive way of storytelling. In the back roads of Cardiganshire, the leading writer of children's books, T. Llew Jones, had a natural feel for a well constructed script, while Mari James 'Llangeitho' was very difficult to stop when in full flow and impossible to cut if recorded. She seemed incapable of drawing breath – but could be guaranteed to bring a dose of common sense and humour to the airwaves in between organising her husband's school buses.

At the time, scriptwriter Wyre Thomas was moonlighting from his day job as a Welsh Office civil servant. One of the brightest of minds, he was equally adept at writing Welsh poetry in the strict metre of cynghanedd as he was knowledgeable in current affairs. He once won the inter-college Eisteddfod Chair having written the poem in one sleepless night. Two years later, when I moved to TV, Wyre replaced me and in 1969 launched *Bore Da* [Good Morning], an early morning news magazine presented by T. Glynne Davies, the first Welsh programme to move to VHF only in 1974.

The political programmes which I inherited on radio could be boring but I was told not to change the formats. The BBC had a statutory obligation to report Westminster politics in both languages. I was landed with organising *Wales at Westminster* and its Welsh equivalent *Yn y Senedd* every Friday evening. Since the most able Labour MPs were in government, I was left with a choice of older members sitting on huge majorities with little incentive to be bothered with interviews when so few people were listening. I had also inherited the *Western Mail's* Lobby correspondent, David Rosser, as the interviewer in English. BBC Wales had no Lobby ticket (which gave selected journalists unique access to the Lobby of the House of Commons) at the time and David was the only Welsh journalist with an inside knowledge of Parliament. He was a safe, unexciting interviewer but at least the English programmes were better than the Welsh-language weekly talks which were scripted by the few Welsh-speaking MPs. I wanted to scrap both programmes and start afresh but the 'Third Floor' had bad memories of an unproven investigation into news bias towards Plaid Cymru in the 1950s and wanted no change until the sensitive elections of 1964 and 1966 had passed.

I improvised by launching several 'specials' to add background knowledge to the Welsh scene, since 1964 marked a new milestone in Welsh politics. The new Welsh Office now had powers over roads, health and education. The by-election victory of Gwynfor Evans in April 1966 and the October General Election which followed it saw a welcome injection of fresh Labour blood as well as a new party, Plaid Cymru, in

Parliament. There was a sense of change and excitement in the air.

There was only one Welsh-speaking Tory, Geraint Morgan in Denbigh, who always complained about his rare appearances on the media in English, inevitable given his monopoly of the airwaves in Welsh. The two Liberals, Emlyn Hooson and Deputy Speaker Roderic Bowen, kept their party alive in mid Wales while Lady Megan Lloyd George, the feisty MP for Carmarthenshire until 1966, was the only Welsh woman MP and, like her ex-Prime Minister father, would take no prisoners in public debate. These were still the days when packed halls listened to the rousing rhetoric of Michael Foot or Lady Megan who relished these events.

My favourite political character was S.O. Davies, a dyed-in-the-wool old-school left-wing socialist who, in his later years, always wore a bowler hat and answered every question courteously in the third person, 'S.O. thinks...' S.O. resigned the Labour Whip when he rejected his party's move to the centre ground. Following his re-election as an Independent MP when well into his 80s, I watched in horror one day as we filmed him walking down Merthyr High Street, his sound lead tied to a moving BBC car which was about to pull him the wrong side of a lamp-post. At the last second S.O. skipped around the lamp-post like a two year old. Not all of the older MPs had the incentive to be that active, such was the size of their Labour majorities.

I once asked Iorrie Thomas how he campaigned during election time in the Rhondda. He was quite brazen in admitting his technique of touring the bingo halls, taking the tannoy during a break and announcing himself as the sitting Labour member with one simple message, 'Enjoy yourselves'. Iorrie saw no need to distract them with talk of manifestoes.

Gwynfor Evans's by-election victory in 1966 following the death of Lady Megan Lloyd George was a total shock outside Carmarthenshire itself. Gwynfor beat Gwilym Prys Davies, a Pontypridd solicitor who was one of the Labour Party's best thinkers and, ironically, one of its most powerful advocates of devolution. He was just not suited to the hustings. Only a year had elapsed since Elystan Morgan, the obvious heir to Gwynfor in Plaid Cymru, had defected to the Labour Party, disillusioned with Plaid's lack of success at the polls and encouraged by the appointment of a Labour Secretary of State for Wales. As a current affairs producer, I too was caught out by the result. I had no research back-up, no communications system other than a telephone, and my office was three miles from the newsroom. At least a BBC crew filmed the actual result, but we had failed to pick up the local vibes. I phoned my old professor Ted Nevin, and we rushed over to interview Gwynfor on the following morning at his home, Talar Wen in Llangadog.

Ted Nevin was a brilliant and challenging economics tutor who had untapped potential in broadcasting. He was unhappy with what he called the 'Welsh-speaking Nonconformist Establishment' of Aberystwyth in the 1950s following the sacking of Principal Goronwy Rees over his involvement with the Cambridge spy ring of the 1930s. As a strong Catholic, Ted 'escaped' to University College Dublin, where he fell out almost immediately with the Archbishop of All Ireland, realised his mistake, and returned to Swansea in order to be nearer the BBC studios. Controller Oldfield-Davies chided me for using Ted too often for his own academic reputation, but I protested that it was the *Good Morning Wales* team which had hired him to comment on the World Tiddlywinks Championship. Ted died suddenly when still only in his late 50s, just as he was emerging as a radical broadcaster and tough interviewer.

Within months of Gwynfor's election to Parliament, he kept the seat in the October General Election of 1966 but he was neither welcome nor comfortable there. I remember having dinner with him in Soho one night. He was happy to relax and reminisce in company away from the Commons and explained his tactic of pursuing the government with a record number of written questions rather than face a hostile House.

However, Gwynfor was nothing if not stubborn. He had

rejected the BBC's offer of an early evening slot for his very first TV Party Political Broadcast (PPB), due for transmission on 29 September 1965. He demanded peak viewing time. As the producer assigned to those recordings, I was dispatched to Llangadog to persuade him to accept the offer. As we talked I could see the controlled anger as his face slowly reddened, and I realised for the first time that he was not one to negotiate. He won the argument just two days after his Vice-President, Chris Rees, broadcast Plaid's first radio PPB. That attitude won Gwynfor a much bigger battle in 1980 when he threatened to fast to death unless Mrs Thatcher did a U-turn over the launch of the Welsh Fourth Channel.

The 1966 General Election resulted in a new intake of Labour MPs in Wales, many of whom were middle-class lawyers who had already broadcast often for me on radio. Alan Williams in Swansea West would, decades later, become Father of the House; Donald Anderson in Swansea East eventually became Chairman of the Foreign Affairs Select Committee; Ednyfed Hudson Davies became my closest colleague in TV when he lost Conway to Wyn Roberts in 1970; William Edwards in Merionethshire complained that I had given airtime to all the new Labour MPs except himself; finally, Elystan Morgan, who became a Home Office Minister.

In public, Elystan oozed genuine old-fashioned courtesy, always dressed in formal jacket and pinstripe trousers, often ready for a court appearance. In private, he was delightful company with a great ability to mimic his closest colleagues, particularly his nemesis George Thomas. Elystan had a rich vocabulary in both languages but he had to be warned in advance about hogging a debate. I recall producing the Welsh-language constituency debate from Felinfach on TV in later years. Elystan, then the sitting MP, arrived late and apologetic. I warned him against swamping the other candidates in his inimitable fluent but wordy style when his main opponent was the quieter, canny and laid-back Liberal Geraint Howells who was known in every farmers' mart in the county. Elystan lost the plot and his seat by 500 votes. I am convinced that he lost the crucial number of 250 votes that evening because he gave so little time to his opponent.

As evidence of Elystan's memorable sayings, although bordering on the pompous, I shared a taxi with him from Paddington station one morning. He was on his way, he said, to an Appeal Court hearing in the hope of overturning the decision of a well-known 'hanging' judge in Wales who, he claimed, 'had the Cromwellian obsession with the eradication of sin'.

There was no love lost between Elystan and fellow Labour Party MP George Thomas who was always looking for self-serving publicity. In 1964, George was both an MP and President of the Methodist Assembly. On one occasion Arfon Roberts, an enthusiastic news reporter with a nasal voice and a distinctive north Walian accent, persuaded me to allow a 30-minute report on prostitution in Cardiff's Tiger Bay. His report was five minutes short. I asked George Thomas to fill the gap in his religious capacity. He said he could not possibly comment, 'because Mam wouldn't like it'. George was the most devoted of sons.

'How do you know? You haven't asked her,' I said, at which point he left the phone to consult Mam.

He returned saying, 'I can do it.'

'What did you tell Mam, George?'

'I said Mam, the BBC want me,' and she said, 'There's nice, George.'

'It's about prostitution, Mam.'

'No, George.'

'It's alright Mam, I'm against it!'

I would spend many hours with George in later years making films about him when he was Secretary of State for Wales and later Speaker of the House of Commons.

One person who was yet to emerge as a parliamentarian was a young female journalist. Ann Clwyd had worked as a studio manager before writing for the *Guardian* and freelancing for the BBC. She offered me an interview with the notoriously reclusive Saunders Lewis, the former president of Plaid Cymru and an acclaimed intellectual. It coincided with the tenth anniversary of the televising of his famous play *Brad* [Treachery] based on the plot to kill Hitler and which had been a success as a *Wednesday Play* on the network. The phone call with Saunders Lewis asking for an interview was short and to the point: 'No!' stated firmly in English despite my approach in Welsh. Ann's response was to go straight to his Penarth home. Saunders opened the door, listened to her request, but she was refused quite curtly. She put one foot in the closing door – and surprisingly he opened it again and gave her the interview. Ann Clwyd eventually became as determined an MP as she was a journalist, not to be trifled with on subjects as varied as the Kurds in Iraq or the National Health Service following the death of her husband, our former colleague Owen Roberts, in 2012.

One largely forgotten event in 1966 had a massive economic impact on the Welsh economy. The opening of the first Severn crossing dispensed with the old-fashioned Aust ferry or the need to drive around Gloucester to get to London. To celebrate its launch, I co-produced a radio programme with BBC Bristol to examine the potential impact of this event on our respective regions. What transpired from interviews on both sides of the river was the dire warning from urban planners that Bristol would flourish at the expense of Cardiff. At the time, Cardiff's current boom years and the dramatic decline of industry in the south Wales coalfield in the 1970s and 1980s were not even contemplated. In the event, Cardiff defied the doomsters, offering job opportunities to a new generation of commuters pouring into the city on all the Valley railway lines. In the 20 years between 1966 and 1986, the Welsh economy would evolve into a nation of prosperous 'haves' employed in the service industries, as opposed to the tens of thousands of 'have nots' discarded with the decline of steel and coal.

Settling into BBC life was easy enough but, within three months of arriving, I was pleased to meet an equally inexperienced producer of my own age who appeared in Cardiff for his induction month. Meirion Edwards had replaced a Bangor producer who had resigned in disgust on learning that my appointment was on a higher pay grade than his. It seemed that the BBC regarded current affairs as a tad more responsible than other programmes. I tended to agree with the protester. Crafting drama or light entertainment required greater skills than that of the jobbing journalist.

Meirion proved to be an intellectual heavyweight. We immediately became the closest of friends and started arguing about the ways of the world – and the BBC – for over 50 years, and have never stopped. We would work together for many years in programme management from late 1976 until I left in 1990.

My two years in radio were spent in one of five offices – mainly in 1 Museum Place, just around the corner from the HQ and radio studios of BBC Wales in 38–40 Park Place. The other four offices were inhabited by an eclectic collection of radio producers. Head of Religion Tregelles Williams, father of future Head of Music Huw Tregelles, had an office above mine. A former Baptist minister and university lecturer in Greek, he was the most genial of companions, a pipe constantly in his hand. At the time he had a fearful if well-meaning white-haired secretary, Lynn Osborne, who was prone to address one bishop on the telephone as 'Bish' and I could hear the banging of a heavy Bible on her desk when she was angry. Having started her BBC career working for the legendary and eccentric light entertainment producer Mai Jones before the war, she was eventually transferred to radio planning where she was less of a danger to the public. It was, however, always wise to keep her on side. If she didn't like you it could be difficult to get studios when you wanted them.

The quiet, highly respected and colourful drama producer Herbert Williams had an office next to mine. He was well connected to stars of the West End stage who could only take part in his productions at weekends. This gave him the run of the studio without prying management eyes and allowed for substantial hospitality before and after work. We were all surprised when he suddenly emigrated to Australia and amazed when he ended up as Head of Religion at the Australian Broadcasting Corporation.

A third office was the domain of a very quiet woman. Marion Griffith Williams was a conscientious features producer with whom I would share a coffee but we never seemed to have much in common. I had no idea then that Marion Eames, as she became known through her remarkably successful historical novels, would write some of the best TV plays during the next decade.

There was one other producer with whom I had much more in common professionally. Elwyn Parry-Jones was Wales's BBC World Service producer, a highly ambitious journalist from Denbigh who was determined not only to get into TV but also to move on to London's current affairs unit. That is precisely how his career progressed, first moving to *Week In Week Out* in Cardiff and then to London in 1971. He finally became deputy editor of *Panorama*, making several important documentaries on the newspaper industry which included the first TV portrait of the young Australian entrepreneur Rupert Murdoch. Elwyn finally became executive producer of *Rough Justice* where he crossed swords with the powers that be. He left the BBC, returning to north Wales with the intention of becoming an independent producer working primarily for S4C. He fell ill in 2002 and 12 years later died without fulfilling his final ambition.

In 1966 Elwyn and I were both transferred to TV. My two-year apprenticeship in radio was too short to contribute anything of significance, and certainly not long enough to understand the varied tastes of Welsh audiences. Other than vox pops, it was difficult to interact with a wide spectrum of the audience because the engineers still frowned on the use of phone-ins. I enjoyed my radio apprenticeship and the pleasant ambience of Park Place immensely, but at the time it was a relatively stagnant backwater compared to the excitement generated by the two-year-old BBC Wales TV service based in Newport Road. Little did I think that eight years down the line I would return to the wireless and help create the buzz of two national radio channels. However, Hywel Davies and Aneirin Talfan Davies had encouraged me to try out a couple of ideas in TV. It was an offer too good to miss.

CHAPTER 4

There's a Story Coming in from...

... ABERFAN. It was October 1966. Those of us who lived through it will never forget the tragedy of Aberfan. There had been terrible mining disasters in Senghenydd, Gresford, Six Bells, and, in the year before Aberfan, 31 miners had lost their lives in Rhondda's Cambrian colliery. The risks of working underground were well known. Aberfan was different. It involved schoolchildren. Sheer horror reverberated around the whole of Britain and much of the wider world at the news. It was the first disaster to unfold live on the BBC's only TV channel, which scrapped its schedule that night and the following day as the bodies of 116 children and 28 adults were dug out of the slimy slurry which slid down the mountain to engulf the local primary school.

When the first reports came through many BBC staff joined people from all walks of life helping the miners who were desperately digging in hope. They came from far and wide, joining the long line of men passing buckets of slurry away from the buried classrooms. The following days required sensitive reporting of a situation in which a whole generation, the future of the village, was nearly wiped out. All the Welsh reporters, including Brian Hoey and Gareth Bowen in English and both Owen Edwards and Gwyn Llewelyn of HTV Wales in Welsh, treated the story with compassion and avoided sentimentality. Cliff Michelmore covered the event with great sensitivity for London's flagship *Tonight*, but had been shaken enough by the scene to ask *Heddiw* producer Geraint Stanley Jones, 'What do I say?' A year later, however, his colleague Fyfe Robertson made a programme entitled *What's Happened to Pity?* which was a total intrusion into the privacy of mourning families and caused considerable local anger. Aberfan became a running story as the negligence of the National Coal Board and the arrogant disinterest of its Chairman, Lord Robens, as well as the inhumanity of Secretary of State for Wales George Thomas added bitterness to the horror of it all.

My contribution to the weekend resulted in the worst programme of my life. Scheduled to produce a Sunday afternoon chat show during my first month as a TV series producer, I pleaded with Head of Programmes Aneirin Talfan Davies to cancel what I believed to be inconsequential chat in the face of so much grieving. Aneirin insisted that the show must go on and named three respected clergymen to offer the audience relevant support. It was fortunate that I added agnostic journalist T. Glynne Davies to the panel because he was the only person to make sense. Some of the clergy found themselves unable to cope with the magnitude of the reality on the ground.

The BBC Wales newsroom came of age with Aberfan. It was stretched as never before and its small staff excelled itself. It was based in a converted chapel in Stacey Road, totally isolated from the rest of the BBC in Cardiff. *Wales Today* had launched in 1962 from a tiny studio shared with *Heddiw* on the first floor. It started as a ten-minute news bulletin directed by documentary producer John Ormond and read by a variety of announcers, including Michael Aspel, the future presenter of *This is Your Life* and *Antiques Roadshow*. The news editor in the early days was the diminutive and lame figure of Tom Richards who called out 'First Class!' at the end of every programme in a hoarse high-pitched voice. Tom had been involved in defending an accusation of news bias in favour of Plaid Cymru in the

1950s by a Tory MP, and was glad to be transferred to Swansea as west Wales representative.

Alan Protheroe, the former industrial correspondent, was now the editor of news, and he presided over the newsroom for the rest of the 1960s. During my two years in radio I visited it often to read the diary of upcoming events. Alan asked me to help out on election nights, basing me in the large London election studio, open telephone in hand, instructing Cardiff when to opt out of the network discussions hosted by Robin Day.

Having thought I now knew Alan quite well, I was surprised to hear that he was the Welsh-speaking son of a Nonconformist minister from St Davids in Pembrokeshire. His commitment to maneuvers with the Territorial Army (TA) seemed at odds with his background, and he never showed his ability to speak Welsh fluently. On one occasion he turned up to work in full TA uniform driving an army jeep. It was promptly 'stolen' and parked around the corner by a wag in the newsroom. Alan took firm editorial decisions in a military manner and was a very good journalist who never lost control of the most difficult mix of individuals in BBC Wales. He was, however, prone to melodrama when big stories broke. During the long weekend of the Aberfan disaster, he installed a bed in his office and refused extra help from London when it was obvious that some people were overtired and making mistakes. One of his overwilling radio staff, Arfon Roberts, was beginning to sound incoherent when taken off air after what seemed like 48 hours of continuous broadcasting on the BBC World Service.

Freelance sports reporter Peter Walker remembered a famous incident when *Wales Today* had an accident-prone evening. Everything that could go wrong went wrong. Protheroe called everybody into his office, sat in front of them with his head buried in his hands, looked up slowly, inhaled deeply of his cigarette and, in a low voice, said, 'What are you doing to me?'

Alan's senior staff did not have his ability to create dramatic

49

silences. His deputy news editor was pipe smoking Wynford Jones, who had a habit of shrugging his shoulders – or perhaps adjusting his jacket – while considering the best way forward and giving his opinion in a very deep voice. It was Wynford who first suggested the title *Wales Today*. It was rubbished immediately but nobody came up with a better idea. It has now lasted over 50 years. Assistant news editor Tudor Phillips was the mild-mannered man who seemed permanently caught up in rescheduling the shifts of the small staff, including Aled Rhys Wiliam who was specifically appointed to translate the news bulletins into Welsh for both radio and TV, an unsatisfactory practice which continued throughout the 1960s. It was Aled who actually read the bulletin – in English – on the first night of *Wales Today* in 1962.

Only one journalist seemed to belong to my generation. David Morris Jones was a news assistant when I first met him, his eyes glued to the typewriter with little time for small talk. During the next 25 years he gradually emerged as the anchor of the newsroom, always in the centre of things and with a tendency to read his own written material aloud before passing it on. I began to admire his single-minded professionalism as he grew in stature and was steadily promoted through the ranks until finally appointed editor of news and current affairs in the mid 1980s. Good news days or bad, 'D.M.J.' was the straight-talking and uncompromising professional, the first to arrive in the morning and last to leave at night. The story of BBC Wales news, as it unfolded in my time, centres to a great extent around David's advancement.

The two studio directors who had to cope with the chronically late running orders were Gareth Wyn Jones and Richard Lewis. Completely different in character, Gareth Wyn was infamous for screaming instructions while standing on the gallery table as the presenters gave viewers the impression that all was under control. Richard Lewis rarely got excited. Both he and Gareth Wyn craved only one thing – to get out of the newsroom and make their own documentaries. I would see a lot of Richard in the future, but I missed the dinner parties of talented chef Gareth Wyn when he turned independent producer and moved to north Wales.

Gareth Wyn and Brian Hoey, the very first presenter of *Wales Today*, were also the first BBC TV news team to beam pictures back from Aberfan. Hoey had only been asked to front *Wales Today* until Head of Programmes Hywel Davies found a suitable permanent replacement. In the event, he stayed for many years, usually standing next to seated newsreader John Darren, the very same who had read my first *Morning Story* in 1964. After a long career as a freelance presenter, Hoey became a prolific royal biographer.

During a protracted steel strike in Port Talbot in the 1960s, one filming location was renamed Kane's Corner where the man who would become Wales's leading news and current affairs broadcaster in English first made his name. Vincent Kane dominated the airwaves like no other of his generation and was in demand for the greater part of his career, presenting *Wales Today* and *Week In Week Out* on TV as well as *Good Morning Wales* and finally *Meet for Lunch* on radio. Vincent's voice and manner immediately signalled authority. He was an incisive interviewer, ruthless in supplementary questioning and took no prisoners. He had won the coveted 'Observer Mace' three times as a mature student debater for University College, Cardiff. I learnt that to my cost when his lightning repartee destroyed my feeble attempt to match him in one such arena. His broadcasting achievements could have emulated that other star interviewer from Cardiff, John Humphrys, had he persevered longer than the short time he spent working in London's current affairs division.

Week In Week Out is still the current affairs stablemate of *Wales Today*. It had been launched during the BBC Wales expansion in 1964. Its first editor, David Bevan, had been transferred from radio current affairs to the *Week In Week Out* office, together with the other TV departments, in Newport Road. His appointment created the vacancy in radio which gave me the opening to join the BBC. David tried to imitate the satirical edge to contemporary issues which was very much in vogue in programmes like *That Was The Week That Was* during the early 1960s, but *Week In Week Out* gradually evolved into a serious issue-led weekly. Bevan eventually left to replace Morfydd Mason Lewis as senior announcer for some years before moving on to a lecturing post.

In the early days his assistant producer was David Parry-Jones, who had started as a journalist on the *Sunday Times*. 'D.P.J.', as he became known, left *Week In Week Out* to freelance as a reporter and then present *Wales Today* while also developing as BBC Wales's rugby commentator. In doing so he and Kane became the best-known voices and faces of Wales for a generation. David was a safe pair of hands, patient and agreeable, a person with whom it was easy to work.

When Bevan left *Week In Week Out*, a number of different people worked on it. Geraint Stanley Jones remembers running it for a season, Elwyn Parry-Jones stayed with it for a couple of years before leaving for London and, after 1966, I made a few 50-minute current affairs 'specials' under the same title.

The longest serving editor of *Week In Week Out*, I recall, was Jeffrey Iverson, a former industrial correspondent on *Wales Today*. Jeff was a tough old-school journalist with slightly impaired eyesight, a condition called tunnel vision. It restricted his ability to see people seated either side of him and he would regale the BBC Club with the embarrassing story of trying to cope with conversation at a Buckingham Palace dinner, with royalty seated beside him on a long table not realising he lacked peripheral vision. Iverson wanted to make as many films as possible on current issues, but the demands of a weekly series dictated that a majority of the programmes would, of necessity, be studio bound. With Kane as main presenter they were a formidable team when conducting studio debates and interviews. Some people felt that they generated more heat than light, but nobody could complain that those in authority, particularly politicians, had an easy ride. When former film editor Brian Turvey arrived as a *Week In Week Out* producer in the mid 1970s, there was more time for investigative reporting on issues such as miscarriages of justice, or memorable major interviews with film stars Anthony Hopkins and Richard Burton. Jeff's most mysterious production involved the Bloxham Tapes, in which a psychotherapist of that name based in Barry hypnotised people and interviewed them about their previous lives. One man was taken back to the Battle of Trafalgar and spoke in the common English of that time. *Week In Week Out* researcher Beata Lipman told of a massacre of Jews in the crypt of a York church. When the crypt was opened up, new evidence was revealed of a massacre. The programme was offered to BBC1 Controller Aubrey Singer who was initially excited by it, bought it, worried about it and cancelled it for lack of scientific authority. Jeff published a book about it privately. Both the BBC Wales transmission and the book were very successful.

Several other reporters and presenters of *Week In Week Out* were prominent but served for shorter periods of time than Vincent Kane. Phil Parry and David Williams were excellent investigative reporters. The Humphrys brothers, John and Bob, worked together when John had already established himself in the hot seat of Radio 4's early morning flagship programme *Today*. They were totally different in temperament and character. John has arguably been the toughest radio interviewer ever on the BBC. His high nervous energy levels and distinct lack of patience at being kept waiting for the next event is in sharp contrast to the laid-back nature of his late brother. Bob always seemed relaxed, friendly and cheerful. He spent more years working on *Week In Week Out* than anybody else except Vincent Kane, but eventually opted to settle for the life of sports correspondent on *Wales Today*.

It was when I was appointed Deputy Head of Programmes in 1974 that I noticed a total lack of news and sports results from Wales on Saturday evening TV, and managed to persuade assistant news editor Tudor Phillips to fill five minutes – called

Sports News Wales – immediately after the short ten-minute network news bulletin. Bob Humphrys was the obvious choice to present the first TV news of Wales at the weekend.

Wales Today naturally employed more people than *Week In Week Out*, including a long list of regional reporters. The genial Elfyn Thomas was an award-winning journalist who covered north Wales for many years as well as presenting well-researched industrial documentaries. The versatile Gerry Monte was based in Pembrokeshire and was also well regarded as a presenter of Radio Wales programmes. George Ashwell on TV, and the extremely long-serving Gilbert John on radio, operated out of Swansea. They were but a few of a group who stood out as consistently dependable professionals covering large areas of the country while ensuring that their films arrived early enough in the afternoon to be processed and edited in time.

By 1970 Alan Protheroe was being regarded as a future candidate for a senior management position in BBC Wales, but he suddenly transferred to London's news division and never returned. Given responsibility for a succession of the BBC's top news programmes, he was eventually promoted to the hot seat of Assistant Director-General in charge of all news and current affairs programmes where he was caught up in the biggest BBC controversy of the 1980s. (See Chapter 18)

Alan's replacement was Owen Roberts, the husband of Ann Clwyd. He was the former HTV Wales editor of the Welsh daily *Y Dydd* [The Day], a successful hard-edged programme with a daring light touch provided by the protest songs of the emerging Dafydd Iwan. Owen had developed an able cadre of young journalists at HTV, many of whom would follow him to BBC Wales, working in the newsroom for *Heddiw* and eventually Radio Cymru. He took *Heddiw* and *Week In Week Out* under the news and current affairs umbrella and was the first person to be appointed editor of both divisions. He looked to be setting out on a major BBC career path. Instead, through no fault of his own, he became embroiled in a major disciplinary problem which was to change everything. (See Chapter 12)

Patrick Hannan was already a respected political journalist when he joined BBC Wales from the *Western Mail* in 1970. He quickly established himself in the dual role of political and industrial correspondent and built up a reputation as the leading analyst of the Welsh political scene for the next 30 years. We had become close friends when editors of the student paper, *The Courier*, in successive years at university in Aberystwyth. 'Pat' had a background in Welsh history from listening to lectures by the charismatic radical Gwyn 'Alf' Williams and was blessed with a phenomenal memory, exemplified when winning Radio 4's *Round Britain Quiz* five times in ten years in partnership with university lecturer Peter Stead. Hannan's coverage of the 1974 and 1984–5 miners' strikes, as reporter and analyst respectively, led him to record Radio 4 documentaries on the issue and write the most authoritative book on contemporary Welsh industrial history, *When Arthur Met Maggie*. He was a sceptic rather than the cynic he was sometimes dubbed by colleagues who were afraid of his acerbic tongue – although even his closest friends never escaped that. Patrick was highly respected by politicians, union and industrial leaders alike for his depth of knowledge and expert analysis. He was a broadcaster who could prick the bubble of hypocrisy and humbug through the use of humorous double entendre to devastating effect. Patrick experienced a decade to remember, from the first coal strike in 1972 and the two general elections of 1974, another election and the referendum on devolution in 1979, through until the end of the seminal second and final coal strike in of 1984–5, although by that time he had left the news department.

A number of Welsh MPs held sway in the Labour Governments of the 1970s but several active backbenchers made a big impact on the contemporary scene. Leo Abse had already made his mark in 1967 with a Private Member's bill on sexual offences which, when backed by Gwent-born Home Secretary Roy Jenkins, led to homosexuality law reform. It was their reforming zeal which made Britain a more tolerant society on a number of human rights issues – but not in relation to the Welsh language.

In the divisive battle of the 1979 Devolution Referendum, which was played out daily on BBC Wales radio and TV, the role of the Welsh language became the central issue. Leo Abse shared the strong anti-Welsh language views of the young MP Neil Kinnock and the older George Thomas, which effectively divided the Labour Party for another 15 years as they resisted the Labour Government's official policy in favour of devolution. Wales-based Government ministers were real heavyweights. They included Prime Minister Jim Callaghan; John Morris, the long-serving Secretary of State for Wales; Cledwyn Hughes, one of his predecessors and the highly respected Minister for Agriculture; Leader of the House and MP for Ebbw Vale Michael Foot. All but six Welsh Labour MPs supported the official policy, yet they failed to carry the people with them. The build-up to the 1979 referendum was bitter, fuelled by Abse's cries of Welsh-language 'fanatics'. Glenys Kinnock's claim that children in her native Anglesey had to ask to go to the toilet in Welsh also hit home. The continuing public protests of the Welsh Language Society and the success of Plaid Cymru in 1974, when three MPs – Gwynfor Evans, Dafydd Wigley and Dafydd Elis-Thomas – were elected for the first time, acted to reinforcce the anti-Welsh element of the 'NO' campaign if not the long-term devolution process. The result was decisive. The rebels won. John Morris famously 'recognised the elephant at the door'. Patrick Hannan told me, 'Welsh politics is dead for a generation.' He was right.

The next referendum would not take place for another 18 years.

Two months' later Mrs Thatcher came to power. The tone of British and Welsh politics would change dramatically. The failure of the 1979 referendum sparked a wave of public protests on behalf of the language and nationalism with no single target. The Welsh Language Society intensified their campaign for a fourth television channel, in Welsh; the farcical Free Wales Army and the sinister Mudiad Amddiffyn Cymru (MAC) continued their sporadic marching and bombing respectively; but it was the mysterious burning of second homes by Meibion Glyndŵr [The Sons of Glyndŵr] which was new. The increasing number of second homes being bought by English people in rural Welsh-speaking Wales were targeted for the next ten years by one or more arsonists who were never identified despite a number of high-profile arrests and considerable embarrassment to the police. One Chief Constable in west Wales invited the Managing Director of HTV, Emyr Daniel, and myself to dinner at the Bridgend Police HQ one evening. He found it difficult to believe that our respective newsrooms had no inkling as to the possible culprits.

It was towards the end of James Callaghan's government of 1974–6, with its wafer-thin majority, which marked the high point of Plaid Cymru's influence when its three MPs could determine or delay events. Before entering Parliament, Plaid Cymru MP Dafydd Elis-Thomas had been a lecturer at Coleg Harlech, 'the college of the second chance' for mature students who had missed out on an opportunity to go to university for various reasons. He moved on to lecture at University College of North Wales, Bangor, but had hardly had time to settle there before Plaid Cymru came calling. Possessing cultural depth and the quickest of minds, Dafydd 'Êl' was an expert at exploiting media coverage, including a crafty habit of sending out press releases on Saturday nights, knowing full well that the Sabbath was usually a weak news day. He quickly became one of the most interesting, entertaining and successful politicians of his generation. As President of Plaid Cymru he was never afraid of going against the flow. He disagreed with Gwynfor Evans's threat to fast to death in the fight for a Welsh TV channel and continued to take an interest in broadcasting matters. He left Parliament and became the highly respected first Presiding

Officer of the new Senedd in Cardiff, giving due weight to the constitutional basis of the devolution process. Now a lord of the realm but out of office, he became a loose cannon on his party's decks and resigned the Plaid Cymru Whip at the turn of 2017. Whenever given a responsible position however, Dafydd Êl has always given of his best.

Dafydd Wigley, who had worked as a manager at the Hoover factory in Merthyr, was a straight-talking interviewee, strong on economic policy, who stood in the pragmatic centre ground of Welsh nationalist politics. The two Dafydds were totally different in temperament and attitude, despite following similar career paths as presidents of their party. Both served as MPs and AMs and were elected to the Upper House. The other strange fact they had in common was that neither was re-elected to lead their party, despite being by far the ablest of their kindred political spirits. Wigley was prone to complaining to the BBC on behalf of Plaid Cymru at every opportunity. On one occasion he complained about the publication on *Wales Today* of a professional poll showing Plaid Cymru in a poor light, and he was proved to be right. He kept up the pressure on BBC Wales, and the number of complaints he made over several years suggested an obsession about a news bias which I never understood. BBC Wales had always been regarded with suspicion by some Labour MPs for an alleged pro-nationalist bias, so we therefore concluded that being blamed by both sides meant that the newsroom must be doing something right.

Patrick Hannan was not the only person to join BBC Wales from the *Western Mail* in the 1970s. The lively Roy Roberts was another experienced journalist from the same stable, a first-class reporter and industrial correspondent whose ambition led him to be promoted to senior programme posts in the English regions. It robbed Wales of potential managerial material. Roy's ebullient personality was such that even a chance meeting would begin with a torrent of rapidly-fired questions. The journalist in him never switched off.

David Morris Jones had by now become a powerful presence in the newsroom. He resented any interference from senior management, whether it was over a change of schedule or a criticism of presentation. He guarded the independence of news vigorously against all-comers, often by just 'forgetting' to implement advice on presentation. David's only blind spot was sport. Peter Walker remembered the difficulty of selling him sports packages on any subject other than the annual Barry yachting races near where David kept his own modest dinghy. Fortunately, we had enough sporting coverage elsewhere.

Very occasionally, in the 1980s, a conflict would arise between David and me on questions of public interest. David had reason to be angry when I instructed him to 'pull' a planned item reporting on armed police in Llanelli. The Chief Constable phoned and asked me to withdraw the item but refused to tell me why the police were armed. I could not censor a news item unless it was in the public interest to do so. He relented and said that they were expecting an armed robbery in the area and wanted to retain the element of surprise. I accepted his argument but it was one of only two occasions I had cause to stop a story in 16 years. The other was over a simple matter of fact.

It was only in the 1980s that women made an impact on *Wales Today*. David reminded me of Jayne Case's contribution in earlier days, but later Noreen Bray and Sara Edwards presented the programme. Vincent Kane was not best pleased when told of the move to dual presentation. Noreen not only shared screen time with him with great success but was sorely missed as a true professional when she decided to go into public relations work. Sara, the daughter of distinguished actress Gwenyth Petty, began presenting the programme in the late 1980s following experience of making documentaries for Capital Radio in London. She was the sole presenter of *Wales Today* until well after I left the BBC in 1990. By that time BBC Wales was in no danger of being criticised for a gender deficit during the constant growth of the services in the late 1970s.

Men still had their place fronting the programme, including the particularly friendly Christopher Morgan, a round-faced presenter of several years standing. Chris started in the religion department as part of the *All Things Considered* radio team, and eventually left *Wales Today* to become religious affairs correspondent for both the BBC and a quality Sunday newspaper. He knew the corridors of Lambeth Palace and the precinct of Llandaff Cathedral very well. Chris brought a modern journalist's insight into the workings of both the Church of England and the Church of Wales on long-running matters of modern theological dispute, such as the ordination of women. Sadly, he committed suicide at an early age, his funeral service in Llandaff Cathedral officiated by the Archbishop of Canterbury, Rowan Williams.

The expansion of broadcasting services – starting with radio services in the 1970s – required the newsroom to be restructured in order to cater for four separate channels. The task was a major managerial challenge. *Newyddion Saith* [News at Seven] was allocated the same length of time as *Wales Today* but with the added responsibility of covering international issues. Both Radio Wales and Radio Cymru had a mandate to prepare packages integrating the news of Wales, the UK and the wider world. From 1978 onwards each service emerged with their own stories to tell.

By the time S4C was launched, Arwel Ellis Owen had followed Owen Roberts as the editor of news and current affairs in Wales, in charge of a newsroom of over 100 people split into five units – an input desk and four outputs, each serving a different channel. When Arwel left to become Head of Programmes in Northern Ireland, David Morris Jones succeeded to the top job at last. David's safe pair of hands continued to guarantee senior management a good night's sleep, and he in turn was grateful for the support of his deputy, Deryk Williams. David's departure to English regional ITV in 1989 marked the end of an era in a newsroom which had grown beyond recognition in the previous quarter of a century. It also heralded a change in the status of *Wales Today* from being the dominant force in the newsroom to being the first – and most watched – among equals.

When *Wales Today* finally celebrated its 25th anniversary, it was appropriate to reflect on the greatest challenges it had faced during that time.

The Falklands War was second in importance only to Aberfan as a single traumatic event. It involved death and terrible injuries to Welsh soldiers on the troopship *Sir Galahad* and elsewhere in the conflict. When Britain goes to war, Welsh foot soldiers have historically taken more than their share of the losses.

The most important running story was, as always, the economy. By the mid 1970s the sudden resignation of Prime Minister Harold Wilson led to a Callaghan Government which failed to control inflation or the power of the unions. In 1979 Mrs Thatcher came to power. Her Chancellor of the Exchequer, Port Talbot-born Geoffrey Howe, turned the economy around with a famous but unpopular budget which cut income tax but raised interest rates, VAT and, as a result, even worse unemployment.

When I left the BBC I worked for Geoffrey Howe for six years. He was the Chairman when I was Director of the Thomson Foundation. Howe was the most courteous of men, a conviction politician who used to tell me of his belief that everybody had to suffer in the short run in order to get Britain back on track after Callaghan's disastrous 'winter of discontent'. He said he had to convince Mrs Thatcher that the pain was necessary but moved from the Treasury to the Foreign Office before the long miners' strike of 1984–5. However, he still exercised his influence on domestic policy as a cabinet minister until his resignation. Geoffrey may have been a quiet, thoughtful and very easygoing companion, but he never flinched from the terminal political pain he inflicted on Mrs Thatcher when he delivered the 17th draft of his resignation speech in the House of Commons which led to her

61

downfall in 1990. It was the ultimate revenge for the public bullying he had received from her over many years.

The Chernobyl disaster's impact on sheep farmers in the hills of north Wales hit the most vulnerable people in the rural community as it lurched from one crisis to another at the will of the market, milk quotas, the vagaries of the weather, or the outbreaks of various animal diseases. In the wider community floods washed away houses, droughts led to water rationing and people continued to be killed on the roads. There were fraud cases, murder trials, and more, much much more.

Wales Today was always dominated by events. As time passed, one obstacle after another to meeting tight deadlines was overcome with the help of new technology. Autocue eased problems for presenters; light video cameras replaced film; computers replaced typewriters; the fax machine replaced the teleprinter, but the BBC Wales newsroom had entered its second quarter of a century before the internet becamse an useful tool.

Only one thing never changes: the quality of the content which has been enhanced since my time by the addition of more special correspondents. The appointment of journalists committed solely to health and education has revolutionised two key areas of universal concern; culture is now given due recognition; the split between business and economics allows for added depth. After 1997, the opening of the Senedd brought an expanded political unit to the newsroom. This was the very time when competition in broadcasting and the press weakened when the influential British daily newspapers pulled all their correspondents out of Wales. It left BBC Wales as the most important source of news for the whole nation, indeed the only provider of news for four of the five broadcasting channels.

5

A Time to Laugh

MOVING FROM RADIO to TV in 1966 involved leaving the engaging gossips of the Park Place canteen for the aptly named General Accident building in Newport Road. All the TV offices, except the newsroom, were located there. The buzz in TV was unmistakable; the dress of the largely young intake of 1964 very informal and the laughter during coffee breaks often generated by the characters of 'Light Ent'.

The brightest star in Welsh was, of course, Ryan Davies, who worked on stage, film, TV, and pantomime at Swansea's Grand Theatre. Ryan was a superb comedy actor capable of playing a vast range of characters which delighted his audiences everywhere. He acted as second voice to Richard Burton in a film of *Under Milk Wood* and his partnership with the often underrated Ronnie Williams attracted big audiences in Welsh and English. Ryan could entertain audiences in mime or song and play the Celtic harp with humour or pathos as required. His hilarious rendering of the Russian 'Kalinka' with the Richard Williams Singers was one of the greatest of his many memorable moments on the screen.

Ronnie Williams wrote many of the sketches for Ryan and Ronnie and, although playing straight man to Ryan, brought a sense of timing and an indefinable chemistry to the partnership which was the hallmark of a classic period of comedy characterised in England by *The Two Ronnies* and *Morecambe & Wise*. Unfortunately, Ryan and Ronnie were never as convincing to an English audience in their three afternoon network series as they were in Wales. They never gave themselves the time or had the back-up required to produce enough material tailored to the British audience. *Morecambe & Wise* were given a whole year and a massive budget to prepare for each of their last few Christmas shows. Ryan and Ronnie were always travelling the length and breadth of Wales performing late night gigs before appearing for TV rehearsals the following morning. It was a crazy schedule which, viewed retrospectively, could never last.

When the partnership broke down in 1974, Ryan continued to star in one-man shows and the Welsh sitcom *Fo a Fe* [He and He]. Ronnie never recovered from the break-up. Their last summer season in Blackpool ended early and had to be rescued by 'King Rat' Wyn Calvin, whose huge circle of friends in the Variety Club answered his call at short notice.

By the mid 1970s three great stand-up comedians emerged representing England, Scotland and Wales: Jasper Carrott, Billy Connolly and Max Boyce. Successful stand-up comedy is the rarest of broadcasting gold dust and all three took turns to entertain network audiences in very different styles. Max's father had died in a colliery accident before Max was born. He had little choice but to follow his father down the pit as an electrician for ten years. That decade underground not only coloured his attitude to life but also inspired him to write two iconic songs loaded with pathos, 'Duw, It's Hard' and 'Rhondda Grey'. An early appearance on the pop programme *Disc a Dawn* [Disk and Talent] in 1971, singing a Welsh folk song accompanied by his simple guitar playing, showed little sign of a future as a great entertainer. Gradually, Max developed into the storyteller who sang of the glories of Welsh rugby in the 1970s. He drew heavily on his 'innocent' boyhood memories centred on his alter ego Billy Williams, stories which could last up to eight minutes at a time. In the halls and on his best-selling records, such as the iconic *Live at Treorchy*, Max could recycle those stories until honed to perfection. If ever there was an essence of Welshness in the English language, it was Max. If ever there was a golden period of laughter in BBC Wales, it was the decade or so between 1966 and 1977 when first Ryan, and later Max, built a momentum in both languages without ever working together.

The dominant figure in creating the Welsh-language team of singers, performers and producers in 1964 was Dr Meredydd Evans. 'Merêd' had returned to Wales from Princeton University armed with a Ph.D. in Philosophy and wedded to Phyllis, an American soprano with the Carl Rosa company. He was already well known in Welsh-speaking Wales from his university days in Bangor where his trio, specialising in humorous songs, had been extremely popular on radio in the 1950s.

Merêd started work on creating a new tradition of Welsh-language light entertainment in TV, spurred on by a huge and restless creative energy combined with a vision so strong that he steamrollered all opposition to his departmental requirements. In his dealings with senior management there were often raised voices and much slamming of doors. Merêd admitted that when he returned to Wales following years in America, the entertainment scene seemed restricted to the popular evening events in the towns hosting the National Eisteddfod. The London Welsh *Noson Lawen* was always best in the late 1950s and early 1960s, and he therefore had no choice but to build his department around a creative young group of mainly teachers based in London. In the course of barely a year, he offered full-time contracts to schoolmasters Ryan Davies and Rhydderch Jones, together with their organisers behind the scenes, brothers David and Bryn Richards, who became their producers. All performers had to justify their contracts by taking part in a variety of other programmes, particularly for a grateful children's department. One versatile presenter and singer was Mari Griffith. She remembers the time as being part of a repertory company moving from light entertainment to children's series before doing a stage tour and then back to light entertainment, working hard and playing very hard. The Ryan and Ronnie entourage included the ubiquitous Alun

Williams, singer Bryn Williams, with actor and bass player Derek Boote boosting Benny Litchfield's orchestra.

Rhydderch Jones separately teamed up with another former schoolmaster, Gwenlyn Parry, to become the greatest writing duo in Welsh TV. Ryan combined with them both to produce the most popular situation comedy ever on Welsh TV. *Fo a Fe* played on the differences of language and cultural behaviour between north and south Walians when a young married couple take in their respective fathers-in-law to live with them. South Walian father-in-law Ryan kept pigeons and drank beer in his local club which shocked the teetotal, organ-playing, chapel-going Guto Roberts from north Wales. Fine comedy acting from Clive Roberts and Gaynor Morgan Rees made up a perfect quartet for a high-quality series which always topped the ratings.

It was so successful that an attempt was made to convert the comedy into English through the introduction of an English – rather than a north Walian – father-in-law, but the script did not work. The Englishman was too stereotyped. *Fo a Fe* continues to be repeated more than any other series in Welsh and was the first Welsh TV programme to be sold as a video.

The sheer creativity of their output was such that a managerial blind eye allowed them the freedom to write whenever the muse took them – or as Rhydderch put it, 'tra bod y ceffyl yn cachu' [as long as the horse shits].

In fact, the light entertainment department always won top marks in the mythology of BBC Wales for its madcap lifestyle. Every Friday lunchtime Merêd would shout 'Staff Outing!' down the light entertainment corridor, then lead a mass departmental exodus, first to the BBC Club in Newport Road, followed by the ritual crawl around the 22 Club, the Spanish Club and wherever else until the early hours. To be fair, they were often in the studio on Sundays, the larger shows recorded in Birmingham because of a lack of studio space in Cardiff.

The light entertainment Christmas party was the highlight

of the social year. It was regarded as an honour to be invited to a loosely structured event in which everybody present had to participate. Top of the bill and compère each year was Rhydderch, who was always expected to recite his version of 'Carmarthen Bridge' *à la* Dylan Thomas, and always an original 'poem' which gently satirised everybody present.

Merêd launched *Lloffa* [Burrowing], a quiet and illuminating panel discussion between four erudite academics challenged with interpreting Welsh words, phrases, place-names or objects of unusual interest. They wore their knowledge lightly and with considerable wit. It featured the diminutive but celebrated figure of poet and professor Sir T.H. Parry-Williams, who had a particularly distinctive and attractive monotone timbre in his voice. 'Parry Bach' arrived in the studio with a briefcase full of research for the programme which he distributed to the other knowledgeable panellists, expecting them to follow his lead. Chairman Frank Price Jones and panellists Roy Saer, Prys Morgan and a dozen other guest panellists always strayed from the great man's brief but the chemistry between them worked to perfection. Studio director Ieuan Lewis remembered how 'Syr Tomos', relaxed after the recording, would sip sherry in the Green Room and hint to his wife, Lady Amy Parry-Williams, that a second glass, poured quietly without being noticed, would not go amiss. *Lloffa* ran for years until the day 'Parry Bach', then in his mid 80s, felt he was no longer able to remember the occasional word. The series died without the presence of its 'X Factor'.

Merêd's successor as Head of Light Entertainment was Jack Williams who had worked for many years in the theatre. He was a friendly, bearded and somewhat bohemian figure who had once lived in a barge on a London canal. Jack was serious and well read, thoughtful and good company. His Welsh-language satirical series, *Stiwdio B*, included a clever soliloquy by Criccieth-based actor Stewart Jones denouncing the ills of the world – and his neighbours – which translated to other programmes for many years. At the end-of-series party held at his Caerphilly home, the cast discovered that Jack and his artistic wife Jean had painted the longest inside wall of the house with colourful naked images of all his performers!

The senior woman in light entertainment was Ruth Price, a former headmistress of the first Welsh-medium school in Pontarddulais. She had made a name for herself in the *Daily Sketch* newspaper for standing firm while fighting to retain a proposed new school building for her pupils. Ruth always cherished the memory of the *Sketch*'s headline, 'Monroesque Headmistress'. Sam Jones, the Head of BBC Bangor, had admired Ruth's spirit and appointed her as a children's radio producer in Bangor before she moved on to work for Merêd in his new TV department. She always claimed to have given a first appearance to Max Boyce and Mary Hopkin, both in Welsh.

Neither Max nor Mary were in any way representative of the 'Swinging Sixties', the decade of American rock, Mick Jagger or the Beatles, a time when many young people broke away from the 'Thou Shalt Not' hanging in the front rooms of their God-fearing parents and the stifling atmosphere of the chapels. A new scene gradually appeared in Welsh as music groups emerged, disappeared, and re-emerged with different drummers and lead singers, depending on their particular brand of folk and rock, or even where their day jobs had taken them to live. Ruth Price latched on to the mood of the times and produced three very different music shows. *Hob y Deri Dando* featured the Welsh folk scene with groups such as Hogia'r Wyddfa [Snowdon's Boys]; another was the first Welsh pop and rock programme *Disc a Dawn*, presented at one time by the serious-minded future Chief Executive and Chairman of S4C, Huw Jones. He had made his name with one angry pop song, 'Dŵr' [Water], a protest against the drowning of Capel Celyn to make way for the building of the Tryweryn dam near Bala. It stands alongside the more numerous protest songs of Dafydd Iwan as a classic of the genre.

Semi-professional bands played gigs in halls all around Wales. 'Bando' and 'Ac Eraill' [And others] were early entrants to the scene. 'Tebot Piws' [Purple Teapot] was one band which really took off when it found Dewi 'Pws' Morris, the anarchic practical joker who could sing and act better than he played the guitar. He ended his career in rock as a lead singer of the phenomenally popular 'Edward H. Dafis'. 'Pws' has been one of Wales's genuinely funny entertainers on stage and screen, including years as a straight actor in soap opera *Pobol y Cwm* [People of the Valley] and comedy actor in the highly popular *Grand Slam*. He brought laughter to a musical scene which ranged from the political and satirical to the romantic and sentimental. Dewi 'Pws' never pretended to be the greatest of musicians. Cleif Harpwood had a better voice, as did Emyr Wyn, another well-known actor with a strong personality regularly seen on *Pobol y Cwm*. The combination of radio and TV, gigs and recording labels produced in particular by Sain in Caernarfon, all added up to a vibrant age of Welsh folk and rock. The Denbigh National Eisteddfod of 2013 featured three different shows by Edward H. Dafis, Hogiau'r Wyddfa and Dafydd Iwan. Most were nearing 70 years of age, having emerged nearly 50 years previously! Many artistes from that era will remain in vogue for decades to come through their recordings and the radio. Dafydd Iwan is the exception. As noted, he originally made his name performing his own protest songs on HTV's *Y Dydd* every week in the late 1960s, and still fills the halls with as many last appearances in Welsh as Tom Jones.

Ruth's favourite male artist was Meic Stevens, an eccentric who inspired many of his peers with his totally original songs and brilliance on the guitar. A notoriously unreliable character, Meic never turned up on time and sometimes not at all. Ruth persevered and played the headmistress all over again. She constructed a safety net of sorts by ensuring two other leading singers and songwriters, Endaf Emlyn and Hywel Gwynfryn, were available to keep an eye on Meic in between rehearsals, both of them students of the huge talent he brought to the Welsh music scene.

Her favourirte female singer said she had merely accompanied a friend to an audition with Ruth Price with no intention of doing anything herself, but did bring a guitar to while away the time. In a break between auditions, Ruth noticed her guitar and asked her to play anyway. Iris Williams passed the audition and her friend failed. Iris walked home happy but on her own. Ruth once asked Hywel Gwynfryn to compose a lyric suitable for Iris to sing but then cancelled it. She had already found something suitable – William Williams Pantycelyn's great hymn 'Pererin Wyf' [Amazing Grace]. It made Iris a household name in Welsh Wales. She continues her career in New York and on cruise ships, following in the footsteps of Alun Williams, Johnny Tudor and Margaret Williams.

English-speaking young people had no outlet for rock and roll in those early days. Instead Iris, Johnny, Heather Jones, Frank Hennessy and Dave Burns (who became the Hennessys) were given their break by learning songs in Welsh. The latter made their name with the evergreen 'Kerdiff Born and Kerdiff Bred'. Their catchy Irish sound added a different dimension to the folk music of the time, although a mystery surrounds lead singer Frank Hennessy's pronounced accent. Was it genuine or adopted? Whatever the truth, Frank became a first-class broadcaster in his own right on Radio Wales and is still going strong 30 years on.

Heather Jones was one of two young starlets to emerge in the late 1960s. Mary Hopkin was the other. Both had that purity of voice which made them an immediate hit. Mary retained her shyness even after reaching number two in the US charts with her most memorable hit 'Those were the Days' in 1968. She retired from the front line to raise a family and never really enjoyed the limelight.

Heather quickly built a leading role for herself on the Welsh scene under the initial influence of husband Geraint Jarman and Meic Stevens. She was doubly talented, equally at home in both rock and folk, as well as a prolific songwriter. The trio lived and worked at Meic's village of Solva for a time, developing a new genre in music-making which Ruth Price claimed helped improve standards of singing on her programmes.

Three other outstanding young women emerged, two from early appearances at the National Eisteddfod: Margaret Williams, and much later, comedienne Caryl Parry Jones. Margaret's voice, combined with perfect diction, prompted the production of several TV series in her name which included recordings of many memorable melodies. The lyric composed for her by Ryan Davies, 'Pan Fo'r Nos yn Hir' [When the Night is Long], is as much hers as 'My Way' is to Frank Sinatra. Margaret sacrificed a possible training in opera in order to make her mark as the leading lady in Welsh light music and as a member of Ryan's travelling troupe of entertainers.

Ruth Price remembered the younger Caryl Parry Jones appearing for the first time in her school choir. She has developed over the years into the leading multi-talented singer and comedienne working in Welsh media. Caryl writes her own comedy sketches and songs and has a gift for mimicking different accents, whether of hippies, teachers of eisteddfod competitors, or the clichés of rugby players' sound bites. Over 30 years on from her schoolgirl start, Caryl remains a national treasure.

Gillian Elisa Thomas also stands out, having taken a very different route with her ability to sing, dance and act. She took the part of Sabrina in *Pobol y Cwm* for years but was equally at ease in Variety, playing the halls as a stand-up comedienne. Gillian Elisa was a favourite on TV's *Noson Lawen* show before breaking into musicals in London's theatreland. This peaked with playing the role of grandmother in *Billy Elliot* for five years from 2011. Gillian's outgoing personality would surely have conquered London earlier if only Wales had a professional tradition in the musical theatre which dominates the West End.

A whole raft of popular soloists, duos and groups became household names through TV and gigs – the all-female 'Y Diliau', Tecwyn Ifan, Tony and Aloma, Aled and Reg, Ar Log and Mynediad am Ddim – all added to the variety of artistes available to Ruth Price in that particular era.

Throughout that time a much more experienced producer had been working quietly in the wings. Hywel Williams was one of BBC Wales's 'apprentice boys' who had joined the army in 1944 and had been recruited by BBC Wales as a 'demobbed' soldier. He completed 40 years of service in broadcasting, mainly as a producer of music series including both *Stuart Burrows Sings* and *Margaret Williams*. He covered the great Albert Hall concerts featuring a thousand Welsh voices and was the first to use Owain Arwel Hughes to present programmes with the BBC Welsh Orchestra.

Merêd, however, was the steamrolling leader of light entertainment. For all his uncompromising attitudes, he created the happiest department in BBC Wales. His outbursts on the office telephone could be heard down the corridor, but they blew over as fast as a cyclone. Everybody kept their head down, knowing it would pass. As he left the office Merêd would call out, 'Os [If] mates, mates.' The departmental bond was always his primary concern. 'Hogia Ni' [Our lads].

When Aneirin Talfan Davies and D.J. Thomas neared retirement, Merêd was invited to take up a six-month attachment as a chief assistant to the management team. It was obviously not to his liking. He was not only compromised by his deep desire to join the public protests of the Welsh Language Society; he was also aware that a rip-roaring lifestyle led him to drink too much. Merêd left the BBC and became a teetotal alcoholic for the rest of his long life. When he died he was rightly lauded for his massive contribution – together with his wife Phyllis – to the cause of Welsh folk music and the Welsh language in general. It was a time during which he climbed the Blaenplwyf TV mast as a protest against the Conservative Government's refusal to countenance a Welsh fourth television channel and he often demonstrated his dislike of the BBC's Welsh-language policies.

Merêd distrusted the word 'British' in the title of the organisation but retained the deep mutual friendships he had forged with all of us working for it.

I argued with him until his death at the grand old age of 95 that he did more to convert larger audiences to the language during the decade he was Head of Light Entertainment than he did after leaving it.

'Arglwydd Mawr, Na!' [Good God, No!] Merêd would bellow in return.

I did not expect him to agree.

6

Trial by Live TV, 1966–70

MOVING FROM RADIO to TV in 1966 felt like going back to school. Adapting to the new medium was difficult in the days when filming on location in monochrome required a team of seven people moving around in a convoy of three cars; when shooting on video involved expensive outside broadcast units, including three bulky cameras and about 30 technical staff; when the two-inch videotapes had to be cut by razors; when presenters had no autocue and had to count down eight seconds and ten seconds to film and video. I had already dabbled in TV current affairs productions with *Week In Week Out*, but the greatest need for new blood was for Welsh chat shows on Sunday afternoons. It would be the TV studio, however, where I would learn a new craft while making embarrassing errors live on air on the way.

My new boss was Nan Davies, the highly respected Head of Welsh-Language Programmes. She didn't make me feel particularly welcome at first. Nan had a formidable record in developing her own team. She had risen from being Sam Jones's secretary in Bangor, moved through general programmes in radio before launching the daily TV flagship *Heddiw* in 1961. Her team consisted of two future Controllers, presenter Owen Edwards and producer Geraint Stanley Jones; a future Head of Light Entertainment, Jack Williams; a future Head of Bangor, John Roberts Williams, and Wales's first independent producer,

William Aaron. The quiet and unassuming Rhys Lewis, a fluent French speaker, was a highly effective producer who converted the grounds of the old British Steel building in Cardiff into the first BBC Wales garden and had directed dozens of Eisteddfod events with Geraint Stanley Jones, including the Swansea National Eisteddfod on that first trailblazing Saturday in August 1964 when they shared the whole afternoon with coverage of Glamorgan's cricket match against Australia from St Helen's.

Producing *Heddiw* as a news magazine was the Welsh equivalent of the network's *Nationwide*. It was originally transmitted five times weekly, live at lunchtime throughout the UK. Presenter Owen Edwards joined it shortly after its launch and was arguably the greatest TV broadcaster in Welsh in the 1960s. He was good-looking, possessed a good short-term photographic memory, and was an expert on the standard three-minute interview, always preparing carefully the last question but one in order to finish on time. He was supported on air by the lively John Bevan, the serious Mary Middleton, and evergreen Harri Gwynn, who used an old-fashioned egg timer during interviews. A procession of presenters passed through *Heddiw* in later years – particularly R. Alun Evans who replaced Owen Edwards in 1972 and was his equal in fluency, especially when he was talking off-the-cuff or 'filling time'. Alun turned out to be the best soccer commentator I ever heard in Welsh but gave it up when appointed Head of Bangor. Emyr Jenkins presented *Heddiw* before joining the planning department, and then became a highly successful Director of the National Eisteddfod. Arwel Ellis Owen was the programme's presenter and editor before becoming editor of news and current affairs for the whole of BBC Wales and, in time, interim Chief Executive of S4C. Emlyn Davies presented the programme in the 1980s and re-emerged as one of S4C's first commissioning editors.

Several journalists came from the equally successful HTV news programme *Y Dydd*, since *Heddiw* allowed more scope for feature items. In the future Gwyn Llewelyn, Sulwyn Thomas, Beti George, Richard Morris Jones and others would bring authority and experience to Radio Cymru and BBC Wales's *Newyddion Saith* on S4C.

Another early escapee from HTV was Deryk Williams whose first job at BBC Wales was to help me during a busy time in 1968 before hungry *Heddiw* soon swallowed him up. Deryk was the most entertaining of companions, a highly intelligent maverick with a wicked anti-establishment sense of humour, a remarkable memory and an impressive knowledge of European history. He became the first editor of *Newyddion Saith* on S4C and was much missed in the newsroom when he joined S4C, eventually as its Head of Programmes.

Aside from Owen Edwards, Nan's best find was Hywel Gwynfryn. While dining out in a local restaurant one evening she remarked on a young waiter's walk and ability to talk and, on discovering he was a student at drama college, invited him for an interview. Hywel never looked back, whether on *Heddiw*, children's programmes, as a song writer in light entertainment or as the most prolific broadcaster ever on Radio Cymru.

The contribution that *Heddiw* made to broadcasting in Wales was just as valuable for the many talents developed there as for the virtues of the programme itself.

Heddiw always opened with a news bulletin prepared in the newsroom, but required a constant flow of feature ideas in a magazine format demanding original human interest stories. I only edited it for two months during a summer break for John Roberts Williams and Geraint Stanley Jones and realised how dependent the Welsh output was on such a slim staff. Geraint Stanley Jones worked punishing hours, clocking up a massive mileage all over Wales, while co-producer John Roberts Williams opted to stay in the office. Nan would oversee her expanding empire while lying back in her swivel chair, her eyes alert, a quizzical look on her face, her head leaning on one hand to control a slight tremor, and one leg curled under her body; always thinking aloud in a quiet voice, always planning ahead.

The only person I knew well when I joined Nan's department was William Aaron who used to visit my family home in Aberystwyth to watch TV when on vacation from Oxford. His father, the ascetic Professor of Philosophy Richard Aaron, had taken no interest in buying a TV set in the late 1950s. William's quiet and engaging personality disguised a huge talent, illustrated best by a lyrical film he shot around the beautiful coastal area of Nantgwrtheyrn near Nefyn in north Wales. It featured the legend of two lovers, engaged to be married until on the eve of the wedding the bride-to-be disappears, her body only found when lightning splits a tree with her body lying inside.

I co-produced one Sunday afternoon series with William before he joined *Nationwide* in London and went to report the war in Vietnam with Max Hastings. Fifty years after becoming Wales's first truly independent producer, William still works when and where his whims take him. Our Sunday show brought together two totally different presenters – the polished and experienced Owen Edwards and first-timer Hywel Teifi Edwards, an uncut diamond who was a hugely popular lecturer at University College, Swansea, and a specialist on the history of Victorian Wales and the National Eisteddfod. Hywel held strong opinions, delivered in a loud voice with great humour, totally dismissive – in a light-hearted way – of all who challenged him, with a put-down heavily laced with choice language. Hywel brought a different dimension to Welsh programmes and was one of the few who forced people to listen. Even when his comments sounded extreme he could make people laugh. He did, however, have his detractors who believed he was loud and opinionated, but I liked the idea of using strong-minded individuals rather than depend entirely on smooth and often bland professionals. The mix of Hywel Teifi Edwards and Owen Edwards certainly contained creative tension between two men of completely opposite backgrounds, particularly when William Aaron insisted that Hywel present an item on Owen Edwards's family tree. That really tested Hywel's professionalism and was worth a laugh at Hywel's expense for a change.

Tied down by the instruction to produce a season of cheap chat shows in a small studio, I decided to escape from safe professional presentation altogether. I teamed Hywel Teifi Edwards up with the unpredictable and much more eccentric John Davies, then a lecturer at Swansea's prestigious Welsh History department who would eventually publish the standard work on the history of Cardiff as well as the phenomenally successful Penguin *A History of Wales*. In the 1970s he became the popular warden of Pantycelyn, the Welsh student hall of residence in Aberystwyth which he ran rather like the father of an extended family despite his demeanour as 'one of the boys'.

The mischievous Hywel 'Aberarth' Teifi Edwards and bohemian John 'Bwlchllan' Davies were joined each Sunday afternoon by what I termed 'contrarian' guests. Their swipes against the cosy cultural norms of British and Welsh society resonated with a younger generation despite being regarded as too extreme and opinionated by some viewers. One week we broke out of the studio and decided on 'living it up in London'. We spent three days with a stills photographer – I had no film allocation – visiting some of the places where the wealthiest top ten per cent looked for entertainment, a landscape largely unknown to a group of highly intelligent but wide-eyed young men from Wales. It was the visit to the risqué Bunny Club and the cracking of a bottle of champagne in the fashionable Trader Vic's of Mayfair which caused 'Old Wales' to protest when we went on air the following Sunday. Owen Edwards, then acting chief assistant to the Head of Programmes, complained that his mother had phoned him in disgust at the waste of money on such frivolities. For that matter, so did my mother-in-law. We enjoyed testing the prejudice and hypocrisy of it all.

Times were changing. The Swinging Sixties allowed for

greater freedom to challenge authority. David Frost's *That Was The Week That Was* had already launched the first wave of satire. The Beatles had barnstormed America and the sexual revolution was creating a generation gap between the young and their elders, particularly among chapel society. Everything and everybody was being questioned.

I recall radio producer Lorraine Davies making a lively series featuring Welsh university students. One group from Bangor included the radical Dafydd Elis-Thomas who would make a considerable impact on the Welsh political scene, as well as the brilliant intellectual Dafydd Glyn Jones who urged broadcasters to distinguish between 'da sâl' and 'sâl da' – in effect concentrate on producing good populist programmes rather than bad worthy ones.

I also liked the idea of encouraging a younger generation with strong opinions and invited another young Bangor intellectual, Derec Llwyd Morgan, to give full rein to his prejudices in his own personal short series *Y Brawd Llwyd* [Brother Grey], the title being a play on Derec's middle name, although he was anything but grey. Derec had a distinguished academic career which peaked with his appointment as Vice-Chancellor of University College of Wales, Aberystwyth.

My studio-based years in TV had already had a terrible start during the Aberfan disaster. There was more to come. Nan Davies acted as my editor when I became producer of another Sunday afternoon chat show, *Disgwyl Cwmni* [Expecting Company]. On one occasion she sent me to Tregaron to audition an old man who was said to have the ability to memorise 100 words, all randomly selected, and then repeat them in reverse order. Nan was right. His memory was phenomenal. I brought the old man to Cardiff to take part in a live programme. Between the Green Room and his seat in the studio, the occasion overwhelmed the poor man and he forgot everything while the sequence of words was actually running on the screen so that viewers could check his progress. Desperate embarrassment all round. My co-producer, the experienced but difficult colleague Ifor Rees, who organised the show every other week, congratulated me on my *faux pas* with a telling smile on his face. He was not the only ageing producer who seemed jealous of a younger generation. The series was presented by University College, Cardiff, Chemistry lecturer Dr Glyn O. Phillips and the ever dependable John Bevan. Glyn 'O.' was one of the most able scientists of his generation in Wales. He published a successful periodical in Welsh, *Y Gwyddonydd* [The Scientist], which popularised a range of subjects for the non-scientific reader. Glyn had a brilliant mind, with an unquenchable thirst for the knowledge of a wider world than his chemistry laboratory. In later life he travelled the world more than any other Welshman I ever knew, with institutes of science named after him in China, Japan, and back home on his native heath of Clwyd at Glyndŵr University where he became Vice-Chancellor.

The moment Nan Davies retired in the late 1960s was always going to lead to big changes. Geraint Stanley Jones wanted to follow his own programme interests. Owen Edwards and Hywel Gwynfryn had both moved on. During the two-month interregnum when I took over *Heddiw*, morale was low because of the uncertain future of both production staff and presenters. The gloom was so obvious that I tried to raise spirits by mounting an interview with Ryan and Ronnie on my first night in charge. Head of Programmes Aneirin Talfan Davies talked to me about my editing the programme full-time. I said I would if I had a free hand in selecting a new team with a fresh image, but he baulked at the scale of the change. I was released with a new freedom to film documentaries.

There was even more change when Richard Burton, Stanley Baker and Wynford Vaughan-Thomas headed the celebrity-laden board of the newly-launched HTV in 1968. They appointed BBC Wales's Head of Documentaries Aled Vaughan as their Director of Programmes. Aled was a great loss to a younger generation of producers, since we had expected he

These six broadcasters attracted the largest BBC Wales TV audiences in my time.

The BBC2 programme *Poems and Pints* combined the rare talents of L–R: Max Boyce, Ryan Davies, Mari Griffith and Philip Madoc in the 1970s.

Interrogator in chief Vincent Kane was a dominating presence on radio and TV in Wales.

Alun Williams was the most popular entertainer and commentator in both languages and both media for over 30 years.

A rare photograph of Dylan Thomas (seated extreme right) and the Kardomah Café circle comprising L–R: poet Vernon Watkins, John Pritchard, artist Fred Janes, composer Daniel Jones and Dylan, with producer John Griffiths (standing).

Swansea studio in the early 1950s.
From L–R: G.O. Williams (later Archbishop of Wales), Saunders Lewis, Brinley Thomas and producer Aneirin Talfan Davies.

Head of Programmes Hywel Davies (left) sees off Nan Davies and John Ormond for the first film on Patagonia.

Living it up in London. A 'shameful' programme in the Bunny Club in 1967, starring John Davies (back, to left), Hywel Teifi Edwards (seated, back to camera), Elfyn Thomas (also seated), while T. Glynne Davies engages a bunny.

The controversial President Makarios III of Cyprus was a courteous interviewee of Ednyfed Hudson Davies (seated) and myself.

Ryan and Ronnie were the most popular comedy duo ever in Wales.

Dr Meredydd Evans created a whole new TV Light Entertainment tradition.

Folk quartet Hogiau'r Wyddfa [The Snowdon Boys], always in perfect harmony.

Max Boyce's expressions had as much impact as his words. His rugby and Billy Williams stories could stretch as long as eight minutes. The most popular stand-up ever to come from Wales.

The popular Hennessys were Kerdiff born with an Irish lilt. Frank Hennessy (centre) and Dave Burns (right) had occasional additions, the first, Paul Powell (left).

Meic Stevens's talent was much greater than his self-discipline. His technical expertise took the scene to a different level.

Fo a Fe [He and He] is the most repeated TV series in the Welsh language. The two fathers-in-law clash. Ryan Davies (left) and Guto Roberts.

Rhydderch Jones, an outstanding writer of comedy drama.

Dewi 'Pws' Morris (left) never stops making mischief, whether on or off the set. Here with Alun 'Sbardyn' Huws (right) and Stan Morgan-Jones in the group Tebot Piws [Purple Teapot].

Versatile Caryl Parry Jones remains the leading comedienne in Wales.

Iris Williams was producer Ruth Price's favourite singer. She is always remembered for 'Amazing Grace'.

Mary Hopkin preferred the quiet life after her hit song 'Those were the Days'.

The young Heather Jones tiptoes towards a long singing career.

Margaret Williams launched her career when winning the Song for Wales in 1969.

The Lloyd George series starring Philip Madoc and Liz Miles was the biggest ever production made in Wales.

Stylish John Hefin, director of *The Life and Times of David Lloyd George*, *Pobol y Cwm*, *Grand Slam* and more.

Pioneer producer D.J. Thomas launched the brilliant career of drama writer Elaine Morgan.

Gwenlyn Parry was the most creative writer/ producer in BBC Wales. *Pobol y Cwm*, *Grand Slam* and his single plays have stood the test of time.

Pobol y Cwm calendar girl Sue Roderick sits in the buff for a good cause.

Actors Emyr Wyn (left) and Huw Ceredig (right) get to grips with Gwyn Elfyn in *Pobol y Cwm*.

L–R: Siôn Probert, Windsor Davies, Cissian Rees (make-up), Colleen O'Brien (costume), Alan 'Treasure' (dresser), Gwenlyn Parry, Beth Price, John Welch (lighting), and Mansel Davies (sound recordist) at the Parc des Princes filming *Grand Slam* after the match was lost.

Kenneth Griffith and a bus full of children starred in *Bus to Bosworth*. The children were beautifully behaved.

Charles Williams, as Mr Lollipop, MA, and Dame Flora Robson starred in a minor classic.

Dic Lewis's biopics, *Dylan* and *Nye*, were outstanding tributes to both men. He always chose to work with Paul Ferris in English and Meic Povey in Welsh.

Penyberth. The trials of three leading Welsh Nationalists for treason was the first time Welsh was subtitled on BBC2. From L–R: John Phillips as the writer D.J. Williams, Dyfan Roberts as the Reverend Lewis Valentine and Owen Garmon as Saunders Lewis.

BBC newsroom in Stacey Road, 1966. News editor Alan Protheroe bends over towards George Ashwell (extreme left), Jock Sinclair (standing with camera). Seated L–R: Hywel Morris, Clive Clissold, Arfon Roberts, PA Rosemary Allen (standing), Tudor Phillips, David Morris Jones and Handel Jones (foreground). Also standing in background is copytaker Mary Evans.

David Morris Jones (left) on his way to become Editor, Wales News & Current Affairs. With Clive Clissold, smoking a cigar, on his way out of the BBC.

David Parry-Jones presented *Wales Today* and rugby commentaries on *Sports Line-Up* for a generation of viewers. They are the most watched programmes on BBC Wales TV.

Winning *Round Britain Quiz* added to Patrick Hannan's reputation for acute political analysis over 25 years.

Editor Radio Wales News Gareth Bowen (in jacket), Robert Orchard (left) and current Head of Sport Geoff Williams (standing) in the modern newsroom with unidentified staff.

Week In Week Out editor Jeffrey Iverson (centre) briefs brothers Bob Humphrys (right) and John Humphrys.

Noreen Bray shared the presentation of *Wales Today* with Vincent Kane.

Sara Edwards came originally from London commercial radio to present *Wales Today*.

Carwyn James took two years off from *Sports Line-Up* analysis in order to win the Italian League with Rovigo and then meet the Pope!

Dewi Griffiths was the best rugby director of his day. His crew covered the Lions tour of South Africa in 1968. Here with cameraman Russ Walker (exteme right), Ken Mackay (assistant cameraman, extreme left) and sound recordist Ted Doull (right of Dewi). Doull was the grandfather of cyclist Owain Doull.

Gareth Charles, currently rugby commentator of the professional game in both languages.

Huw Llywelyn Davies and Ray Gravell made a great team covering S4C's first Wales–England match in 1983.

John Hardy, the long-serving soccer commentator, who has the memory to exploit the radio archives.

Former Wales rugby captain Onllwyn Brace motivated his young staff as Head of TV Sport for over 20 years.

Geraint Jones, newsreader and snooker commentator, partnered John Evans on S4C.

would be our new boss when Nan retired. Aled had a caring and sensitive nature who would often answer 'Why not?' when new ideas were tested in the canteen – a positive attitude of support we needed.

Aled had some distinguished programmes to his record including the documentary *The Shepherds of Moel Siabod* which recorded the tough communal lifestyle of Welsh hill farmers which was fast dying out. His most memorable series was a riveting six-part biography of nonagenarian writer and raconteur Jack Jones, delivered straight to camera. Jack's long life allowed him to reflect on the turbulent social history of Wales spanning two world wars and the Great Depression of the inter-war years, all presented as a seamless sequence of stories.

Following Aled's defection to HTV and Nan's retirement, I now had a new boss, the highly intelligent but contrary senior producer Selwyn Roderick. Only the third person to be appointed a TV producer in Wales, Selwyn had started as an outside broadcast director of rugby, religion and even *Come Dancing* in the mid 1950s. He had since built a deserved reputation as a film-maker, but he was no manager. Selwyn was totally disorganised, expecting his PAs to save him at every turn. In 1970 I was his junior co-producer covering the Ammanford National Eisteddfod. It did not go well. Despite his vast experience in outside broadcasts, Selwyn told his PA Rosemary Allen to 'shut up, woman!' when she reminded him twice that presenter Carwyn James was one link short for the 15 items tied to only two reels of videotape. The inevitable happened. Halfway through the show Selwyn ran in front of the live cameras, hurriedly scribbling words for a bemused Carwyn. It was a total shambles. We were never asked to cover the Eisteddfod again.

It was too late for Selwyn to change. He was an individualist who knew what he wanted when filming but operated on a whim rather than a plan, but his films on the Welsh in Patagonia, edited in both languages, matched the standards set by John Ormond's earlier expedition. A 1968 film, called *Tamed and Shabby Tiger*, shot on location in Cardiff's Tiger Bay, demonstrated Selwyn's ability to cajole the great characters of a unique ethnic community into talking brilliantly on camera. It included a fascinating insight from Shirley Bassey on her early life in Cardiff's dockland. Selwyn's most sensitive film exposed the reality of the crippling disease which shortened the lives of so many ex-miners. *Pneumo* was a powerful tribute to a generation of colliers dying slowly from 'the dust', helped only by the large cylinders of oxygen delivered to their front door, but with no sympathy or compensation from the National Coal Board.

Selwyn's tantrums, however, made a working relationship impossible. No idea was good enough for him, particularly any mention of filming abroad which he considered his personal fiefdom. In the end several of us bypassed him and went directly to Head of Planning Owen Thomas who needed a full schedule of programmes without further ado and allocated the resources required. Selwyn, with great panache, continued to build his own distinguished portfolio of films which were never boring or predictable, in fact rather a reflection of his own character.

Socially, Selwyn could be both engaging and entertaining, even caring in private. The music at his funeral service mixed Welsh hymns with the left-wing anthem 'Internationale'. It was the last request of a memorable maverick.

Selwyn's most senior colleague was the award-winning film-maker John Ormond. If Selwyn had been the first full-time outside broadcast producer, John was a pioneer documentary maker who built the BBC Wales film unit. It was the first group of really professional film editors and camera crews to be appointed in Wales.

John had already made two award-winning films when I first joined the department. The best was *Borrowed Pasture*, featuring two Polish soldiers and their struggle to scrape a living over the four seasons of the year from their run-down and isolated farmstead in Carmarthenshire. John used the first cameraman he had appointed, the tiny, busy Billy Greenhalgh on the project. He wrote his own verse commentary which was read by Richard Burton. He asked Arwel Hughes to compose a musical score based on the songs he had heard sung by the Polish farmers themselves. It was a truly outstanding 'handmade' film, and the one of which John was deservedly most proud.

John was always surrounded by a group of friends with varying cultural interests in his favourite watering hole. He engaged his listeners with his background in Swansea, followed by several years on the magazine *Picture Post*, a gap year spent in the world-renowned National Film Board of Canada, and two slim but superb volumes of poetry. Several poems, including 'The Cathedral Builders' and 'Salmon', count among the best writing in the canon of Anglo-Welsh literature.

I was grateful for the couple of weeks John spent on location trying to teach me the craft of shooting film. His last burst of film-making comprised self-portraits of some of the great artists and musicians he had befriended in Wales – Kyffin Williams, Graham Sutherland and Daniel Jones included. In 1983, when I was Head of Programmes, he came to my office clutching a bottle of sugar-free lager to say that he had run out of new ideas. He was too near retirement to offer him redundancy. It mattered not. He left a legacy of beautifully drawn programmes and a film unit which helped build programme standards at BBC Wales. John was never suited to being a slave of a modern schedule. His generation of producers made programmes with care, cash and conviction, but were allowed the freedom to do so regardless of when their documentaries would see the light of day.

The third member of that generation was the meticulous Gethyn Stoodley Thomas, brother of popular *Western Mail* sports editor J.B.G. Thomas. Gethyn produced a seminal series of films on his native Rhondda – *The Long Street*, and a telling portrait, *Ill Fares the Land*, on the depopulation of the Welsh countryside in the 1960s. However, he will be better remembered as the first producer of *Songs of Praise* which still runs on BBC1 to this day.

It was a generation which gave birth to a tradition of making documentaries in Wales which set a standard for future generations to emulate. The difference was that they were part of a cottage industry. The one-off documentary of their era gave way to programme series which had to build audiences over successive weeks. From now on we were expected to be the servants of a production line which existed to feed a constantly demanding schedule.

7

Freedom to Film, 1970–74

AN OLD MAN in a cloth cap cleaning somebody else's false teeth was not the most elegant shot to kick-start a career in filmed documentaries. T.E. Nicholas was not even a properly qualified dentist, but he was one great character, seemingly committed to two diametrically opposed faiths – Communism and Christianity. He was over 80 but was still preaching a unique brand of socialist theology as an ordained minister on Sundays while practising as a dentist during the rest of the week. As students we used to visit his house and listen to his view of the world order, always receiving the latest Chinese magazine illustrating the glories of 'the Great Leap Forward'. When asked why he enjoyed being a dentist his answer was, 'If you see something rotten you must pull it out.'

In reality it was his wife who was the qualified dentist but he had a small coterie of admirers who would risk an abscess in order to keep his company in the unhygienic shed 'down the back'. 'Niclas y Glais' had been jailed in Swansea during the war as a conscientious objector, and there he had succeeded in writing populist left-wing and patriotic poetry on toilet paper. He was known as 'Niclas y Glais' in memory of a chapel he had served in the Swansea Valley. During his long life he had not only had a 'calling' to a chapel in the United States, but also stood as an Independent Labour Party candidate in Aberdare in 1918, thereby continuing the campaign of his late friend

Keir Hardie in Merthyr and Aberdare. During his ageing years in Aberystwyth, however, he probably knew nothing about the young Aberystwyth graduate and *Western Mail* journalist Gareth Jones who first exposed the truth about the Ukrainian famine when Stalin was in power in the 1930s, and was murdered by bandits in Manchuria one day short of his 30th birthday.

There were several ageing, fascinating and colourful personalities who belonged to a bygone era and were living history, natural storytellers who had never been near a university. Under the title *The Changing Years*, I invited several people of a certain age to recount the stories of their lives. Albert Heal, a retired miner, recalled with great vigour the battle to establish the Independent Labour Party and extend trade unionism in Wales between 1900 and 1920. At the other end of the social scale Sir William Gladstone, then the Chief Scout of the UK and great-grandson of the nineteenth-century Prime Minister, maintained the memory of the 'Grand Old Man' on the family estate at Hawarden Castle in Flintshire where William Ewart Gladstone used to cut down trees by his own hand as his hobby.

Sir Julian Hodge was Wales's most prominent entrepreneur in the 1960s. He built a banking empire centred in a signature building bearing his name across the road from our Newport Road TV offices. Hodge had been much criticised for the controversial introduction of expensive second mortgages. Unfortunately his was the worst programme in the series, as he was determined to use it as a public relations exercise for his company. Even more embarrassing, Hodge wrote to all his shareholders urging them to write and congratulate me after transmission.

My two favourite men in the series, however, were Sir Archie Lush, the former agent of Aneurin Bevan, and Leslie Illingworth, one of the leading cartoonists of his age. They were both short in stature and impishly long in humour. 'Illingworth' was the signature on his artistic political cartoons in the *Daily Mail* and *Punch*. He lived in the Sussex countryside next door to Malcolm Muggeridge, but spent his days in the famous Fleet Street watering hole El Vino's thinking about his next target, the pictures and words drafted in pencil. Illingworth's best friend was the well-known broadcaster on archaeology, Dr Glyn Daniel, who went to the same Barry County School for Boys and said of Leslie that 'he suffered from two sad illusions; that he was ugly and that he was ignorant. He could not think of himself as a genius. The world will remember him as one of the great political cartoonists and draughtsmen of the twentieth century.' Leslie's personality and sense of humour was more than enough to 'talk my face away' as the radical John Wilkes once said of himself. I cherish the political cartoons he sketched so quickly on the programme, but I can imagine the furore he caused over the depiction of Churchill sitting listlessly at his desk, published in *Punch* on 3 February 1954, which cruelly underlined the call for the aged prime minister to resign. It was Illingworth's most telling testament.

Sir Archie Lush was Aneurin Bevan's alter ego. His cheeky chappy personality included a talent as a mimic, particularly of Nye himself. Archie imitated him, stammer and all, while recounting his stories of Nye practising his speeches high on the moors above Ebbw Vale to an audience of bemused sheep. Archie's humour was such that while recounting tales to me on one occasion at a Cardiff restaurant, he slumped over the table with a heart attack. Ironically, he was Chairman of the Welsh Board of Health at the time and, as he was stretchered into the ambulance, he could be heard threatening the paramedics on what they would suffer if they didn't treat him well. His half-humorous description of how he and Bevan searched for the levers of power was a classic. Together they looked in vain for it when on the local council, and again as county councillors. Bevan failed yet again in the search for power when he first entered Parliament – and only found it when he became Minister of Health.

It was a very special lady who graced the series, one Michael Foot called 'one of the most influential women of the twentieth century'. Frances Stevenson was the long-term mistress and private secretary of former Prime Minister David Lloyd George from 1913 until 1943 when he married her just two years before his death. In 1970 she had been difficult to locate, a reclusive figure living in small but beautiful cottage in Churt. Nearby, in the Surrey countryside, is a hostelry called 'Pride of the Valley', sporting the face of Lloyd George as its most famous former resident. Frances, still a handsome 82 year old, half-Scottish, half-French, had been aggrieved by an interview with Fyfe Robertson on the *Tonight* programme some years earlier when asked to name the father of her daughter Jennifer, born out of wedlock in 1929. It took me three visits to build a position of trust before she allowed me a lengthy interview for a 50-minute documentary on BBC2. She gave a unique insight into her influence on and relationship with Lloyd George during the whole of the First World War and the breakdown of the post-war coalition in 1922. Whatever the success or otherwise of that post-war government, Frances described how Lloyd George had guided the nation successfully through the 'war to end all wars' in three distinct stages; first by reorganising the munitions factories as the minister in charge, moving on to run the War Office after the death of Lord Kitchener, and finally replacing an 'indecisive' H.H. Asquith as Prime Minister in 1916. Frances talked of her attraction to Lloyd George.

'It was his eyes,' she said, and then a pause before she dropped her voice dreamily, 'He was a great lover.'

Her final thought about him ended the programme.

'He was different from all the others. He was Welsh and they weren't.'

She did not mention the obvious difference, that 'all the others' were from wealthy public school backgrounds and left Oxbridge expecting to rule an Empire armed with an effortless air of superiority.

Frances lived with her sister Muriel and near her daughter Jennifer. Muriel told me quietly that Jennifer was the daughter of one of Lloyd George's employees, Lieutenant-Colonel Tweed. Jennifer told me equally quietly she 'felt' she was Lloyd George's daughter. He had brought her up as his daughter and she called him 'Taid' – the term for grandfather in north Wales. The old lady said nothing. I suspected by this time she did not know herself. Research on possible dates of conception suggested that Frances probably slept with both men in the same month. She had certainly never told her own family. After Frances's death Jennifer told *Woman's Hour* she would take a DNA test, but I doubt that she did. The mystery has occupied the minds of historians to this day. I went to Frances's funeral in a Guildford crematorium. Only a small group of us were present – her immediate family and Lloyd George's old political friend Lord Boothby. In her will Frances made me a trustee of the Lloyd George Museum in Llanystumdwy near Criccieth, which was later transferred to the good care of Gwynedd County Council.

Illicit relationships were common enough in Lloyd George's day but they were never revealed in the press when he and Asquith were in power. Asquith used to write letters to his mistress Lady Venetia Stanley while chairing Cabinet meetings. I recall trying to interview an old lady in Criccieth who had once worked as a maid in No. 10, one of many installed by Lloyd George's wife Margaret to keep an eye on him. The old maid sent me packing, shouting after me, 'Whatever you say about Lloyd George – remember Asquith was worse!'

Making that programme on Frances Stevenson made me acutely aware of the greatness of a flawed genius who held his nerve during the most traumatic of times. Even before she knew him Lloyd George had launched the first old-age pensions in 1909 and won his other bitter battle against the landed gentry with the passing of the National Insurance Act of 1911, two acts which launched the British welfare state. Lloyd George had many faults and made many mistakes – the creation of the Black and Tans in Ireland, meeting Hitler, the Marconi scandal and more, but the sum of what he contributed to our lives in the long run outweighs that of any other British politician during the past century.

Reacting to current events in the 1960s, I had already come across Port Talbot-born Cardiff West MP George Thomas during my radio days. He was one of the best-known politicians of his day – much loved and hated in equal measure. His career took off when appointed Secretary of State for Wales during the run-up to the divisive Investiture of the Prince of Wales in 1969 before being elected Speaker of the House of Commons in 1976. George had bigoted anti-Welsh and anti-nationalist views, delivered to both colleagues and public, heavily laced with a sly and dismissive humour – and then the laugh, always the bronchial laugh. When conversing in company his innocent jokes were always delivered with great natural timing. He had the acumen of a streetwise politician, particularly when he saved the mid Wales railway line in a Cabinet meeting by interjecting: 'Prime Minister, one, two, three, four, five marginal constituencies.'

George was, however, deeply distrusted even by many of his own senior parliamentary colleagues, Michael Foot, Cledwyn Hughes and James Callaghan included. On the other hand he loved Margaret Thatcher and, after introducing me to her on one occasion, whispered in my ear, 'Isn't she a beautiful woman?'

George had great support from Harold Wilson. He enjoyed being at the centre of planning the Investiture. It split the nation in two. Choirs such as the Cardiff Polyphonic sang there with half their number missing. It even divided two prominent brothers – Elystan and Deulwyn Morgan – during the Urdd National Eisteddfod in Aberystwyth when Prince Charles accepted an invitation to speak there.

Around this time Charles took a break at Picton Castle, the home of Pembrokeshire's Lord Lieutenant. Charles had promised to introduce a scientific lecture on TV, the details of which I have long since forgotten. I arrived for the briefing meeting to be told by his secretary, 'Mr Price, please remember to walk out of his presence backwards when you leave.'

HRH was seated behind a desk in a large semi-circular room with the door disguised by bookshelves. The meeting was brief and civilised, but my mind was on my exit from his presence. Reversing, with one hand hoping to grope a hidden doorknob, reminded me of Charles's hero Spike Milligan singing 'I'm walking backwards for Christmas!' I am told that this goonish practice has long since disappeared but it indicated the degree to which the royal family led a surreal existence.

Meanwhile, George Thomas told me privately he saw the Investiture as a showpiece which would, as he told me, 'see off the Welsh nationalists'.

It has since emerged that Prime Minister Harold Wilson was more worried about the security of the whole operation, given the known activities of the mysterious MAC (Movement for the Defence of Wales) and the harmless nine members, arrested in 1969, who made up the Free Wales Army. He contacted Home Secretary James Callaghan and wondered whether it was wise to allow Prince Charles to attend Aberystwyth for a university term at all. Unusually, Callaghan and George Thomas agreed with each other and the Prince was taught Welsh. I thought it was highly irresponsible to gamble anybody's life in such a pointless exercise. Charles was a pawn in a high-risk political game. In the event two men, said to be from MAC, accidentally killed themselves on the evening before of the Investiture while plotting to create an incident. Charles was in a vulnerable situation throughout the summer of 1969.

At the time I was making the first film on the workings of the Welsh Office. George was happy to co-operate regardless of the feelings of his reclusive senior Welsh Office civil servants. He was filmed signing expulsion orders on behalf of the Home Secretary and talking to civil servants desperately trying their best to keep a low profile. It was the first time I met Sir Goronwy Daniel, the department's Permanent Under-Secretary who would become the first Chairman of S4C. We filmed him leaving Pembrokeshire in his mud-splattered Land Rover, dressed in morning suit, top hat and wellingtons, totally unaware of how incongruous he looked. We would meet often in the future, but he never told me what he thought about his former political boss.

George and I never trusted each other. The fact that I could speak Welsh was enough to put him on guard. I knew he thought BBC Wales was crawling with 'Welsh Nats'. What we did have in common was a tacit professional understanding. George wanted maximum publicity for himself while I wanted to make a film which threw first light on the hitherto hidden world of our devolved parliamentary powers.

Many National Union of Mineworkers (NUM) leaders in Wales were unavowedly Communist. Dai Francis was one of its secretaries who broadcast often in Welsh. Dai was honest, direct, rough with interviewers on air but the warmest and caring of human beings in private. I recall one special occasion when his son Hywel and fellow historian Dai Smith launched their seminal history of 'The Fed', the rousing story of the Welsh miners' union in the twentieth century. Dai was a proud father that day, relaxing with a large whisky with the greeting, 'nothing is too good for the workers!'

Former NUM General Secretary Will Paynter was in constant demand when back in Wales. He was one of the finest natural speakers I ever heard, such was his mellifluous flow of language. Ideological Socialism still existed through the ballot box in the 1960s not only with S.O. Davies but also with the highly respected Rhondda councillor Annie Powell. It was still possible to produce a debate between those who believed that Socialism owed more to Methodism than Marx, as opposed to many who had drunk deeply of all the Marxist literature in the local workmen's library and took a very different view.

As the mines gradually closed, historian Hywel Francis created the South Wales Miners' Library – having scoured the collections of the workmen's institutes of south Wales before they were lost to posterity. Hywel left the library at University College, Swansea, to become Labour MP for Aberavon until 2015, maintaining a proud family tradition of left-wing thinking as his party moved ever nearer to the political centre.

Both my grandfathers were miners working in the Gadlys and Aberaman districts of Aberdare. They were caught up in the desperate 156 days of the long strike of 1926 with its 'summer of soups and speeches'. Political correspondent Patrick Hannan's father was our popular Irish family doctor in Aberaman. We combined to produce a 50-minute documentary, *Not A Penny Off The Pay; Not A Minute On The Day*, the war cry of miners' leader A.J. Cook. The programme concentrated on the real suffering of the majority – the kids queuing up outside the soup kitchens, often without shoes on their feet; the male voice choirs collecting money on their tours of Britain; the women supporting the morale of men scrabbling for coal on the tips which surrounded the tightknit communities, sharing what little was available to maintain a modicum of normality. Fortunately, the sun-drenched summer of 1926 encouraged outdoor entertainment – the jazz and bazooka bands; the majorettes and the carnivals all alleviating the approach of the inevitable failure of the strike in a world changed by international competition and the increasing cost of mining the seams. It left communities embittered and in debt for a generation before the miners became essential again, this time for the war effort just 13 years later.

At the other extreme of the Welsh political spectrum, the reclusive right-wing President of Plaid Cymru, Saunders Lewis, made no bones about his total disdain for all things industrial, as epitomised in his savage poem, 'Y Dilyw 1939' [The Deluge 1939]. Saunders was no natural democrat. A distinguished university lecturer in Welsh, he retired to his Penarth home, keeping his silence in public for years at a time, often refusing interviews. Years had elapsed since his famous radio lecture of 1962 which had spurred Welsh students into launching

Cymdeithas yr Iaith [The Welsh Language Society]. I asked Head of Programmes Aneirin Talfan Davies to phone him for a filmed interview. Aneirin had been the only person to interview him on TV some five years earlier. This time Aneirin invited him for lunch at Cardiff's Angel Hotel to discuss possibilities. Saunders was a short man with pointed features who spoke slowly and sparingly in a distinctive nasal tone of voice. His conversation was reactive, never proactive. Saunders was a wine buff and a terrible snob. When I handed him the wine list he deliberately handed it back to me and I was forced to order on the basis of cost given my total lack of knowledge at the time. The somewhat tense discussion ended in a promise to be interviewed for only three minutes. Interviewer Meirion Edwards joined me in planning for a whole half-hour, just in case. Saunders spoke for 33 minutes. We sent the transcript to the BBC lawyers in London, who cleared a possible inflammatory reference to the need for social 'terfysg' or 'unrest' in pursuit of saving the language. Meanwhile, Lewis wrote me a letter stating that either the programme went out as a whole or not at all. Aneirin Talfan Davies asked him in to discuss the need to cut three minutes and I advised that a relatively unimportant piece on the University of Wales could be removed. There was a long silence and then Saunders uttered the words 'Ewch ymlaen' [Go ahead]. He left without a further word. Only former Conservative Prime Minister Edward Heath struck me as a colder man.

Most of the early Welsh Language Society activists belonged to my generation of university friends at Aberystwyth. The place was a hotbed of nationalist debate in the early 1960s.

Even before the Welsh Language Society had developed momentum, the issue of Welsh water became a major political problem. Emyr Llywelyn Jones was fired up by both issues and was one of three people jailed for a year. They were caught attempting to plant a bomb in the Tryweryn reservoir, being built by Liverpool Corporation, as a protest against the forced removal of all the local inhabitants of the Welsh-speaking village of Capel Celyn as well as the drowning of their homes, school and chapel.

The two issues of language and water merged at a time when many Welsh-speaking students were disillusioned by the failure of Plaid Cymru to gain ground in the polling booths. I first befriended Emyr 'Llew' when he was editor of *Llais y Lli* [Voice of the Sea], published as one half of the Aberystwyth college newspaper when I was English editor of *The Courier*, the other half. Emyr, now a retired teacher, remains to this day both a popular radical and the most likeable of men. Always easygoing in private, his political convictions made him a fiery and passionate public speaker and activist. Soon after his release from prison, he did tell me how difficult that time had been but took comfort from the fact that he helped make the prosaic issue of water a massive political issue. It even forced pacifist Gwynfor Evans to join the chaotic riot which ruined Liverpool Corporation's insensitive attempt to hold a celebration on the day the dam was opened. The importance of the issue in the 1960s was reflected in a now famous piece of contemporary artwork, 'Cofiwch Dryweryn' [Remember Tryweryn], painted on a derelict wall on the side of the road between Aberystwyth and Aberaeron by another university friend, Meic Stephens, who would later become Director of Literature at the Welsh Arts Council.

The Welsh Language Society developed momentum from 1963 onwards despite internal disagreement over tactics. There were long-running debates over the acceptable degree of damage to public property. The first memorable media event was a sit-down blocking the busy Trefechan Bridge in Aberystwyth, but some of the early leaders thought that was the wrong way forward. The faces I recognised on the network TV news during my two years in Belfast included historian John Davies; future MP and AM Cynog Dafis, who had been a friend of mine since schooldays in Aberaeron; Gareth Miles, a committed Communist who became a leading dramatist; Twm 'Trefor' Jones, a man devoted to his community and the brass band in the village of that name in Gwynedd; and later, Emyr 'Llew' himself. They were not the hooligans as often portrayed in the media but highly intelligent and principled people thinking seriously about ways to shake the political establishment out of its complacency over the state of the language, and heavily influenced by a Gandhist strategy of non-violent law breaking. They knew their disruptive tactics would make them unpopular, but they wanted to bring a sense of urgency to the situation. Inevitably, a couple of their successors did 'go over the top' in direct action against government ministers in particular, but no-one can deny that they succeeded in many of their goals.

When I tried to sum up the main events in Wales over the whole decade of the 1960s in a major review on Boxing Night 1969, Emyr Llywelyn, Welsh water and the Welsh Language Society loomed large.

In the previous year I had attempted an ambitious survey of contemporary Wales – a series of films on the state of the body politic, the economy, the arts, the language, sport and religion. It was an exciting project shot in both Welsh and English. I had the luxury of the highly experienced journalist and writer T. Glynne Davies as my presenter and consultant for six months. What the lovable, generous, but insecure T. Glynne sometimes lacked in timekeeping he made up for in the depth of his knowledge of Wales as an experienced journalist for both BBC Wales and the short-lived Welsh channel WWN. As the writer of a major historical novel, *Marged*, based on family life in his native Llanrwst, and a poet who had won the National Eisteddfod Crown in 1951, Glynne had seen it all but would never forget following the story of the Six Bells colliery disaster in 1960 as the most distressing of his life. He had a pessimistic and unsentimental view of life which often ran counter to mine. I needed his daily opinions as much as he needed the trek to the pub at day's end.

We called the Welsh series *Dan Groen y Genedl* [Under the Skin of the Nation] but my mentor in shooting film at the time,

John Ormond, insisted on the more prosaic title of *Check-Up* in English. In truth, Wales was in a fairly healthy state in the second half of the 1960s. James Griffiths and Cledwyn Hughes had protected the interests of Wales very well in the relatively new Welsh Office; unemployment never exceeded four per cent and would never be as low again; the Labour Government had invested heavily in the steel industry; light industries were attracted into newly designated development areas to combat the gradual closure of the mines at that time; the Labour Party in Wales held 32 out of 36 seats in the 1966 election. Its concern grew with Plaid Cymru in by-elections after Gwynfor Evans's breakthrough in 1966, followed by two by-election frights for Labour in Rhondda West and Caerphilly later in the decade, but even that faded temporarily in 1970. The fight to save the language was firmly on the political agenda, helped by the Welsh Language Act of 1967, a dramatic increase in the number of Welsh-medium primary schools and the escalation of Welsh Language Society protests. The Swinging Sixties in Wales gave a younger generation the impetus to rebel against their parents. They deserted the chapels in favour of gigs in the pubs and sex before marriage. In fact, referenda were still being held every few years on the issue of the Sunday closing of public houses in those parts of rural Wales where Nonconformity still had a hold on voter sentiment. In the end, the issue descended into total farce because those who wished to drink on the Sabbath merely used the local clubs. It was a time when there was every expectation of increased prosperity for all. Gambling on slot machines had taken hold among working people flushed with higher wages. To prove how wasteful a pastime gambling really was, T. Glynne Davies, who indulged regularly himself, insisted on being filmed operating a machine with five pounds in coins in one straight take. When the third coin was inserted, money poured out all over the floor. It made a great end to the programme.

The wider political implications of devolution were not even on the radar outside Scotland and Wales, despite the fact that the announcement of the establishment of the Welsh Office in 1964 would inevitably lead to a demand for an increase in democratic accountability sooner or later. Twelve years before the first referendum in 1979, I planned a major debate involving Wales, Scotland and Northern Ireland with the title *The Disunited Kingdom*. There was a fluttering in the dovecotes inside the BBC before I was allowed to go ahead. The networks turned it down flat. The newly appointed English Controller in Northern Ireland tried to dissuade me from pursuing the matter on his fragile territory, but realised that I had lived in the province longer than he had. It was agreed to present the programme from Glasgow, with film inserts from each of the three nations, with the well-known Canadian presenter, Professor Robert McKenzie, in the chair. It went well enough but the event itself caused hardly a ripple. It was a decade too early for such a debate.

There were much newer and more popular programmes to enjoy when colour TV was gradually introduced from 1969 onwards. It coincided with the growing interest in overseas holidays. Colourful international travelogues drew large audiences. It was a great opportunity for Welsh-language TV to embrace internationalism in a different dimension. When experienced broadcaster Ednyfed Hudson Davies lost his parliamentary seat in Conway in 1970, I asked him to present a new 26-part series called *Cywain* [Reaping] which ran for four years. Ednyfed was a polymath, with degrees in PPE from Balliol College, Oxford, and in Philosophy and Welsh from University College, Swansea. A lecturer in Economics at the Welsh College of Advanced Technology in Cardiff, he was a jack of all trades, 'a dabbler' in his own words, a dilettante in mine. I thought of him as one of the last of the great amateurs who was interested in how everything worked: from car engines to advocacy; from identifying poisonous mushrooms to edible snails; from broadcasting to photography; from cooking to eco-tourism. He practised at the Bar for a year without losing a case. He could have made a living as a gardener, chef or car mechanic, but satisfied himself in the end as Chairman of the Wales Tourist Board and then a chain of commercial radio stations while creating the first butterfly farm on the UK mainland. Ednyfed had both a butterfly mind and a phenomenal memory to go with his formidable intellect. During our first assignment abroad in Israel, he recited whole passages of the New Testament from childhood memory although he had long since become an atheist. During the same visit Ednyfed interviewed the ageing first Prime Minister of Israel, David Ben-Gurion, in his cramped one-bedroom flat in Tel Aviv. Warming to our information on how many Bethels and Bethanias existed in Wales, Ben Gurion ended a long conversation with the core policy of every Israeli government: 'Settle the land! Make the desert grow!'

It was said in 1970 that Israel still had the backing of the international community for its right to survive as a nation while living at peace with its Arab neighbours. Since then they have achieved wonders in growing the desert but have created hell on earth while settling more and more land.

When Prime Minister Edward Heath led Britain into the European Economic Community in 1973, it was a must to explore on *Cywain* the nature of a new level of bureaucracy which was bound to have implications for Wales. Three old college friends of mine were already working in Brussels. I had first befriended Gwyn Morgan when he was a junior deck chair attendant on Aberystwyth's promenade in 1957. He was a born politician and gifted public speaker but had been robbed of the Labour Party General Secretary's post in 1972 through the casting vote of anti-European Tony Wedgwood Benn. Gwyn switched to Brussels, first as Chef de Cabinet to the first British EEC Commissioner for Regional Policy, George Thomson, and followed it with ambassadorial postings to Israel and Canada, as well as being Head of the Welsh Information Office in Cardiff in the late 1970s. He ended his career with responsibility for the EU's diplomacy in nine Asian countries but had the capacity, given better luck, to go much further in the diplomatic world.

Aneurin Rhys Hughes surprised me when he joined Gwyn in Brussels despite his eventual appointment as an EU ambassador to both Norway and Australia. I well remember Nye's highly successful production of *The Crucible* at the National Student Drama Festival and always thought he would have done well in the BBC regardless of the fact that he was somehow related to Huw Wheldon.

The third member of the 'Welsh Taffia' in Brussels eventually became Director-General, Employment, Social Policy and Industrial Relations for the European Commission. I had noticed that Hywel Ceri Jones was a good administrator when President of the Aberystwyth Students' Union and I was the NUS Secretary. His fluent French was certainly of great advantage in Brussels's Berlaymont building. During this uncertain era of Brexit, it is good that Hywel is remembered as the founder and manager of the EC's important Erasmus Programme, a major educational project which Britain should, if necessary, pay to retain membership of in our post-Brexit world.

At sundown on most evenings, all three members of the Taffia could usually be found in the Irish pub where they resided in Brussels, and were a source of helpful advice to the Welsh media for upwards of 30 years.

Back in my office, Ednyfed scrutinised my scripts and was meticulous to the point at which he would often send me up the proverbial wall. He behaved like a dog with a bone, querying every sentence but infuriatingly he was usually right.

We portrayed a variety of exotic destinations long before they became tourist traps. Israel provided material for four memorable programmes, given Welsh interest in both its politics and religion. Hong Kong had many Welsh residents, the best-known being the banker J.R. Jones who had been driven out of Shanghai when the Communists took over. He left without his two Chinese servants and thought he had seen the last of them. It took them a year to track him down in his wealthy Hong Kong apartment, stuffed full of the most expensive jade. He had always been employed as an executive of the Hongkong Shanghai Bank (HSBC nowadays) ever since Lloyd George advised him to 'Go East, young man'. In Wales he was known as a philanthropist who supported many Welsh causes.

We travelled to countries which had no Welsh connections. Sierra Leone provided a portrait of a former British colony which was desperately poor yet rich in diamonds. Its capital, Freetown, had been created for the resettlement of former slaves released when the barbaric trade was abolished. The inhabitants further inland were the indigenous peoples living in the malaria ridden 'bush', without access to the prosperous diamond mines. My abiding memory is of filming the ceremony of turning on the first water tap in one village near Freetown. Little wonder that the country is a prime source of diseases such as Ebola over 40 years on.

One BBC executive wished to know what was Welsh about a programme on Iceland. Ednyfed snapped back, 'What's the English connection?' We wanted to prove that in Welsh you needed no excuses to reflect the whole world. In fact, it was schools' producer J. Mervyn Williams who asked us to share the costs of his project on volcanoes and glaciers in Iceland which led us there.

My motto for *Cywain* was, 'Go global, Go local'.

At the other end of the geographical scale, villages from all over Wales were portrayed for the same series. The traditional notion in Welsh of the rural *Milltir Sgwâr* [Square Mile] assumed a stronger sense of community than was possible in the cities. Cultural activities were still thriving in villages as diverse as tiny Trefor in Caernarfonshire with its brass band, or Felinfach's multi-purpose theatre in Cardiganshire.

The only incongruous fact of life was that we were recording with big outside broadcast vehicles which dwarfed the houses, and I usually had to choose locations near the main roads on which the vans were travelling from a *Songs of Praise* in north Wales to a rugby match in the south. Only two locations managed to make the outside broadcast vans look small. One was the copper mountain near tiny Amlwch on Anglesey which helped develop Swansea into the world's great Copperopolis. Known as Mynydd Parys, incredible orange craters were gouged out of the earth, leaving the deepest open holes in Wales to impress the modern tourist. The second location was Bethesda, its Penrhyn slate quarry the stage for the longest strike in British industrial history. Between 1900 and 1903 it was the scene of the battle between a moderate union and the intransigent owner Lord Penrhyn, whose family money had been made largely from the port of Liverpool's Jamaica slave trade. He sat in his forbidding castle overlooking the Menai Straits while enhancing his wealth in the quarries. In terms of numbers, slate employed less than ten per cent of those who worked in the south Wales coalmines but the slate workers represented the heartland of the Welsh language and a rich cultural heritage. A strike of three years was so long that many went to work in the south Wales coalfield. Others joined choirs which toured Britain and North America to raise money in support of their families. What was different about this strike was the enormous split between those who stayed out and the blacklegs who went back to work. The hatred of the 'scabs' led to posters being placed in the windows of houses proclaiming 'there is no traitor in this house'. A whole street in the nearby village of Tregarth was dubbed 'Stryd y Cynffonwyr', the best translation of which is 'Yes-men Street', an image which stayed in the memory of the community for at least a generation.

Problems always arose when out filming. Rain when you wanted the sun, noise when you wanted good sound, but only once was I caught endangering my crew. When interviewing Richard Burton's brother Graham Jenkins at his Channel Islands home, we were invited to visit Sark on a yacht owned by Graham's friend. A fine day of walking and filming ended with a sudden storm brewing and, as we left harbour, we heard an incoming boat captain shouting on his radio, 'There are fools going out to sea now!'

The next noise we heard was our loose anchor bumping into the side of our small motorcraft. It had to be pulled in by cameraman Martin Saunders with Ednyfed hanging on to his legs in what was now a gale force storm. By the time we entered the quieter waters of Guernsey dusk had fallen. The harbour lights had been switched off. We were not expected to return that night. The captain made for a light on a headland but, to our horror, it was only a house light. Too late, he was heading for rocks just below the surface of the clear sea water and we all had to shout 'rocks' as he tried to avoid them. A lucky escape for all of us but a huge lesson for me, endangering the lives of my crew of five people in the days before health and safety legislation changed our gung-ho behaviour for ever. Martin Saunders went on to work for Bristol's natural history unit and is credited for the most famous sequence of film featuring David Attenborough interacting with a family of mountain gorillas.

Having survived Sark, *Cywain* completed four series totalling over 100 programmes in the early 1970s. Thursday evening slots at 7.30 or 8 p.m. attracted large semi-captive audiences, even if many English speakers were irritated when their three-channel choice became even more limited. That social divide ended only with the launch of S4C in 1982. By that time I had long since moved from the 'face' to become a foreman.

8

Team Spirit

THE ACTORS, PRESENTERS and contributors seen on screen and heard on radio are only the tip of the iceberg. They conceal the very large numbers of staff who work behind the scenes in support of the production process. In 1964 these performers, with notable exceptions such as Alun Williams and the presentation unit itself, worked on short-term BBC contracts which took the insecurity of their tenure into account through paying them about 15 per cent more than to pensionable staff. All production operations were conducted in-house. Outsourcing canteens or hiring independent producers did not begin in earnest until the 1990s. The making of programmes was entirely reliant on specialist teams of staff in the studio, on film and on outside broadcasts. Skilled technicians and crafts people were backed up by an administrative staff, from secretaries to top management, with further support from in-house canteen staff, a team of garage mechanics, another team to build the sets and strong riggers who hauled the thick camera cables. All were charged with the sole aim of supporting the much smaller body of producers. The unwritten mantra was, 'The producer is king'. Permission was required from the producer or director to enter the gallery, even if you were the Director-General. In the early days of broadcasting, however, staff producers were often frustrated by the limitations imposed on them by the engineering department. Radio presenters were surrounded by studio managers until commercial radio demonstrated that allowing presenters the freedom to play in music themselves made for greater fusion of word and music. Early on there were limits to low lighting on TV shows as well; trade unions insisted on larger film crews than were required, although the BBC was much healthier than ITV in that respect. Gradually, those limitations faded as new technology forced a cut in the numbers of technical staff – only to be replaced by the rise of the accountants.

Regardless of all such constraints, a great team spirit prevailed most of the time and in every part of BBC Wales. It was a team which included a wide range of characters who stamped their personality on broadcasting for a generation. The technology they worked with, one now realises, belonged to the age of the dinosaur but the creativity of those involved in the production process is now best demonstrated by the growth in the use of today's precious BBC Archive.

The staff of the TV film unit were considered to be an elite. It included only four film crews and about 12 film editors, all part of a prestigious department built on the foundations laid by documentary maker John Ormond in the late 1950s. The four lighting cameramen were responsible for the filming of everything on location. They were always on the road, moving from the demands of one producer to the next, anywhere in Wales or beyond. Russ Walker was the thoughtful Scotsman who would ask, 'Don't you think...?' when his practised eye had noticed a better shot than the one originally selected. He dominated the work of his four-man crew with quiet authority. Their numbers increased with the scale of the production, particularly in drama, when Russ's expertise at lighting was particularly important.

All four lighting cameramen had their little quirks. The portly Charles Beddoues could be cajoled into a good mood by being offered a boiled egg by the PA in the middle of the morning. The amusing Cockney Tom Friswell hid behind his camera when he was in a naughty frame of mind. When asked to shoot a reel of what life was like on a university campus, all 400 feet of film gave the impression that it was an all-female college. Assistant cameramen were regarded as the future inheritors of a proud tradition. Hugh Maynard and, as mentioned, Martin Saunders, our saviour during our escapade from the island of Sark, had such incredibly sharp eyesight that they were promoted to the natural history unit in Bristol. It was only gradually that Welsh speakers appeared in the film unit. Robin Rollinson and Gerald Cobbe were the first to be appointed to full cameraman status and, over 40 years later, Robin was still working as a director on *Pobol y Cwm*.

Sound recordists were a breed apart, rightly obsessed with the problem of extraneous noise which could interfere with recordings. Ted Doull (grandfather of international Welsh track cyclist Owain Doull) was oblivious to delays which would irritate even cameramen once they had set up the shot they wanted but Ted, soundproofed behind his earphones, was always the first to pick up the sound of approaching low-flying aircraft.

Film editors sifted through all the new material dumped in their cutting rooms prior to the long and detailed process of choosing and assembling a rough cut, often working to a producer's guidelines on their own. They were allocated productions by a Head of Film Unit who treated them all as if equal in ability. Only slowly were producers allowed to select the editor of their choice. The bearded Chris Lawrence was regarded as the doyen of the unit by those responsible for the big drama productions. Totally trusted and self-confident, while working on the last long interview with Richard Burton he asked me when I was Head of Programmes for an extension of five minutes to an agreed 50-minute placing on BBC1 at peak time. Fortunately, I was on good terms with Controller Alan Hart who reminded me that, 'What the audience doesn't see, the audience doesn't miss!' Chris eventually moved on to become chief film editor at the major Welsh facilities company of its time, Barcud Derwen.

Different producers had their own ideas when it came to working with their favourite film editors. Richard Lewis preferred the workmanlike Bill Mainman who was the only editor in the film unit to wear a suit to work. I enjoyed the company of jolly John Brewser who nearly always wore a colourful summer shirt which I thought had been bought in Thailand. Much later I discovered they had been made by his wife. I was to see a lot of John as he was the Wales Association of Broadcasting and Allied Staffs Union (ABS) representative. He always made his arguments firmly, courteously and well. He was patient and persuasive when wearing both his union hat and in his normal job, particularly when working on very old and dangerously inflammable archive film and laboriously synchronising old footage of steam engines with original sounds.

The newsroom operated with a film unit of its own. They were a totally different breed, dedicated to speed rather than finesse. The aim of the news cameraman was to get to the incident as soon as possible, and return to the laboratory with the footage a.s.a.p. in order to develop the film before it could be edited for the same night's *Wales Today*. Shooting on combined magnetic film was the time-consuming predecessor of the video camera but was much faster than the 16mm separate magnetic film being used for timeless programmes such as drama or documentaries.

The news cameramen were members of a 'smash-and-grab' brigade with no interest in arty-farty filming. The news films of the 1960s and 1970s were mainly shot by the gung-ho quartet of Jock Sinclair, Eric Warrilow, the young Dave Jones, and Harry Hynam who had been a member of Bomber Command during the war.

When the film arrived in the cutting room, news film editor Peter James and his assistant Peter Maby were put under huge pressure, with the news producer looking over their shoulders and the programme deadline getting ever nearer. Peter James always remained cool, knowing full well that the panic to get the item on air would be no different tomorrow.

The TV producers' closest colleagues were their female

PAs who guarded the gateways to their bosses – most with welcoming warmth, a few with suspicion of motive, all fiercely loyal to the BBC and its ethos. None had been to university, yet their standards of both written and spoken Welsh and English were impeccable, likewise their typing and shorthand skills. They were experts at continuity in studio and on film, were nerveless in countdowns for the presenters and were expected to find and book contributors, cast minor drama parts, research libraries and manage the office. Discreet and proficient liars when required to protect their immediate bosses, they were also the first to criticise them if they felt things were wrong. This army of some 40 TV PAs, one for each producer, were no shrinking violets. One notable illustration occurred when a PA known as Jean O. applied for a transfer to London's light entertainment department. During the interview, light entertainment boss Bill Cotton Jr asked her rather condescendingly: 'How do you pay your contributors down in Wales?'

Quick as a flash, back came the answer, 'With little green notes with the Queen's head on them, just like you do in London.' Jean O. Davies got the job.

Her colleague Margaret Price was the first TV PA to be appointed in Wales and the first secretary to have learnt the basic skills of typing and shorthand in Welsh. The daughter of a policeman with the intriguing telephone number TUMBLE 2, she joined the BBC as a secretary in 1946 and worked on the first BBC TV programmes produced by pioneer producer D.J. Thomas in the early 1950s. She worked on location with a host of famous names, from Dylan Thomas, Richard Burton and Richard Dimbleby in the early days, to Ryan and Ronnie 30 years later. As the senior PA to Head of Light Entertainment Meredydd Evans, her wicked sense of humour fitted in well with the high jinks associated with that department.

Surprisingly few PAs ever married. Some were married to the job; others claimed they had met so many really interesting men on the set that they had become fussy!

Some could be as eccentric as their bosses. The PA for *Heddiw*, responsible for the picture archive, was on holiday when there was an urgent demand for a photograph of Gwynfor Evans. The team searched the library and failed to find it under E for Evans, G for Gwynfor or P for Plaid Cymru. It took a phone call to establish it was hidden under A for 'Arwr', the Welsh for Hero!

Video cameras were the preserve of studio and outside broadcasts where cameramen trained in technical knowledge understood the insides of their large pedestal video cameras which moved around their allotted space rather like Daleks. Their operators spent months at a time either in the studios shooting *Pobol y Cwm* or talk shows, or on location manning cameras tied to the large outside broadcast vans as they travelled all over Wales broadcasting sports events, hymn singing programmes, the summer festivals and whatever else could be fitted in to justify the expense of such labour-intensive vehicles on the road. The cables alone required a small army of riggers to move the bulky cameras around.

When in the studio, senior engineers such as Peter Stanton knew how to inform producers quietly that they only had ten minutes left to finish recording before the whole technical crew broke for the day. Soft talk, but sound advice. Running out of time could mean massive overtime payments or even the crew downing tools if the director had lost their sympathy. In the early days tensions could arise from the gulf between the highly-trained cameramen, almost exclusively English speaking who knew about TV technique, as opposed to the early Welsh production teams who knew their Wales but little or nothing about TV. Gradually, mutual respect grew with the passing of time, both in the studio and at the BBC Club, which certainly resulted in several marriages between cameramen and PAs.

Differentiating between identical names in Wales has always led to the creation of nicknames which stick when they become immediately recognisable. At one point there were three men on the BBC Wales staff named Philip Davies. The first Phil, the cool, quiet Head of Finance, was dubbed 'Phil the Till'; the producer with copperplate handwriting was called 'Phil the Quill' and the third, a member of the technical staff who had suffered a car crash, was called 'Phil the Spill'. Inevitably, there was confusion at times. Two people with the same name who never checked their monthly pay certainly had a problem. A clerical error resulted in one of them receiving double pay, the other nothing. The staff member with double pay spent it, the other went into debt. That caused Phil the Till a minor headache. It was the price one paid for being Welsh.

BBC Bangor was well known as a breeding ground for budding broadcasters. As noted, its first head was the remarkable Sam Jones who built a small empire of young people enthused by his love of broadcasting. One of Sam's earliest appointments was Victor Williams, the office boy who ended up in Cardiff as one of the senior outside broadcast floor managers. Vic was another of the 'apprentice boys' recruited by the BBC after their war service. There were about five outside broadcast managers, including Elwyn Jones and Wyn Jones. All were masters of communication between the large outside crews of up to 60 people and the very different directors. Whatever the weather or the difficulties at the location, or however animated the disagreements between camera crews outside the big outside broadcast vans and the directors inside in the warmth, the outside broadcast floor managers were the indispensable link. They had to be authoritarian in their determination to get the job done within the allocated time but their firmness was always laced with a bonhomie which held the whole team together.

A later arrival to their team was the popular gnome-like figure of Brydan Griffiths, a Welsh speaker who affected a fake posh accent when speaking English, picked up from trying to get work as an actor at the start of his career. He found his niche much later as a trusted studio director. Brydan spent all his off-duty time travelling the world on his own, carrying only one plastic bag containing just one change of clothing.

Ralph Evans was a junior member of the house staff, partially sighted but with the sharpest of brains for practical jokes. When a member of the public asked the whereabouts of a doctor outside the Newport Road TV offices, he was directed to Doctor of Philosophy Meredydd Evans in the light entertainment department. Ralph was, however, deadly serious when sitting on the Association of Broadcasting and Allied Staffs Union committee. When the ABS was asked by management to share facilities with HTV during the Pope's visit, it was obvious that some people were unhappy with the idea of working with commercial counterparts earning more than double their wages. A lengthy silence was broken when Ralph spoke up, stating that everybody should cooperate in a great day for the BBC, for Cardiff and for Wales. He was the lowest paid person in the room.

The house staff were often the proudest members of the staff before the steady growth of BBC Wales from 1977 onwards. Eddie the carpenter had access to all the offices and knew everybody. He was proud of his handiwork in keeping the offices in good order and would respond as soon as possible to a request for help – and a chat.

Then there was the motherly figure of Maureen Bennett who served food and drink in the small hospitality room. Maureen moved around with a quiet efficiency and total discretion, never disturbing the middle of a tense discussion or a silence at a critical stage of a contract negotiation while she served coffee.

The most senior engineering managers controlled the studios and outside broadcast lorries, and were committed to their central role in getting the productions recorded or on air. They managed large crews, all of them no-nonsense bosses bent on producing a Rolls-Royce service for producers. Tony Barnes Sr led a team of cool-headed people including Geoff Alford, or long-serving Laurie Owen and Stan Jones, both of whom stood out in the department as the tiny minority of Welsh speakers in the early years. They dealt with equipment which was heavy to move, inflexible to use and fragile in temperament. Laurie and Stan were pioneers in the industry who carried their huge knowledge lightly but firmly. I only stretched Stan's experience once. Setting up cameras in Anglesey's Rio Tinto plant, Stan discovered that the magnetic field was so powerful adjacent to the aluminum smelter that the pictures wobbled uncontrollably. It took him quite a time to work out how to minimise the retreat from certain areas before the cameras stabilised. One of his staff was an engineer whose expertise was best illustrated trying to balance the pictures in sports stadiums as the director cut between cameras as the ball moved from sunlight into shade and back again.

One Head of Sound, Radio, was the communicative and sociable Colin White who was always asking the editors whether they had problems in the technical areas, always choosing to check the answer at 5.25 p.m. when he knew Teleri Bevan or Meirion Edwards would open their drinks cabinets!

Supporting the technical and production teams was the bookings unit which allocated resources according to the demands of programme management. The soft-spoken John Wallis was the head of the unit and, for 20 years, had as his 'admin' assistant the colourful and popular figure of 'Blod' Jones, a striking woman with jet-black hair, a face that seemed permanently tanned, complete with bright red lipstick. I always imagined her dancing, Mexican-style, around the corridors. Blod moved to the public relations department and organised the ticketing and public seating plans in concerts and major events with great precision, sharing an office for a time with the young ex-teacher Eddie Butler who honed his writing skills in the public relations office before moving to the sports department. Such was Blod's loyalty to her colleagues that she has continued to organise the Ryan

Davies Memorial Fund to this day, long after leaving the BBC for pastures new.

I first worked with the cheerful and smiling Sid Roe when I was serving my first month's apprenticeship in Swansea in 1964. He had joined BBC Swansea in 1946 as a studio manager and it was claimed that he had recorded Dylan Thomas's last broadcast at the Alexandra Road studios before Dylan made his final, fateful trip to New York in 1953. I was surprised when Sid resurfaced in the 1970s as Harry Hynam's freelance news sound recordist in Cardiff. I learnt later that his war was as interesting as Harry's. Posted to a top-secret radar station near Dover, Sid witnessed the Battle of Britain as he plotted the incoming waves of German aeroplanes. After D-Day he helped maintain the Allied air defence system in support of the troops advancing into Germany.

The design department was full of creative and sensitive people who loved the challenge of designing a brand-new set, whether building a street for *Pobol y Cwm* at the back of the Llandaff premises, or the ingenious dual set for *Wales Today* and *Heddiw* which involved reversing the background image in five seconds with the touch of a finger. Necessity was the mother of invention, because at one time *Wales Today* and *Newyddion Saith* followed each other within 30 seconds on two different channels. It was the minimum time required for presenters and production teams to change seats. That small Llandaff news studio C2 was regarded as the most productive corner of the whole BBC, with recordings of children's programmes most weekday mornings and rugby's *Sports Line-Up* live every Sunday afternoon.

Designers were experts at building drama sets which stretched their imagination, although it was a drama producer who asked for a budget to include an Elizabethan mansion when the real thing existed between Crickhowell and Brecon.

One of the first designers appointed at BBC Wales was also the funniest of storytellers. Julian Williams, a jazz-mad law graduate from Aberystwyth, wore his college scarf daily for decades before it dropped off him. A large man, he regaled colleagues, in between loud sniffs, with stories of minor catastrophes in his previous role as a studio manager. When asked to reproduce the tinkling of a teacher's bell in a school yard during one edition of *Wales Today*, Julian found a sound more akin to the big bell of Kiev. It was a hilarious image, much repeated and extended at Christmas parties.

Costume people really knew how to throw parties. One of Julian's large circle of friends was elegant Judy Tarling, one of the BBC's first costume designers who left to run the family's Bear Hotel, a famous hostelry in Crickhowell. For years after leaving the BBC, Judy threw a large and sumptuous summer feast in the beautiful grounds of her house for local friends and former colleagues fortunate enough to be invited.

The Head of Costume and Make-Up was Pearl Setchfield, organiser of annual Hogmanay parties with haggis, neeps and tatties, while Scottish husband and Head of Personnel, Andrew McCabe, saw to thirsty guests. Pearl would hire students in the summer holidays to sniff her stock of costumes and check whether they needed cleaning – one way of testing a young person's desire to join the BBC!

Her staff included two senior make-up artists, Marina Monios and Cissian Rees. Both were experts at chatting up VIPs or calming inexperienced interviewees. They always offered the best possible welcome to studio contributors.

Tucked away in the darkness of a tiny film theatre was dubbing mixer Robin Griffith, a person with endless patience in getting the commentary to hit the picture at exactly the right place. Rob had been a conscientious objector and spent the war in the X-ray department of a Liverpool hospital. He then worked as a photographer on the Welsh weekly newspaper *Y Cymro* before joining the BBC as a studio manager.

No programme was complete without graphics, the design of which became more and more sophisticated by the day. Roger Fickling was nothing less than a genius. For one General Election on S4C, he devised a simple and thoroughly acceptable system for less than £1,000, on a night when London was said to have spent £400,000.

Peter Morgan excelled in the growing sector of TV promotions. He won several awards for the short, sharp, tightly-edited packages which had to make an immediate impact. The most memorable one, for a forthcoming rugby international between Wales and England when we were considered no-hopers, won an award. The caption, 'WINNABLE', flashed over a sequence of Welsh tries and, shown regularly throughout the week, caught the imagination and lifted the spirits of Welsh viewers as well as, it was widely claimed, the team. Wales won the match.

In the early days before the creation of researcher posts, studio management was the obvious route to promotion. Geraint Stanley Jones was a studio manager at the same time as future Labour MP Ann Clwyd. Drama producer Lorraine Davies terrified them both as she shouted and bawled her way through a production. She would only trust the straight-backed figure of senior studio manager Mostyn Jones who would ignore the tantrums, press the talkback switch and say 'Let's try it again' in a quiet and unruffled voice.

The Head of Contracts had the sole responsibility for paying freelancers and contributors. One such boss was Marion Jenkins who served the full 40 years, having started out as a junior secretary. When Marion reached retirement in the 1980s, I hosted a small lunch in her honour, surrounding her with friends and favourite people. As I led her out to the foyer she slipped on a wet floor and broke a hip. We tried to persuade her to sue the BBC since the Corporation found it cheaper to be sued than insure every member of staff. Marion suffered painful years in retirement but refused to take the organisation she had loved so much to law. Her successor, the lively and genial Bryn Roberts, defected to the independent sector as Chief Executive of the facilities company Derwen, his head full of sensitive BBC commercial information. It expanded and became known as Barcud Derwen and flourished for many years, but foundered when the company invested too much in its Caernarfon studios and bought too many companies outside Wales. The irrepressible Bryn then became manager of the first city TV station in Wales, 'Made in Cardiff', before moving on after a year.

In the personnel department senior PA Barbara Ellis worked for Head of Department Andrew McCabe, a constantly cheerful combination. Barbara had once been a member of Cardiff's famous Sybil Marks dance troupe which regularly appeared on *Come Dancing*, the 1950s predecessor of *Strictly Come Dancing* when Alun Williams used to compère and Selwyn Roderick direct it from Wales. Whether deliberate or not, even Barbara's dress sense made everybody think of her as the spitting image of Richard Burton's wife Elizabeth Taylor.

Iris Cobbe, wife of cameraman Gerald Cobbe, was the first person to provide a proper archive service to radio producers in Cardiff. She created order where there had always been chaos. Critically significant programmes had been lost. Saunders Lewis's 1962 Radio Lecture, an extremely important historical record, was only rescued by copying the tape of a friendly listener. Iris brought not only intelligence and professionalism to the archive but she also anticipated the needs of the services in a pleasant and caring manner.

The situation in Bangor was even worse. There seemed to be no official archive at all. Through sheer good fortune, one loyal and long-serving studio manager, Tudwal Roberts, had created his own private archive. Tudwal saved considerable embarrassment to an organisation which came late to the value of contemporary Welsh history. BBC Wales owes him a great debt.

The vast majority of the small BBC staff before the great expansion of the late 1970s were well known to each other. Few were attracted to join TWW or the early years of HTV. Aneirin Talfan Davies's dismissive dictum was, 'We are here to make programmes; they are only there to make soap'! Only after the growth of the services was there a significant movement of people between the BBC, HTV, S4C and the independent sector. When a diehard BBC man told a departing Emyr Daniel that he earned £15,000 and would never leave the BBC, even if offered £30,000, the immediate riposte from the clever and cheeky Daniel was, 'Neither would I!'

The launch of Radio Wales, Radio Cymru and S4C meant that it was no longer possible to know 1,500 people scattered around the different sites, let alone larger entities such as the newsroom which had grown to a unit of about 100 people. Departments became more self-contained. Radio Wales and Radio Cymru people saw themselves as members of their own clubs once they had separated out into individual channels. Radio Cymru, based as it was in Llandaff, had more in common with Swansea and Bangor than with Welsh TV units based elsewhere in Cardiff, whether in the General Accident building on Newport Road or later in the former British Steel premises in Mynachty. The cosy club of the 1960s split into several close-knit units on different sites. The pace of growth had undermined BBC Wales as a single entity, but within each new and separate unit a host of interesting characters would emerge.

9

'It's a Thinking Game'

CARWYN JAMES WAS presenting a National Eisteddfod TV programme for me in 1970 when, to his genuine surprise, he heard news of his selection to coach the 1971 Lions rugby team. He thought he would be rejected because he had stood as a candidate for Plaid Cymru at the recent general election. Instead, his selection by the Lions' hierarchy marked his emergence on the international stage. Carwyn James was the only Welshman to inspire an All Black defeat three times – as coach of the British and Irish Lions in 1971, Llanelli in 1972, and an unusual pep talk given to a Barbarians team in 1973 which included 14 of his 1971 Lions. He was respected throughout the world as simply the best – yet he died a disappointed man on his own in an Amsterdam hotel room.

Carwyn was different from the rest of the rugby world. He combined teaching Welsh literature at Llandovery College, and then Trinity College, Carmarthen, with coaching Llanelli to consistent success, culminating in the famous win against the All Blacks on 'the day the pubs ran dry', as told by Max Boyce.

In the years since his death a host of myths and misconceived opinions accumulated about him in TV drama, radio interviews, books and newspapers.

By 1974 Carwyn needed to escape from his west Wales base where he was trapped in the impossible situation of being both in the centre of a macho male rugby world and a chapel secretary where 'Thou Shalt Not' was still etched in the mores of the older generation. He desperately needed freedom from his in-built Nonconformist conscience. His old boss at

Trinity College, the outspoken Miss Norah Isaac, accused me of causing his death through spiriting him to Cardiff. She knew nothing of the tortured sexuality which impelled him to escape from her world. In fact, Carwyn behaved as if freer the further he travelled from Wales – out of sight, out of mind. Still an ambassador for his country, his years coaching in Rovigo, according to Alun Richards who spent many weeks with him there, gave him so much more satisfaction than anywhere else except New Zealand. He stayed more relaxed in Italy – without even a telephone – for two years when he had planned to return to Wales after only one. In the end it gave him his escape from the crazy round of invitations in Wales and beyond, but his guilt complex still kept him eating little and drinking too much.

In 1974 his only declared ambition, he told the commentator John Arlott, was to emulate the writings of Neville Cardus on cricket. There were no fully developed radio channels in Wales at the time and we could not afford a full-time rugby reporter, but Carwyn readily accepted a freelance retainer as a sports reporter. He did not wish to be tied down to any one employer but relished the opportunity of covering different sports, comparing notes with coaches of different disciplines and spending summers covering Glamorgan. He became well known for his early morning rush for the studio, often still dressed in pyjamas. He never knew as much about time management as about game management and knew even less about money, so much so that my secretary took over the collecting of his BBC cheques. It was his acceptance of dinner invitations from even minor rugby clubs from all over Britain which was a major element in his demise over which the BBC had no control. Those who claimed that the BBC did nothing to help him in his darkest days never knew that Carwyn was the most pampered broadcaster in Wales. He was treated like a china doll by his two main producers, Head of TV Sport Onllwyn Brace, once his closest friend in the Llanelli team, and the strict teetotal non-smoking Head of Radio Sport Thomas Davies, who even tolerated his presence at meetings while

'C.J.' leant against the open office door, puffing considerately in the opposite direction. His quiet charm and vulnerability conquered the rest of us and I was expected to allocate him 'rest periods' for his own good.

Never a great broadcaster and more nervous than most before transmission, Carwyn tended to speak too fast and swallow his words on air. Yet he always communicated a sense of personal integrity, authority and wisdom beyond his years. As a cultured devotee of the Welsh poet D. Gwenallt Jones and the Russian playwright Anton Chekhov, or as President of the Day at the National Eisteddfod, his varied interests and singular achievements earned him charismatic status and everywhere an open door as he smoked his way through life.

On Sunday afternoon's *Sports Line-Up* he taught his biggest regular audience to watch rugby with new eyes through his invention of post-match TV analysis, the clips identified with the help of ex-international Alun Pask hidden away with the videotape machines.

Carwyn's mantra, 'it's a thinking game', demanded cool calculation as a coach, treating each of his players as individuals, as opposed to the emotional cry of 'calon' [heart] espoused by his equally successful contemporary Clive Rowlands.

On only one occasion did Carwyn lose his temper with the selectors live on air, and that for dropping his great favourite Phil Bennett in favour of the young David Richards (my wife's second cousin). In the event Phil was reinstated through David's injury, an event celebrated in song by Max Boyce as 'Divine Intervention'.

Carwyn's normally placid personality hid many regrets and unresolved issues. He had played for Wales only twice. When he scored his one and only drop goal for his country and returned to meet his team-mates while basking in the roar of the crowd, he told how one senior player hugged him and said, 'Make the most of it boi bach, you may never have that feeling again'. When he was only 30 years old, Carwyn delivered an illuminating talk on radio on the subject of 'Joy and Sadness'. There was more of both emotions to come in his life.

The joy of beating the All Blacks was followed by the sadness of never being asked to coach his own national team. In 1974 I pleaded with him for three hours one evening to keep his name in the frame as the next Wales coach and try to persuade the 'Big Five' selectors of the day to fall in with his ideas. In the early hours of the morning he showed me the letter which he had already sent to the Wales Rugby Union (WRU), stating as its very first point that 'the National Team Coach, as in some other countries, should always be the Chairman of selectors'. He was a man before his time, but that letter ended Wales's hope of having the world's greatest rugby brain as its coach. That was probably the moment he decided to leave teaching. Did the WRU letter really resolve the issue as one of the many on his mind? We shall never know.

Later that year he joined the BBC and within months asked for four days off to be the guest speaker at Wellington Rugby Football Club's annual dinner, all first-class expenses paid. That is how much he was respected in New Zealand. I told him to take two weeks off.

He found it difficult to cope with fame but always enjoyed calling on friends without warning. Carwyn loved visiting families with children, taking the boys to Saturday matches or playing them at table tennis, although his ruthless competitive instinct never allowed them to win. His tiny coterie of genuine female friends would be taken home on a rota to visit his sister Gwen for Sunday lunch. They knew he would have loved a family of his own but the woman to whom he proposed marriage knew she could never cope with his shambolic lifestyle. Another sadness?

Although he himself was always well turned out, the boot of his car was always full of unpaid parking fines and uncashed cheques from his non-BBC activities. He used his friends shamelessly; the generous Swansea rugby journalist Clem Thomas once drove him all over South Africa, rushing him to the studios in time for a broadcast while 'C.J.' catnapped all the way. He would forget his dress suit when on the way to a rugby dinner, but there was always somebody who would get it to him. His friends did what he wanted without him even asking. Somehow his company was always enough.

When Rovigo won the Italian title the team was greeted by the Pope. The Welsh weekly newspaper *Y Cymro* printed a photograph of Carwyn with the Pope, with the caption reading: 'The Pope (right) meets Carwyn James.'

That joke appealed to 'C.J.' since he had a wicked sense of humour, particularly when shared with his close friend, the writer Alun Richards. They delighted in gentle but malicious word games designed to offend, such as, 'your contribution is appreciated, however small' and the riposte, 'Just because you scored one drop goal for Wales,' etc.

In constant demand from radio and TV, the *Guardian* newspaper and the endless rugby dinners at which he never ate, Carwyn's indisciplined way of life could not last; he succumbed to a virtual diet of gin and water. A skin disease covered his bloodied body, leading to sleepless nights – and more gin. Halfway through his final rugby season in 1983, he was booked into Hotel Krasnapolsky in Amsterdam by my secretary for another rest. On the day before he flew out I was asked by his sister Gwen to join her and brother Dewi in his flat where they were puzzled by his attitude. When I saw the rubbish Carwyn was writing for some paper I told him not to go. He swayed as he demanded to know what right I had to stop him. Gwen did not believe me when I declared him drunk, because they thought there were no alcohol bottles in the place. The empties were found later that same day, his last in Cardiff. He died in Amsterdam, having fallen into a scalding bath. I was particularly sorry that a major Welsh-language film on his life was written as if he had deliberately gone to Amsterdam to die. The myth of suicide was born. I have always believed that he accidentally fell into a bath of scalding water, so prevalent in expensive European hotels, while in an alcoholic stupor.

Suicide was never mentioned by the doctor or the police. They only talked of natural causes. He was certainly drunk when making his last phone call to Teleri Bevan wanting to know the score of a match involving his beloved Llanelli.

Carwyn died in an alcoholic haze but I believe his demise was rooted in the complexes seeded in his early years, an angst which nearly caused the suicide of referee Nigel Owens over a quarter of a century later. Nigel conquered his demons. Carwyn never did.

He was only 53. We organised a memorial service at Broadcasting House in Llandaff on the day of an Ireland international. 'Wee' Willie John McBride paid a great tribute. In the foyer the bust of Carwyn's head stands next to that of Ray Gravell – the great teacher side by side with the student he once called 'the last Prince of Wales'.

If Carwyn's glass was half empty, Ray Gravell's was always topped up by the flow of constant praise he required to boost a vulnerable soul. 'Grav' was an extraordinary and emotional personality, totally different from his mentor. As a youngster he had found his father's body after his suicide, but had survived that terrible trauma to build a physically strong character on the field and a totally natural communicator off it. Grav developed a successful career as a broadcaster on both Radio Wales and Radio Cymru, and was the most excitable rugby commentator on S4C. He was also an actor whose greatest experience was working alongside a Peter O'Toole even more impressed that his on-screen chauffeur was a Welsh rugby hero! If Ray was a guest speaker at a dinner with 100 people in attendance, every person present would be greeted individually with a word or a hug. Grav made sure he was never lonely, and gave his all either on air or in the dressing room. His Welsh team-mates did sometimes get fed up of having to listen to the protest songs of Dafydd Iwan before every international, particularly since he had to be reassured in the middle of a match, according to Gerald Davies, that he was not suffering from flu or a sudden twinge. Yet his passion for his country was an inspiration to all around him. As captain of Llanelli he packed his pre-match talk with so much emotion he exhausted himself going into the match itself. Ultimately, Ray needed to be loved and everybody responded to his call. One woman, who knew nothing about rugby and had known him only from listening to his English radio programmes, cried when she heard of his sudden death on holiday in Spain with his close-knit family. Eight thousand of us packed into the old Stradey Park to pay homage at a funeral service like no other – the tributes from Gerald Davies and Hywel Teifi Edwards, the singing of his hero Dafydd Iwan, the heavy ceremonial sword which he had held aloft so proudly over many years at National Eisteddfod ceremonies now borne steady as a rock by his successor Robin McBryde, nowadays the Wales Forwards coach. It all seemed so soon after an unforgettable night of merriment at Carmarthen's Ivy Bush Royal Hotel when we celebrated Grav's marriage to Mari, looking radiant in the only possible colour, a scarlet wedding dress. The morning after is best forgotten. Ray Gravell will never be forgotten.

The Head of Sport at BBC Wales for 25 years was Onllwyn Brace, a 'hands-on' producer preferring to be on location rather than in the office. He was particularly good in the constructive criticism of commentators and presenters, instructing them when not to talk on air or guiding new young assistant producers, reporters and commentators such as Huw Llewelyn Davies, Gareth Charles and director Ceri Thomas in rugby, while John Hardy, Ron Jones and Ian Gwyn Huws were hugely successful in soccer. Gareth Charles now wears the mantle once owned by Huw Llewelyn Davies in both languages, and John Hardy remains a significant presence in soccer's commentary box.

Short in height, light in weight, fleet of foot, the diminutive Brace was akin to a scarlet pimpernel on and off the field, always somewhere else when wanted. He was drafted into the Wales team following a famous Oxford win in the 1955

Varsity match when partnering England fly-half M.J.K. Smith.

'Onkers', as he was known at Oxford, played inside Cliff Morgan for Wales on several occasions but they were never soulmates on or off the field. Morgan, the senior partner, wanted the ball passed straight to him with no frills; Brace wanted to indulge in reverse passes and scissor movements which were ahead of their time. The story is relevant because Onllwyn replaced Cliff as Head of Sport in Wales when Morgan moved to London, eventually as Head of BBC Television Sport and Outside Broadcasts. Instead of communicating directly with each other as managers, Onllwyn relied on me as the middleman. They were totally different in temperament and character. Onllwyn was a private person, a teetotaller who found showmanship somewhat distasteful, an ironic trait in one surrounded by some massive egos.

Cliff had an outgoing and generous personality, but even his friend Gareth Edwards once noted his 'abrasive' side. He had his critics who dubbed him a 'professional Welshman'. However, Cliff was a first-class commentator, his most famous match the occasion when he took over as a last-minute substitute for Bill McLaren when the Barbarians beat the All Blacks in 1973; it was even repeated on the American TV networks. As interviewer or presenter, Cliff prepared meticulously and had a deep respect for the spoken and written word, best illustrated by his thoughtful, long-running Radio 4 Saturday morning series, *Sport on Four*, the links delivered in his distinctive and mellifluous Welsh voice. He made many memorable live programmes with Teleri Bevan on Radio Wales, including the first live five-hour *Morning of the Match* on international rugby match day from a Cardiff hotel. Cliff never forgot his debt to BBC Wales and, in particular, to Hywel Davies for launching his career. He continued to work as a network commentator in tandem with his closest Welsh colleague, director Dewi Griffiths. Together with Alun Williams, they entertained Lions squads on several tours in the southern hemisphere with their eclectic repertoire of Welsh hymns, jazz and comic routines on the piano.

In Dewi Griffiths BBC Wales had the best rugby director in the world. A flamboyant former TV engineer who had joined Cliff Morgan in the sports department as a like-minded man from the Rhondda, he was confident in directing just three or four cameras with consummate skill, even if the noise he made shouting at cameramen from the gallery drowned the noise coming from the stadium. Dewi held the unique record of directing Wales–England internationals in Cardiff over a period of 25 years without Wales losing once. When he retired he presented his own hugely popular radio series, *A String of Pearls*, until just past his 80th birthday, surely a record length of no less than 60 years' service to BBC Wales.

Retaining Welsh rugby contracts and helping the BBC TV sports department in London with international sporting negotiations was always easier if the Head of Sport was a former rugby international. Negotiations over the Welsh clubs' contract involved a lunch for Wales Rugby Union Secretary Ray Williams and Treasurer Ken Harris, who was merely asked over coffee to name their sum for the following year. Ken was always fair, recognised the BBC Wales track record and we had no need to bargain. We paid under £100,000 a year for all Welsh club rugby matches even in 1990, albeit in the days before the advent of the professional game.

The craft of commentating on rugby and soccer has been of a consistently high standard over the years. Cliff Morgan and David Parry-Jones had only one peer in English. Bill McLaren, the Scotsman hailed as an honorary Welshman by the Arms Park crowd, was armed each international match day with notes on each player in different colours. Only on one occasion did we wonder about his research. It was the constant reference to Welsh second-row forward Geoff Wheel as 'the man from St Thomas's', a suburb known to few outside his native Swansea. We were criticised for costly duplication when insisting that David Parry-Jones should commentate on Wales internationals sitting next to network colleagues doing exactly the same work. But the accents of a couple of English commentators lacked the right tone for a Welsh rugby audience. In any case, it would have been wrong to exclude the regular club match commentator from the big occasions. When the time came for David to step down, following 17 years of consistently great service to BBC Wales, he took it badly. David was not the only freelancer to be shocked at times of change. I took full responsibility for the decision, but in all such cases the views of the relevant departmental heads were always paramount. Claiming sole decision taker always saved embarrassment when close friends were involved. Broadcasting is, after all, a team game.

The story of Huw Llywelyn Davies was very different, and belongs mainly to the chapters on Welsh-language radio and TV where he was the outstanding commentator of his generation. I had enticed him from his journalism job at HTV in 1978, with a view to a future in the upcoming Radio Cymru and S4C. He was so good that when an English commentator fell ill just before an international, he was transferred to the network without notice and carried it off in English as to the manner born and to huge plaudits all round.

Each summer, BBC Wales continued with its Glamorgan cricket contract. Wilfred Wooller was the dominant figure in the 1960s, a Welsh sporting character like no other. A product of Rydal School in north Wales, Wilf was the only person to have captained Wales in rugby and been a cricket Test selector for England. Imprisoned by the Japanese in Singapore during the Second World War, Wooller returned to captain a highly disciplined Glamorgan to win the Championship in 1948. He was a burly and intimidating man who commentated on rugby and cricket when the sports unit expanded in 1964, but also ignited many a political rough-and-tumble as a defender of apartheid in South Africa and as a right-wing Tory on *Week In Week Out*. In 1964 Wooller was on air again when Glamorgan famously beat Australia at St Helen's in Swansea where, four years later, the outside broadcast crew were on a break during their match against Nottinghamshire and only their personal interest ensured that the cameras kept rolling to record Garry Sobers's unique six sixes.

Don Shepherd, arguably the best bowler who never played for England, also graced the commentary box well after Wooller's day but his team-mate Peter Walker, who did play for England as a fine all-rounder, became an integral part of the BBC Wales newsroom and sports department for 20 years. Peter was a particularly complex person, a self-styled loner and roamer who was fair-minded, a good listener and sociable when off-duty. He was the hardest working of freelance journalists, always first off the mark to chase a story. He wrote skilfully and his soft South African accent went down well with audiences. Peter was born to anti-apartheid parents with Newport connections. As a teenager he ran away from home in South Africa and made his way to Cardiff. He was spotted while playing cricket by Wooller, who instructed him on the 'madness' of fielding close to the wicket. They were an unlikely duo, the young liberal South African and the extreme right-wing Tory who promoted sporting ties with the pariah state. By the time Wooller retired from commentating, Walker was already doing pieces for *Good Morning Wales* and was chosen to follow Cliff Morgan into the chair of *Sports Line-Up*. Peter went on to present BBC2's Sunday League 40-over competition each summer, returning to the hectic life of the newsroom and sports department each winter.

The 'three musketeers' of Glamorgan who won the County Championship in 1969 were Peter, Ossie Wheatley and Tony Lewis. Tony introduced *Good Morning Wales* for a whole year, while Ossie analysed the cricket with Don Shepherd and the emerging, ever-present reporter Edward Bevan who has stayed the pace. During these halcyon days it was possible to follow Glamorgan cricket through thick and thin each summer because daytime TV was still in its infancy.

Football fans were frequently fed up with BBC Wales for

concentrating on rugby at the expense of soccer. It was hard not to sympathise but there were formidable constraints. The first was technology. The 1964 studio-based *Welsh Sports Parade* was the only weekly programme of its kind, its contents reflecting a wide range of sporting activities, but mostly on film. Discerning audiences could easily tell the difference between the coverage of rugby as opposed to the other '57' varieties of sport. When the large and expensive outside broadcast units arrived, rugby was given priority as the nation's most popular sport. Even that statement was considered controversial by soccer lovers. However, we had a monopoly contract for rugby, big audiences and a successful national team.

We were excluded from coverage of the four major Welsh clubs in the English Football League. The Welsh Leagues, the FA Cup and European Cup authorities gave us access and the Welsh national team always featured, but the coverage was never good enough to satisfy the sizeable football-following public. In any case, as one who travelled far to follow the star-studded Swansea Town team which included ten Welsh internationals in the 1950s, only rarely have the Welsh national teams excited since the era of the Charles and Allchurch brothers, and it was depressing to hear of Wales players dropping out of successive squads because they placed club before country – until the coming of Gareth Bale and company!

Boxing had lost much of its appeal since the heyday of radio audiences in the 1930s when Tommy Farr had become Wales's greatest sporting celebrity when matched with and after his narrow defeat by Joe Louis. That was a time when mothers would refer to their growing boys as 'a real Tommy Farr'. However, there was a revival in the 1960s with the emergence of the great Merthyr boxer turned trainer Eddie Thomas, and his stable of Howard Winstone, Eddie Avoth, Colin Jones and Ken Buchanan, although audiences became ambivalent about the future of the sport, particularly after the tragic death in the ring of the young Johnny Owen. It became a big current affairs issue on *Week In Week Out*.

If boxing went into temporary decline, another sport much loved in the workmen's institutes took its place when colour TV was introduced. Although playing snooker used to be regarded as a classic sign of a mis-spent youth, the close-up possibilities in such a confined space were 'made' for the medium, and Welsh stars were there from the beginning of the BBC2 – and later S4C – coverage. Llanelli's Terry Griffiths won the world championship in 1979 before becoming a TV commentator as a new batch of younger Welsh players emerged, including another world champion, Mark Williams. The sport also attracted thousands of female viewers who enjoyed watching smartly dressed men playing a game many of them did not even try to understand.

The BBC Wales Sports Personality of the Year was always held in front of an invited audience at which the stars and their teams from the whole sporting world of Wales could receive recognition for their achievements. Boxer Howard Winstone and Lynn 'the leap' Davies were early winners; Lynn, following his gold medal at the 1964 Tokyo Olympics, became a regular contributor to weekly programmes which tried to provide a flavour of as many sports as possible, including athletics. BBC Sport, in general, was woefully weak on women's and disabled sports but the department was a powerful force in the sporting world before the advent of Sky TV. Ultimately, we knew an audience existed for the '57' varieties of human endeavour but we had neither the hardware nor the money to do justice to them all.

Instead, we relied on the Wales rugby teams of the 1970s to generate a national feel-good factor and excited discussion way beyond Monday mornings; they provided a platform for Max Boyce and the brilliant comedy drama *Grand Slam*; bards claimed that being chaired at the National Eisteddfod felt like winning a cap for Wales. Women regretted walking their dogs just because they were too nervous to watch. The nation still basks in the glory of defeating England but, in Max's words, losing does 'cast a gloom over the whole proceedings' even if you heard the score 'in the middle of a funeral'. The audience figures for the repeat showings always plummet with the disappointment of defeat but we always come back for the pleasure – and then more pain. It is, after all, our national game, played in our largest national theatre, or as the brilliant *South Wales Echo* cartoonist Gren would describe it, 'An area of outstanding natural beauty!'

10

The Script Comes First

FROM THE VERY beginning of *Pobol y Cwm* in 1974, one person stood out as central to the success of the most popular TV series ever in the Welsh language. Script unit editor Gwenlyn Parry wrote the first episode of *Pobol y Cwm* with the help of his one assistant Meic Povey while also enjoying the continuing success of his sitcom *Fo a Fe* with co-writer Rhydderch Jones in light entertainment. When one adds Gwenlyn's already established status as a leading dramatist of single plays on stage and on screen while still a young man, he surely stands alone as the most creative writer to work at BBC Wales for over 20 years until his untimely death in 1991 at the age of only 59.

The launch of *Pobol y Cwm* was a ground-breaking event, made possible by Gwenlyn's partnership with drama producer John Hefin and the backing of Head of Programmes Owen Edwards. It is almost certain that Owen and John had discussed the project with the newly retired assistant Head of Programmes, D.J. Thomas.

John Hefin had already partnered Gwenlyn in the adaptation of two brilliantly researched historical novels for the screen, *Y Stafell Ddirgel* [The Secret Room] and its sequel *Y Rhandir Mwyn* [The Fair Wilderness]. The author was the rather reticent radio producer Marion Eames who, as noted, had occupied the office next door to me for two years from 1964 without my realising that she was writing novels in her spare time. Both series showed costume drama at its best. It was the seventeenth-century story of a Quaker gentleman,

Rowland Ellis of Bryn Mawr, Dolgellau, who hid from religious persecutors before sailing to America with his followers where they founded a new settlement in the 'Welsh Tract' of Pennsylvania and established the famous Bryn Mawr College named after his small Merionethshire mansion.

John Hefin would go on to make a distinguished name for himself as the director of landmark programmes in the English language during the next 15 years, and his relationship with Gwenlyn would reach its peak with the production of *Grand Slam* in 1978. John had great charm and style, the sort of person who kept a cache of tasteful greeting cards to send friends and colleagues when they celebrated personal events or success. He was both persuasive and patient, mild-mannered but determined, committed to a first run of 30 episodes for *Pobol y Cwm*. The second series was commissioned before the first came to an end.

There had been previous attempts at a continuing Welsh TV 'soap'. The leading Welsh novelist of the 1960s and the early 1970s, Islwyn Ffowc Elis, had great success with the serialisation of his published works, but his single plays were never turned into a successful original, long-running serial for TV. The history of TV is littered with similar stories. In 1974 the series *Dai Macaroni*, a comedy on a Welsh-Italian family running a café, never found favour with the management of the day, although I thought it worth a second run. The long-term commitment to *Pobol y Cwm* was an important key to its success.

One of the first decisions the team had to make was the location of Cwmderi. An area in Carmarthenshire, once known as 'Gwlad y Pyramidiau Du' [The Land of the Black Pyramids] around Gorslas and Cefneithin, was selected as a mixed semi-rural community which combined coal mining with smallholdings, although the rural dimension never loomed large in *Pobol y Cwm*.

The composer of the programme's signature tune was easier to find. It was the year singer and songwriter Endaf Emlyn published his original and ground-breaking compositions in the album *Salem*, named after the best-known painting of a Welsh chapel scene. Over 40 years of listening to Endaf's tune for *Pobol y Cwm* played over scenes of the rolling hills of Ceredigion for most of that time makes it the longest running signature tune on Welsh-language TV.

The drama department had access to a young staff capable of directing the studio-based series, but Gwenlyn faced difficulties over scriptwriters. Plenty of ideas and storylines were offered, and scripts were initially accepted from a team of mainly well-known literary figures. There was, however, a dearth of younger professionals capable of writing dialogue suited to an ongoing 'soap' which had to reflect the everyday speech of the man on the street. Gwenlyn saw the necessity of developing a team of young writers who would learn to write dialogue based on storylines delegated by his script editors.

Potential criticism of different accents between north and south Wales were minimised through mixing a number of characters and actors from different regions. Gwenlyn was a north Walian by birth and accent but had married Joy, who came from Pontyberem, a short drive away from *Pobol y Cwm*'s mythical location of Cwmderi. He had an incredible ear for different patterns of speech and had spent enough time in the south to absorb the challenge of writing for the accents of different actors.

There was one further important requirement, and it was arguably the most difficult challenge of all – the need for humour. There would have to be plenty of that.

Gwenlyn's great success lay in maintaining a momentum for *Pobol y Cwm* through nurturing his cadre of talented young 'apprentices' who developed their writing skills in the series before they flew the nest to write single plays which benefited BBC Wales and S4C. Meic Povey, Siôn Eirian, William Jones (Will Sir Fôn) and Dewi Wyn Williams (Dewi Chips) were regarded by Gwenlyn as his four 'blackberries' – all carefully handpicked!

His first apprentice, Meic Povey, has always been an engaging and multi-talented personality, a fine actor and writer in both languages, having taken prominent parts in series such as *Minder* and written major TV plays as varied as *Sul y Blodau* [Palm Sunday], *Taff Acre* and the police comedy *Glas y Dorlan* with John Pierce Jones.

Meic's first job in his native Criccieth was reading aloud the autobiography of the centenarian brother of David Lloyd George, William, to the author himself. It was the office's way of keeping the aged man from interfering in the work of the family law firm. Meic's own autobiography is a searingly honest survey of high life in his early years, followed by a moving account of the tragic loss of his greatest influence – his wife Gwen. Ultimately, Meic shows his sensitivity as a playwright in the use of the word 'malio'. If the audience for his work doesn't 'malio' [care], then there can be no point in the writing of it in the first place. Meic earned the huge regard of his colleagues as an all-or-nothing personality.

One of his early single plays in Welsh, *Sul y Blodau*, was based on the scandalous story of police raids and detention without any charge of some 50 people with nationalist sympathies on Palm Sunday, 31 March 1980. The CID, desperate to discover who was behind the burning of second homes during the previous decade, made the ill-fated moves against local police advice. Everybody was released within days and compensation was paid to certain individuals for the disruption caused to their family life. Nobody was ever caught. Producer Richard Lewis cast Povey as an actor as well as a scriptwriter in what was an early bilingual drama.

The young Siôn Eirian proved to be the second formidable talent in Gwenlyn's armoury. His cherubic face and polite manner was only to be expected of a son of the manse but he lost no time in living life to the full as he learnt his trade on *Pobol y Cwm* and then wrote the highly popular detective series *Bowen a'i Bartner* in 1985. It included the most violent scenes to date on Welsh TV, but escaped censorious outbursts from

Mrs Mary Whitehouse's friends who were then in their heyday as the keeper of Britain's morals. The Broadcasting Council for Wales was much more enlightened and gave it high praise. In the 1990s Siôn followed on with an extensive range of TV work in both languages, including *A Mind to Kill* in English and *Gadael Lenin* [Leaving Lenin] for S4C.

T. James Jones was not a 'blackberry' but did join the chosen few to become a highly successful script editor in the early days of *Pobol y Cwm*. He was older than the others when he joined the series, a member of the well-known 'Parc Nest' family of three National Eisteddfod major poetry winners. All three became Congregationalist ministers, an occupation which Jim was probably glad to escape in favour of a liberal life of writing, freed from the Nonconformist constraints of the 1970s. Jim will always be best known for his brilliant translation of Dylan Thomas's *Under Milk Wood* into Welsh which lost nothing in translation. In later years, serving time as the Archdruid did not stop him continuing to write TV scripts with a penchant for drama-documentary.

Will 'Sir Fôn' Jones and his assistant script editor Dewi (Chips) Wyn Williams emerged as the unsung heroes of the 1988 expansion of *Pobol y Cwm* to five times a week. Will 'Sir Fôn' wrote the outstanding drama *Penyberth*, the first in Welsh to be transmitted on BBC2 with subtitles. Unfortunately, he was yet another member of a hugely creative circle who died at an early age.

Dewi Wyn Williams claims to have written over 100 episodes of *Pobol y Cwm*. His outgoing nature, complete with ready smile and rapid speech, is only contained when cycling or running. That fitness regime and his strict control over alcohol gave him a lifestyle very different from his closest colleagues. His abiding memory is that of rewriting scripts on the day of transmission, usually due to the illness of a key actor. Once, two different writers had been asked to write the same story. This meant that there was no script for another episode. Will, Dewi and Jim wrote the missing episode themselves in blocks, which allowed the recording to continue without the actors realising the extent of the panic. The credits ran with the new name of Nesta Wyn Jones on the closing titles. Nesta Wyn Jones stood for Jim 'Parc Nest', Wyn for Dewi Wyn Williams and Jones for Will 'Sir Fôn' Jones!

Dewi left the BBC to become S4C's drama consultant and then retired to write plays for Radio Cymru and the stage, earning high praise for winning the prestigious drama medal at the National Eisteddfod.

It is impossible to count or name the dozens of scriptwriters who have been hired by *Pobol y Cwm*, but as the series grew, alongside the newsroom, it became one of the two biggest production units in BBC Wales. Yet within the department, the 'bread and butter' nature of the series sometimes made those working on it feel like second-class citizens compared with producers working on single plays or network programmes. During its first 16 years, when I was associated with it as a senior manager responsible for its resources, *Pobol y Cwm* was the most popular Welsh-language programme ever to grace BBC Wales or S4C, yet never won an award of any kind.

Peter Edwards, son of film star Meredith Edwards, was one of several long-serving directors and producers on *Pobol y Cwm*, his serious no-nonsense approach also earning him accolades for producing Siôn Eirian's *Bowen a'i Bartner*, directing the award-winning drama *Penyberth*, as well as producing and directing more episodes of *The District Nurse* than anyone else during its three-series run. His experience of working with Julia Smith and Tony Holland on that production was undoubtedly responsible for his selection as one of the launch directors of *EastEnders* in 1985. At one time Peter even branched out into light entertainment as the innovative director of the pop programme *Twndish*, and eventually left to become Head of Drama at ITV Wales and then an independent producer, during which time he built a huge portfolio of work until his untimely death in 2016.

In 1988 I appointed another experienced producer/director

of *Pobol y Cwm*, Gwyn Hughes Jones, as its Senior Producer not long before he carried through its expansion to transmission on five days a week.

As a small child I had fond memories of Gwyn's father, a caring man with a mop of white hair and a pronounced north Walian accent who had baptised me at his Saron, Aberaman, chapel before Gwyn was born. Gwyn had the same quiet and engaging manner as his father, but he also had the self-confidence to manage a large group of people following extensive experience of working on both *Pobol y Cwm* and single plays. He was faced with a truly massive mountain to climb, the most enterprising gamble since the original launch of the series in 1974.

Recording and transmitting an episode of drama on the same day had never been done anywhere before to the best of our knowledge. 'Thankfully,' Gwyn recalled, 'in Will Sir Fôn I had a wonderful and tireless Tenzing! The journey would not have been possible without him. It was the moment when Will inherited Gwenlyn's mantle.'

By this time some of Gwyn's colleagues had established themselves as an integral part of the *Pobol y Cwm* production team. Alan Cook, David J. Evans and Rhiannon Rees had been appointed to the growing children's department when *Yr Awr Fawr* [The Great Hour] was launched in 1979. In addition, Robin Rollinson had emerged from the film unit where he had shone as a cameraman. The sudden growth of the *Pobol y Cwm* unit required their experience to head up four separate production teams. They worked in pairs – one of the four teams recording the bulk of the episode in the studio, the second responsible for the exterior shoot for that day's transmission; another would be preparing for the following week, liaising with the script unit and assisting at the end of the week with editing in order to maintain continuity between the four groups. Small wonder that I was less than pleased when Mervyn Williams poached Gwyn for his drama unit at Opus Productions just when the new pattern of production had gained momentum and when we had no ready replacement.

Head of Programmes Teleri Bevan had noticed the ginger-haired postgraduate student Glenda Jones during a radio appointments board and recruited her as a TV researcher a couple of years later. Young, inexperienced, energetic and enthusiastic, Glenda went from making documentaries as an assistant producer and helping direct a couple of episodes of *Pobol y Cwm* to taking charge of the series. She used her intelligence in understanding the primacy of teamwork and organisation for all of ten years. An all-action woman, Glenda has never found enough hours in the day to fulfil all her interests, whether studying for a Ph.D., helping out at the Cardiff Blues rugby academy, singing in Eisteddfod choirs, joining Estyn's schools inspectorate as a lay member, or sitting on the boards of S4C and the National Museum Wales – although only some of these at the same time!

Producing *Pobol y Cwm* every weekday exposed the actors to a daily regime of recording on the day of transmission with only one safety net – going live if necessary. A calculated risk was taken on the capacity of the actors to memorise their lines. There was the further risk that winter snow would lead to empty screens. Neither actors nor the weather ever let the viewers down.

Launching the series back in 1974 had involved problems with the availability of experienced actors. During the first five years the action centred around the old people's home 'Brynawelon', because the best actors of that era were approaching a certain age. The most prominent figures were Rachel Thomas and Charles Williams. 'Rach' was the most famous of Welsh female film stars, having appeared in films such as *The Proud Valley* and *Blue Scar*. She had made the part of the strict Welsh 'Mam' her own, an obvious choice to play the equally stern Matron Bella Davies in *Pobol y Cwm*. In fact 'Rach', as she was fondly known, toned down the myth of her stereotype closer to her much gentler real-life character.

Charles Williams, who played Harri Parri, had long been the outstanding male actor of his generation in Welsh and had worked on Radio 4's *The Archers* for many years. His leg-pulling of less experienced actors did not make him popular on the set of *Pobol y Cwm* but everybody admired his acting. It was a happy community with few other personal tensions, even if some actresses insisted on choosing with whom to share a dressing room.

Five other actors established themselves in the series from the very first episode: former headmistress Harriet Lewis as Maggie Post, Lisabeth Miles as Megan Harries of the Deri Arms, Islwyn Morris as Dai Tushingham, Dillwyn Owen as Jacob Ellis and Dic Hughes as the Reverend T.L. Thomas – the last three as residents of Brynawelon.

Only as the series progressed did a younger generation come through strongly. The rough, gruff, rugby-loving Huw Ceredig played Reg behind the bar of the Deri Arms as 'one of the boys', a role which made Reg indistinguishable from his own personality for nearly 30 years. Lisabeth Miles, as his wife Megan, was certainly no hellraiser, acting the loyal and long-suffering wife as she did when taking the part of Mrs Margaret Lloyd George in John Hefin's later epic.

Gillian Elisa Thomas's character Sabrina formed one half of a wonderful double act with Harriet Lewis's Maggie Post in the post office cum village shop. Some actors had better memories than others. Gaynor Morgan Rees earned plaudits from the production team for the best memory on the set, but the older Harriet was always afraid of forgetting her lines. She often hid a crib sheet on a cereal box in her shop – until one day a 'props' man moved the box and left her stranded. Even the cast gradually confused reality with fiction. Sabrina and Maggie Post were not alone in referring to each other by their stage names when off duty.

The earliest scripts were written to suit the ability and even the character of the actors. The belief of the viewers in the series was astounding. Fiction somehow merged into reality on a parallel universe. Many in the audience looked forward to *Pobol y Cwm* as the highlight of their day. As the expanding troupe of actors gained experience, they were capable of dealing with challenging emotional situations – the death of a baby or a father, the weddings and funerals, the innumerable love affairs and the family rows which all strengthened the credibility of the series.

By the time *Pobol y Cwm* celebrated its 40th birthday, Gareth Lewis had been associated with it for 39 years, 36 of them acting as Meic Pierce. He just grew old with his character. Olwen Rees appeared four different times in four different parts. Leading actor in the TV series *Hornblower* and Hollywood film star Ioan Gruffudd started his acting career in *Pobol y Cwm* as the son of Reg and Megan. The inimitable Dewi 'Pws' could be guaranteed to lark around behind the scenes, but was totally self-disciplined on the set playing Wayne, the lively brother of Reg Harries, while Dic 'Deryn' Ashurst was the arch womaniser. Arwyn Davies, son of the great Ryan, is one of many actors who saw *Pobol y Cwm* through the Millennium years and may yet beat Gwyn Elfyn's record of 28 consecutive years in the role of Denzil.

The production team underlined the reality of life in Cwmderi through introducing prominent characters from time to time – Alun Williams and Ray Gravell included. A bounce in the audience ratings was guaranteed when Gillian Elisa got married. A birth was a source of pleasure; death, or the threat of it, attracted a mix of morbid interest and genuine sympathy as characters left or were written out for one reason or another. A substantial section of the audience came to believe that the characters were a part of their own family and empathised with their travails as community life in Cwmderi concentrated less on old people and changed with the times.

There were three directors in the drama department with the surname Owen. The eldest producer in the department, George P. Owen, belonged to that generation which took no notice of the time taken to complete several works by Saunders

Lewis, as well as several of Gwenlyn's single plays, including the TV version of *Y Tŵr* [The Tower] which explored the relationship between a married couple as they moved up the 'tower' of life. Taking the only two roles in *Y Tŵr* gave John Ogwen and his wife Maureen Rhys the greatest pleasure of their acting career, since Gwenlyn had been one of the actor's mentors when they were teachers and taught at Ysgol Dyffryn Ogwen in Bethesda.

John Ogwen was already emulating Charles Williams as the most accomplished Welsh actor of a younger generation and had even taken part in *The Archers* as his son. More than 25 years after playing *Y Tŵr*, John has a massive portfolio of work behind him and much more to come.

Pipe smoking George P. Owen spent his later years producing and directing English-language productions, including *Hawkmoor* and *The District Nurse* for the network.

His namesake, Myrfyn Owen, was the jolly sporting type, always ready for company and a laugh. He worked on *Pobol y Cwm* for many years and also directed several episodes of *The District Nurse*. He spent much of his leisure time playing squash to a high standard until he died very suddenly while jogging on a canal towpath. Yet another friendly personality who died young.

The third Owen, Ron, had been a floor manager in studio and outside broadcasts, working on *Pobol y Cwm* in that capacity for so long that transferring to life in the gallery was relatively easy. Ron's disciplined approach brooked no change once he was in recording mode, a habit taken from his previous life mediating between the floor and gallery. This became increasingly necessary when the series changed gear from the early days, a time when one episode was given a whole week to record.

John Hefin had lost interest in the series given the new network challenges which took over his working life. This was not entirely a bad thing. Every so often there was a need for a transfusion of new blood and new thoughts from editors, directors and producers.

Gwenlyn guaranteed continuity to the series while continuing to write his single plays, first for the stage and then for TV, of which *Y Tŵr* was the second to be staged before being recorded for TV. The first, *Saer Doliau* [Doll Mender], was a cultural sensation and signalled a break from the plays of Saunders Lewis and John Gwilym Jones. It was a piece of total theatre, containing several possible allegories and open to endless interpretations. Its performance at the Aberafan National Eisteddfod in 1966 left the audience perplexed as to its meaning. Most cognoscenti thought it the theatre of the absurd with echoes of Harold Pinter, Samuel Beckett or Pirandello. One theory emerged that the scene of the older man talking to the doll was influenced by the fable of Pinocchio. It unquestionably broke new ground in Welsh drama and stimulated considerable debate to which a wicked Gwenlyn enjoyed listening to without comment. It led to his plays being the subject of a philosophical tome by University College, Swansea, philosopher, Dewi Z. Phillips, postulating that all the plays reveal a dichotomy between the good and evil in all of us. It emerged that Gwenlyn merely wanted audiences to make up their own minds given the choice of possible allegories in the script, and he followed it up with two other plays in the same genre. *Y Tŵr* was one and the other, *Tŷ ar y Tywod* [House on the Sand], was equally open to interpretation as the author explored the frailty of human relationships built on flimsy foundations. The idea for his last play, *Panto*, came to him while watching his other close friend Ryan Davies preparing to go on stage at the Grand Theatre in Swansea. *Panto* had considerable overtones of autobiography for those of us who knew something of his complicated personal life. *Panto* was the commissioned play at the Fishguard National Eisteddfod in 1986, again starring John Ogwen with the strong female cast of Sue Roderick, Christine Pritchard and Morfydd Hughes. The incidental music was composed by Huw

Chiswell. Gwyn Hughes Jones recorded the play for TV during its two live performances at Theatr Felinfach and described the presentations as 'demanding emotionally, and, I fear, shocking in parts for much of the audience in Fishguard'.

All Gwenlyn's works were eagerly awaited when launched in the theatre or when broadcast on both radio and TV. His character was as complex as some of his single plays. Any attempt to understand what was really going on behind his walrus moustache was heavily disguised behind an exhausting lifestyle of writing and then enjoying afternoons of convivial company and hilarious storytelling with Rhydderch and a variety of like-minded colleagues in several watering holes, including the Castell Mynach pub outside Cardiff which they called Studio 4. I recall acting as his chauffeur the night a farewell dinner was held for Head of Light Entertainment Jack Williams. It was particularly memorable for Gwenlyn's mimicry of Wil Napoleon and friends, the unique circle of 'Cofis' in working-class Caernarfon which fascinated him when he lived near the Roman site of Segontium. He could reel off innumerable stories about other people but never revealed anything about himself.

Gwenlyn and Rhydderch had no regard for normal working hours. They were known to work into the early hours and end their day at lunchtime. Gwenlyn always claimed he could not write for more than three hours a day. Yet, when programme deadlines called, they were more than capable of maintaining self-discipline. Gwenlyn never lost the regard of his script unit. They knew he was the sharpest of them all at spotting even the smallest weakness in a script.

Rhydderch was totally different, an open and lovable bear of a man with huge creative ability, a hangdog look on his face, his shambling gait and unkempt appearance often signalling a night working hard or sleeping on somebody else's sofa, at least until he tied the knot with the caring and stable Irene in later years.

Rhydderch's single plays and even comedies, like *Glas y*

Dorlan, used actors and sometimes directors with experience of *Pobol y Cwm*. He himself had spent a short time on attachment to the series, but his usual day job was producing and directing comedy programmes.

When, in late 1985, Ruth Price retired as Head of Light Entertainment, I had to withstand the pleading look in his eyes when I told him that he was more useful to Wales writing comedy than managing people. It was time to have fewer departmental chiefs and I closed the iconic department down with great sadness. In effect, Rhydderch became another distinguished member of Gwenlyn's brood.

Rhydderch's single plays were written with film in mind but there was one notable exception. He will always be remembered for the poignant drama *Mr Lollipop, MA*, produced in both languages. In English it starred Dame Flora Robson and Charles Williams. It was the story of a man losing his mind and believing he was teaching a class of children in his living room. When he says the school inspectors are coming, Flora Robson tells him there is no inspector and no children. Charles claimed that the biggest acting thrill of his life was seeing the great actress telling him the truth of the situation with genuine tears in her eyes. Rhydderch became great friends with Flora Robson after that production.

He wrote three single plays in Welsh which were televised, all of which involved Gwenlyn as script editor, all produced and directed by Gwyn Hughes Jones. *Man a Lle* [Place and Place] has been somewhat forgotten, perhaps because Rhydderch depicted a strange state of disorientation, a loss of time, place and belonging inspired by the noise of cranes demolishing buildings outside his Newport Road office. The impact of the other two highly personal films was so much greater because they were deeply rooted in time, place and belonging. *Gwenoliaid* [Swallows] related the story of wartime evacuees arriving in his native Merionethshire. Set mainly in Rhydderch's home village of Aberllefenni and nearby Corris, it starred the young Rolant Ellis Thomas and was a lyrical evocation of growing up in the most peaceful part of Britain during the war. Rhydderch wrote it with his own boyhood memories in mind and Gwyn Hughes Jones remembers filming his boyhood home at the end of the row of quarrymen's cottages 'which added to the intensity and emotion' of the shoot. It won Best Regional Drama at the Pye TV Awards.

Lliwiau [Colours], filmed in the same area with the same team, focused on the relationship between a quarryman, his family and the owner of the quarry. It used the technique of the colours on a snooker table to portray the different phases in the life of a quarryman – the life of Rhydderch's own father.

It was in production during the week of Rhydderch's funeral in 1987. Gwyn had to break the news of his death to Rhydderch's great friend Stewart Jones who was playing the role of the father. 'His performance the next day in the pulpit of the little chapel in Abergeirw had a sincerity and depth beyond Stewart's usual professionalism, while Bryn Fôn was inspiring in the leading role.' The production won the best Fiction and Drama trophy at the Celtic Media Festival in Roscoff in 1989. Gwenlyn was present, 'desperately trying to hold back the tears, as were we all'.

The funeral itself was packed to overflowing for a man without an enemy in the world. Nearby was the pub where 'Rhydd' used to welcome all his friends but that day the normally genial landlord, Danny Rowlands, felt as flat as the rest of us.

The death of Rhydderch in 1987 and Gwenlyn in 1991, both before they were 60 years old, was a tragic blow to Welsh broadcasting. It was equalled only by that of their close friend Ryan Davies in 1977. Their combined canon of work in drama and light entertainment created more enjoyment for the many, and so many thought-provoking plays for the few than before or since. Yet they were both inexplicably ignored by those who selected the white-robed great and the good at the National Eisteddfod.

The fact that they worked and played so hard together must

have contributed to their early deaths. Their writing, however, has outlived them by more than a quarter of a century already. They combined their talents in delivering Rhydderch's films. They were often two sides of the same coin, both protesting that their partner was merely sharpening pencils for the other. Yet they both had separate full-time jobs, Rhydderch in light entertainment while Gwenlyn was nurturing more 'apprentices'. Whatever his thoughts were when he edited that first script of *Pobol y Cwm* in 1974, neither he nor John Hefin could have dreamt that the series would have outlasted them both and still dominates the S4C schedule more than 40 years down the line.

11

Under New Management, 1974

THE YEAR 1974 was not only when *Pobol y Cwm* was launched; two general elections were held on the theme of 'Who Runs Britain?' and it was also the year it was decided who should now run BBC Wales. This followed the retirement of Controller John Rowley, just two years after that of long-serving Head of Programmes Aneirin Talfan Davies and his deputy D.J. Thomas. The last vestiges of a pioneering generation of producers\managers had gone – but had not been forgotten.

Chance, luck, or being in the right place at the right time are often real factors when people are promoted. Ten years after joining the BBC in 1964, I was appointed deputy to Head of Programmes Geraint Stanley Jones when Owen Edwards was promoted to the Controllership. It led to 16 years on the third floor of BBC Llandaff in all three posts, following Geraint in each one.

Within weeks of my appointment I formed a close working relationship with Teleri Bevan, an experienced senior producer in radio who would eventually follow me into senior management – the first woman to do so in Wales. Geraint Stanley Jones and Teleri Bevan would become my closest colleagues and friends for the rest of our lives. We were the programme team headed by Geraint and assigned by the Broadcasting Council for Wales, its Chairman Glyn Tegai Hughes and Controller Owen Edwards, to build the four branches of the future BBC Wales. The work came to a head during an extraordinary period of six years between January 1977 and November 1982 which changed the landscape of broadcasting in Wales. It was the busiest and best of times, at once exciting, frustrating and fulfilling.

The most fulfilling part of the job was the privilege of appointing a new generation of broadcasters who would serve Wales and beyond with a host of notable programmes for the next quarter of a century. The frustrations were caused by the slow receipt of funds from London during the radio development, as well as some of the crazier proposals for the Welsh Fourth Channel by some politicians who should have known better. The excitement was engendered through trying to anticipate which potential problem or possibility awaited us every day of the week.

The genuine surprise of becoming a manager at the age of 34 was all the greater because an older generation of very experienced colleagues had been expected to succeed to senior management, but all of them had moved on within a period of five years. Dr Meredydd Evans, the strong-minded Head of Light Entertainment, decided to go back to academia and become politically active as a guiding light in the Welsh language movement.

Aled Vaughan, the equally cultured and sensitive senior documentary producer, had been appointed Director of Programmes at the new commercial station HTV.

My old boss Nan Davies, the powerful Head of Welsh-Language Programmes and mentor of so many young producers, had retired and then died within a very short time.

Alan Protheroe, the dominant force in news and current affairs, was spirited off to run the network news operations in 1970, on the way to becoming Assistant Director-General in charge of all BBC news and current affairs outlets.

It only left the youthful Owen Edwards to become Head of Programmes in 1972 and Controller in 1974, just as Nan Davies had predicted. Owen was already well known to Huw

Wheldon, the influential big beast in London who appointed him Controller with the blessing of the Broadcasting Council for Wales. Only Geraint Stanley Jones, who had been Owen's deputy for less than two years, was regarded as a serious candidate for the Head of Programmes post. When I became Geraint's deputy, a new, young and inexperienced management team had arrived at a time when there were signs of significant development, certainly in radio and possibly in TV.

There was, however, one experienced person still in place from the previous management team. Owen Thomas was the small, physically frail but powerful Head of Planning and Finance. A highly educated native of Fishguard, with a razor-sharp mind and a deep love of classical music, Owen had enjoyed working with Hywel Davies immensely and was a massive support to his successors Aneirin Talfan Davies and Owen Edwards. He would prove just as valuable to the new programme team.

Geraint Stanley Jones had eclectic tastes. During his National Service days he had played the organ for the religious services at Plymouth Barracks and had taught a unit of the Army's young miscreants how to calm down by expressing themselves in painting on canvas and through energetic cycling. He enjoyed that time so much that he nearly signed on for another three years in the Army's Education Corps. Instead, he joined the BBC as a radio studio manager, progressing to become a mainstay of the *Heddiw* team throughout the 1960s, producing films and outside broadcasts from the four corners of Wales as well as the production of all the major summer festivals in Wales. He edited *Week In Week Out* for a season, and made a major documentary with Vincent Kane, *The Night the Bridge Caught Fire*, about when Brunel's historic railway crossing over the Menai Straits was severely damaged. Geraint was keen to pursue his wider interests in features, music and light entertainment. He contributed to the network series *Look, Stranger* which included the memorable story of Gregynog Hall near Newtown in the company of Dora Herbert

Jones, the kindly, well-spoken woman who had worked for the art collecting Davies sisters, and for its unique Gregynog Press. Geraint turned to entertainment in English, with Alun Williams as one of his compères, recording innumerable programmes on Welsh male voice choirs and devising *Poems and Pints*, *The Singing Barge* series and *Stuart Burrows Sings* for BBC2; all before becoming deputy Head of Programmes in 1972. He continued to produce the St David's Day concerts for the network. The singing of massed north Wales choirs congregated around the circle of the newly-opened Liverpool Metropolitan Cathedral thrilled him. He just loved the sounds of big bands, music in the great cathedrals or the differing tones of refurbished cinema organs, even buying a Wurlitzer which he played noisily in his own house.

As the new Head of Programmes, Geraint believed that the BBC's role as a public broadcaster was to serve the whole of Wales and resist pressure from the educated and vocal middle-class opinion formers, if necessary. He was always thinking of the next 'big' idea, the 'hammer blow' aimed to stand out from the ever-demanding regular schedule. Ideas would be thrown around to test reaction. He recoiled from heated debate, preferring to take time to probe different options, often punctuated by bursts of hilarity when, as often happened, ideas descended into the surreal or absurd. We had strong differences of opinion about the presenters we liked or disliked which merely demonstrated the highly subjective nature of broadcasting. Geraint avoided people who were trenchant in their views. He hated personal satire and could be totally unforgiving when offended. We formed a partnership based on mutual trust and an understanding of each other's weaknesses and strengths. I sometimes played the hawk to his dovelike approach when disciplinary problems arose. When a discussion became animated he would note the views around the room in silence, stroking his bearded face slowly from brow to beard while making up his own mind. A final decision sometimes resulted from having slept on it overnight, but he was never afraid of going against the herd. Above all, Geraint had emotional intelligence, a sensitivity to the feelings of others and an outer calm which heavily disguised strong feelings below the surface, a temperament rare in the broadcasting business. As the new Head of Programmes he was fortunate to inherit a staff of some 800 people which included some of the most creative people in Wales in light entertainment and drama. As noted, Ryan Davies, Gwenlyn Parry, Rhydderch Jones and John Hefin stood out as the writers, performers and producers of popular shows such as *Fo a Fe*, *Ryan a Ronnie* and *Pobol y Cwm*. Max Boyce had emerged as the talisman of the great rugby teams of the 1970s, reinforcing a growing sense of national pride. Geraint would now build on that inheritance on both TV and radio.

When he first asked me to concentrate on radio development in 1974, I only knew Teleri Bevan by reputation. She was by far the most experienced senior radio producer in Wales, having started her BBC career in 1955 working as an assistant producer to the most demanding, often tyrannical, but highly professional Lorraine Davies when editor of children's programmes. Working for and with children was always a great training ground for an all-round producer. It offered Teleri the opportunity to direct the best-known Welsh actors or use the small BBC Welsh Orchestra (as it was known then) and commission music from composers such as Grace Williams. When she left to raise a family, Teleri freelanced on entertainment shows for TWW, gaining valuable experience on TV for the first time. On returning to the BBC in 1967, she became presenter and producer of women's programmes – *Merched yn Bennaf* and its English equivalent, *Woman's Hour*, transmitted once a month on Fridays from Cardiff, a programme which was always followed by a demanding inquest down the line.

Having returned to radio management after an absence of eight years, I discovered that Teleri had already started expanding the putative radio services and was pondering the impact of the competition provided by the launch of Swansea Sound that very year. With limited resources she was forging ahead with an early Monday morning show in English and the experimental launch of *Bore Da* on VHF in Welsh. Teleri had sat on a working party with Lorraine and Brian Evans, editor of *Good Morning Wales*. They had proposed the future division of the two languages between VHF for the Welsh language and Medium Wave for English. Teleri was the only person in a position to drive the new strategy when I arrived on the scene, and we immediately formed a close working relationship based on a mutual support system which would be of enormous benefit during some of the more difficult days ahead.

Controller Owen Edwards was more aloof as a colleague at the beginning, although I had known him since he had started work as a junior member of staff at the National Library of Wales in Aberystwyth. He was certainly the pre-eminent TV presenter in the Welsh language, as witnessed by large audiences watching *Heddiw* during his heyday on the programme in the 1960s. It went out at lunchtime to the whole of the UK. Owen received a large postbag of personal letters, even from England, including a regular correspondence with a lady living in Newcastle who watched him every day because he reminded her of her dead son. In those days presenters had no autocue. Owen used his short-term photographic memory to perfect countdowns to film and videotape. He accepted the Controllership in 1974 with that sense of entitlement born of supreme confidence, coming as he did from a dynastic family background. He came into his own as the fluent public voice of BBC Wales not only to the Welsh public but also to management in London. In 1981 he walked into S4C as its first Chief Executive in what was seen as a seamless career progression. Everything he said in public was well prepared and based on thorough briefings. When a new Chairman of the Independent Broadcasting Authority, Lord Thomson of Monifieth, came on his first public visit to Cardiff knowing nothing about Welsh broadcasting, he confessed to me later that when asking naïve questions about S4C during his visit, 'I was put in my place by this young man I had never heard of.'

Owen's confidence, however, was only skin-deep. He became progressively more dependant on the support and briefings he was getting from Geraint Stanley Jones at BBC Wales and, later, Euryn Ogwen Williams at S4C. Owen never pretended to be a creative broadcaster. He was a natural performer with the ability to ask the right questions carefully prepared beforehand. The Wheldon and Edwards families were both regarded as members of a fading Welsh Establishment. Huw's father, Sir Wynn Wheldon, and Owen's grandfather, Sir Owen M. Edwards, had been pioneers of Welsh education. Huw's word would have been enough to anoint Owen as Controller, but first he had to serve apprenticeships in the planning department and a couple of years as Head of Programmes, neither of which really suited his ability or temperament. As Controller he demonstrated his mastery of a brief in discussions with the Broadcasting Council for Wales and top management in London, but he was not one for formulating a programme strategy, although he did have a strong Welsh-language schedule and took the decision to launch *Pobol y Cwm*. Gradually, however, Owen seemed to lose confidence in the major projects still at the development stage. He lacked conviction in the potential success of Radio Cymru. He asked me: 'Are you sure it will work?'

Geraint realised that Owen was suffering from depression, often followed by bouts of euphoria after a successful performance in public or in committee. The evening before he agreed to let his name go forward as the first Chief Executive of S4C, Owen called in my office and said, 'I want you to know that I am NOT going to apply for the S4C post.'

The following morning he did the exact opposite. I had not realised until then how depressed he was and how little self-confidence he had in facing the launch of a new channel with no staff and without the security offered by BBC Wales.

By the time he joined S4C, Owen Edwards was not a well man but he was fortunate in having Sir Goronwy Daniel as his Chairman and Euryn Ogwen Williams as his programme chief. Nevertheless, Owen Edwards set a standard of performing excellence in the Welsh language which others have tried to emulate but no-one has surpassed. Above all, he was at the helm of both BBC Wales and S4C when the greatest advances were made in the Welsh media landscape.

When the new management team was appointed in 1974, radio development was already part of a new BBC nationwide policy to advance national channels in Scotland, Wales and Northern Ireland. The Welsh Fourth Channel idea was different, a politically charged project specific to Wales. The Welsh Language Society's campaign of the TV channel gathered pace throughout the 1970s. It was a constant background sound as we began the task of building Radio Cymru and Radio Wales.

12

The Radio Builders, 1974–77

IN LATE 1974 the recently installed Head of Programmes Geraint Stanley Jones determined on a new and different sound for each of the two new national radio services. In essence, the strategy was to appeal to the majority of listeners in Wales who had never been attracted to all-talk radio. He devolved the detailed planning to me as his deputy while he concentrated on the TV output. I immediately turned to senior producer Teleri Bevan who knew more about radio than anybody else in Wales.

It involved building on the foundations of the existing Welsh regional programme which carried programmes in two languages and used Radio 4 as a sustaining service, a situation which had barely changed since 1946. The aim was to build two semi-detached services called Radio Wales and Radio Cymru, designed as distinctive channels for very different linguistic audiences. They would always be semi-detached because of the fully integrated nature of BBC Wales, with news, sport, religion and music departments supplying their wares to all radio and TV channels with their own specialised programming. It took four full years of slow growth before we could afford to appoint full-time editors in November 1978.

The funding promised from radio management in London was exactly the same as was allocated to Scotland, despite the fact that it required only one service while Wales had two distinct language channels. The London argument was that Scotland had double the population of Wales and deserved the same investment per listener.

The problem, however, went deeper than money. The Broadcasting Council for Wales had to decide which channel stayed on Medium Wave and which was to be placed on VHF (Very High Frequency). There were risks whatever the decision. The service on Medium Wave might wait for years before being allocated a VHF wavelength. The service on VHF had the problem of persuading its potential audience to buy new receivers since the take-up to date had been low. The waters were already being tested in 1974, as *Good Morning Wales* was already well established on MW when *Bore Da* was launched on VHF only. That experiment led to the Broadcasting Council for Wales decision to develop Radio Wales on MW in the hope that one day it would be allocated its own VHF wavelength as well. Radio Cymru was allocated the wavelength of the future but it required a massive marketing campaign in order to persuade Welsh listeners to buy VHF sets. That marketing campaign took many different forms. Advertising on our own TV channel cost nothing and it was used extensively. It was also obvious that *Bore Da* suffered from being the only Welsh programme on VHF. There was not enough output to justify buying new radio sets which involved a real financial cost to listeners. At the same time, it was too dangerous to move all existing Welsh programmes to VHF at a time when transmissions in 1974 amounted to little more than 20 hours a week.

It was only at the Criccieth National Eisteddfod of 1975 that Teleri came up with the answer. She had teamed up presenter Hywel Gwynfryn with producer Gareth Lloyd Williams in the first extensive coverage of the event on radio. The idea of *Helo Bobol* [Hello People] was born. An entertaining early morning show, supplemented by news packages, would sound different from the serious fare usually heard on air at that time of the morning. It would include 15 minutes of news every hour with 45 minutes of music and chat. Geraint Stanley Jones and the Broadcasting Council for Wales backed it, although its members were serious-minded people who were much more likely to be listeners of all-talk radio themselves. It was a big gamble whichever way one looked at it.

In order to stiffen the marketing of both Radio Wales and Radio Cymru, it was decided to run experimental community radio stations in English, and Radio Bro in Welsh. In 1976 a radio van, borrowed from RTÉ Dublin which could broadcast live to small communities, was located in carefully selected large villages and small towns in north and south Wales. The neatly designed mobile radio station spent three days in each of ten different locations: Pwllheli on the Llŷn peninsula; Rhosllannerchrugog near Wrexham; Llwynhendy, a village near Llanelli; Llanrwst in Clwyd and Tregaron in Cardiganshire were the five chosen to broadcast in Welsh. In English the studio pitched up in the Rhondda, Merthyr, Wrexham, Newport and Pontypool. Each one of these exercises worked so well that we were invited to several other places and asked to stay on everywhere. The secret of its success was down to a simple formula – they were all communities talking among themselves. The Broadcasting Council for Wales was so impressed that thought was given to BBC Wales having its own mobile studio, but London turned the idea down. In any case, such a move could have compromised the growth of the national services which was the purpose of the whole exercise.

One of the most complex problems to be faced was the restructuring of the newsroom. It was not geared for two fully developed radio services, or the longer term possibility of providing a news service for a Welsh-language TV channel. By late 1975 I was worried by the lack of forward planning in the newsroom. It had always been centred around the TV flagship *Wales Today*, but the expansion of new services could not work as mere add-ons to the existing structure. Worse still, an insidious influence on the newsroom staff was undermining the authority of Owen Roberts as the editor of news and current affairs. Roberts was the first outsider to have been appointed to run all the news outlets of BBC Wales. He had been a highly successful editor of *Y Dydd* on HTV, and had built his own team of first-class reporters and interviewers in Welsh. He arrived at the BBC in late 1971 with everybody anticipating he might well be the 'next Controller but one'. Owen Roberts radiated a natural sense of intellectual aloofness and had an encyclopaedic knowledge of the political scene. However, he never succeeded in mastering the established journalists he inherited in a newsroom which was full of strong-minded individuals. One such person was Clive Clissold, a clever but indisciplined journalist who was organising shifts to suit himself. He survived a near sacking for indiscipline in 1974 but in the following year began a deliberate campaign to denigrate Owen Roberts. First, an anonymous and vitriolic 'Obituary' for Owen was pinned on the newsroom noticeboard but there was no proof of authorship. Months later a cartoon of my face, drawn to resemble Henry VIII in a contemporary TV drama, was pinned on the same board with a caption reading, 'Who will rid me of this troublesome editor?' Enough was enough. Geraint Stanley Jones and I marched down to the newsroom, cartoon in hand, and made everybody deny having drawn it. The suspect was present and, as expected, denied it with the cynical comment, 'not my style', but we signalled our intent to hunt him down. Nine days later the mischief-maker wrote a flawed news bulletin. It forced duty announcer John Evans to go on air and take an editorial decision himself. Clive Clissold was celebrating his birthday at the BBC Club. We pounced. He was sacked immediately and lost an appeal at an industrial tribunal. However, Owen Roberts's health was already failing from an illness, possibly ignited by a traumatic car accident some years earlier. The Clissold affair did nothing for Owen's health, which never recovered, or for the morale of the newsroom.

During this whole sorry episode I needed help in planning the future newsroom radio services. Owen Roberts had already expanded the news and current affairs empire by taking the well-established *Heddiw* and *Week In Week Out* under his wing as separate entities. A fully integrated newsroom was now required to cater for all four future channels. The department had several excellent managers, particularly the thoroughly professional and single-minded David Morris Jones who was now Chief Assistant, News. However, I feared that all the senior editors would just want a costly increase in staffing in their own units, resulting in the potential waste of four journalists covering every major story. I turned to political correspondent Patrick Hannan in private. A close friend since university days, Patrick had worked on two newspapers before joining the BBC and advised me to create a large input desk and four small output desks, one for each service in the future. As I suspected, the senior editors resisted the idea of a large input desk common to all, but I managed to agree a small such unit as a first step in the right direction. I could not blame news editors determined to control the whole of their output and maximise their small staff numbers, but every additional journalist meant one less general producer for the channel editors and their general programme schedule.

General programme budgets were extremely tight, since the funding from London arrived in dribs and drabs. It meant that even as late as November 1978 the two new editors of Radio Wales and Radio Cymru only had nine general producers plus a few researchers at their disposal. Each service also had a similar number of journalists manning their dedicated output desks in the newsroom, in addition to the increased programming from the specialist sport, religion, music and presentation departments. Programme budgets were small, but it was possible to recruit freelancers on a minimum contract in the expectation that several different departments would use them. It was that flexibility which allowed me, for example, to promise enough work to Huw Llywelyn Davies and poach him from HTV in 1978. It was possible to exploit Huw's ability to present a wide range of content on radio and TV and he became one of Wales's star broadcasters in both media.

Chris Stuart had the light touch at the right time of the morning.

Roy Noble attracted the highest morning audiences.

An always cheerful Frank Hennessy (left) takes cover 'on the road' with Roy Noble.

Cliff Morgan, Teleri Bevan and Geraint Stanley Jones (right). Cliff always made the time for Radio Wales.

Vincent Kane (left) could laugh on *Meet for Lunch*, here with BBC Governor Alwyn Roberts (right) and Council member Dudley Fisher.

Hardy Wynford Vaughan-Thomas – one of the greatest of Welsh broadcasters – walked and rode over the roof of Wales for Radio Wales.

© Roger Vlitos

Long-time presenter Peter Johnson has the best memory for Welsh events.

Merthyr DJ Owen Money is still staying the pace.

Megan Stuart was made third Editor of Radio Wales directly from maternity leave.

Vaughan Roderick started as a researcher; he's now BBC Wales's Welsh Affairs editor.

Rob Brydon – the one that got away. And the rest is history.

Radio Wales staff and presenters, date unknown. But several well-known faces are there.

Hywel Gwynfryn and Gwyn Llewelyn in Llangefni on a road trip to launch Radio Cymru and the early morning *Helo Bobol*.

Dei Tomos – a seasoned and respected broadcaster. Been there. Done that.

Richard Rees started as the announcer and the most popular DJ with a stammer – but never on air. He is now a successful independent producer.

The poets engage in a war of words with laughter as the only weapon. Chairman of *Talwrn y Beirdd* Gerallt Lloyd Owen (left) with T. Llew Jones (right).

T. Glynne Davies, a lovable pessimist whose cup was always empty. Father of a 100-year broadcasting dynasty.

T. Glynne's son, Aled Glynne Davies, was the third Editor of Radio Cymru.

And another son, composer Gareth Glyn, spent 34 years of afternoons presenting *Post Prynhawn* [Afternoon Post].

Sulwyn Thomas's *Stondin* [Stand] was a popular and personal daily interaction with the audience.

Betsan Powys, currently Editor of Radio Cymru, has an excellent background in political journalism and wide cultural interests.

Lyn T. Jones, effectively the last head of the Swansea studios, became the second Editor of Radio Cymru.

L–R: Meirion Edwards, the first Editor of Radio Cymru, with Head of Programmes Geraint Stanley Jones and myself.

Beti George, long-time presenter of a talk and music hour, each with an individual guest, has stamped it with her own identity.

I.B. Griffith, Caernarfon's mayor during the 1969 Investiture, presenter of *Rhwng Gŵyl a Gwaith* [Between Work and Play], could turn indifferent material into memorable talk.

Garry Owen travels anywhere, anyplace, any time for the BBC in his Garryvan.

Ruth Parry, producer of *Merched yn Bennaf* [Mainly for Women], holds the buggy. Ruth opened a crèche when she left the BBC.

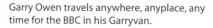

BBC Bangor staff, October 1965. Head of BBC Bangor, R. Alun Evans (third from left, front row), hosts a welcome gathering for me (second from left) as Acting Controller and Andrew McCabe, Head of Personnel BBC Wales (fourth from left).

Tadaaki Otaka conducting the BBC Welsh Symphony Orchestra in the Gewandhaus, Leipzig, May 1987.

Bryn Terfel, winner of the Lieder Prize in the thrilling *Cardiff Singer of the World* final of 1989. The launch of a great career.

Head of Music Mervyn Williams ponders the problem of publicising *Cardiff Singer of the World* with me.

The popular Japanese conductor Tadaaki Otaka conducting the BBC Welsh.

The great Latvian conductor Mariss Jansons was chief guest conductor of the BBC Welsh in the 1980s.

The 'voice of an angel' Aled Jones with Benjamin Luxon at Westminster Cathedral, Christmas Eve 1985, for the BBC2 programme, *The Newborn King*.

Radio 3 organist Huw Tregelles Williams turned BBC producer and became Head of Music in 1986. He was appointed the first director of the renamed BBC National Orchestra of Wales in 1993.

John Watkin (right) and Iwan Thomas gave great support to the big BBC Wales events.

The BBC's Presence after the Launch of S4C.

Dewi Llwyd (right) presented S4C's *Newyddion Saith* for over 30 years, with Editor, Wales News & Current Affairs, Gwilym Owen.

Gwyn Hughes Jones launched *Pobol y Cwm* as a daily series.

Meilyr Ellis Thomas on his horse with an unidentified actor, but the filming stopped on Rhydderch Jones's *Lliwiau* [Colours] on the day of his funeral.

Arwel Ellis Owen went from Editor, Wales News & Current Affairs, to being interim Chief Executive of S4C.

Producers Gareth Rowlands (left) and Ieuan Lewis with PA Eirwen Davies in the ancient Studio B gallery. In the background Head of Light Entertainment Ruth Price briefs Carwyn James for a Sunday afternoon show.

Controllers Owen Edwards (left) and Geraint Stanley Jones (right) became Chief Executives of S4C. Alwyn Roberts (right of centre) sat on both boards. I stayed put at the Beeb!

Head of Programmes Teleri Bevan and Head of TV John Stuart Roberts took two separate channels, S4C and BBC Wales, forward from November 1982.

Peter Edwards directed the popular serial, *The District Nurse*, starring Nerys Hughes, which ran for three series.

John Geraint's film on the Hungerford massacre was powerful. He is now head of leading independent company Green Bay.

Senior producer Dr Barry Lynch broke the taboo of silence about 'the big C'.

Phil George's documentary on Swansea's binmen was hilarious. He is now Chair of the Arts Council of Wales.

Indian Prime Minister Indira Gandhi was killed six weeks after Teleri Bevan interviewed her. Here with Tom Friswell (camera, extreme left) and Shaam Verma, an influential Indian from Cardiff. From extreme right, producer John Watkin, sound recordist John Welsh, PA Brenda Thomas.

Controllers come and go. The five has-beens are L–R: Owen Edwards, Geraint Talfan Davies, Menna Richards, Geraint Stanley Jones and myself.

While I was concentrating on the structure, finance and recruitment for the new radio services, Teleri opened up new strands of programming. As noted, the growth of both services was painfully slow because the flow of funds from London came in small annual tranches which had to be divided up between the technical and programme areas; then a secondary division between the languages – and finally between the general programmes and the newsroom. The radio directorate in London had accepted Wales's need to provide two separate services but never fully understood the implications. The importance of a complete channel in the Welsh language was beyond their ken, and they gave up trying to work out how we were dividing the promised funding between a new English slot here and a Welsh producer there. What they did not know was that we were increasing the hours faster than the official figures revealed, and borrowed TV money at the end of one financial year which was cancelled out by inflation in the next. Otherwise, it was difficult to argue that we were underfunded and then explain away our faster growth.

If we had to keep our heads below the parapet on money, the greatest responsibility was recruiting researchers and producers of the future. In this task Teleri and I were eventually reinforced by another senior manager. In 1976 Meirion Edwards had returned to the BBC as Head of Bangor. He had developed a first-rate track record in radio in a very short time with the production of a stream of in-depth features on literary figures in both languages, as well as a seminal series for the BBC Third Programme, *The Welsh Poetic Tradition*. During his years as a lecturer at University College of North Wales, Bangor, he freelanced as a presenter and an incisive interviewer on the daily evening current affairs programme *Cymru Heno* [Wales Tonight], before fronting the schools TV series *Hyn o Fyd* [This World]. In his new role he would form a troika with me and Teleri in progressing the growth of the Radio Cymru service.

Sometimes the three of us sat together on staff appointment boards for Radio Cymru; on other days Teleri and I did the same for Radio Wales. We would always be joined by one of our personnel officers and an independent chairman from London to ensure each candidate was treated fairly. We spent six hours a day for several weeks appointing future talent, not only for our growing radio production teams but, later, a second time around, when filling the posts vacated by those who moved on to BBC Wales TV, HTV, S4C and the Independents, as early as the beginning of 1982, leading up to the expansion in TV. These appointments added up to a high proportion of the Welsh broadcasting intake of young people in the late 1970s and was the most important legacy we left to the industry in Wales. One fascinating scenario emerged during this time. More women were appointed than men, particularly to the new posts in Radio Cymru. Women, with an average age of around 23, seemed more mature than men of the same age. We never knew at the time of a notorious BBC memo, circulated as late as 1973, warning of the possible limitations in employing women 'suffering from premenstrual tension'.

One woman who found a novel way of getting into the BBC was young Menna Richards, originally from Maesteg. Menna asked to see assistant news editor Tudor Phillips one morning with a view to observing the newsroom at work for a week. Tudor told me she didn't sound like a Welsh Language Society agitator and I agreed to the request. Within a week, sickness left a gap in the radio shifts and Menna was given her chance. She never looked back. A bright and quick learner, with common sense and an ambition to graduate into current affairs, Menna left for HTV when such possibilities were on offer after the launch of S4C. She returned to BBC Wales as Controller at the turn of the Millennium from her post as Managing Director, HTV Wales. Nobody else has achieved the distinction of running both those very different organisations.

There was a constant demand for extra hands to help overstretched departments. On one such occasion, assistant film editor Paul Turner won an attachment to work on *Heddiw*. Controller Owen Edwards received a phone call from London to protest the appointment because Paul was classified as a Communist. Owen asked me what right I had to allocate the attachment to Paul. I told him it was my job to organise attachments and, yes, Paul had attended an East Berlin Communist rally. Furthermore, I regarded Paul highly, and the paranoid executive in London whose job it was to sniff out Communists (and IRA sympathisers) should be told to mind his own business. It reminded me of the treatment of my old mentor John Griffiths in Swansea. A couple of years later the *Observer* exposed this practice of McCarthyism in an article which named Paul among others. That article probably ended the career of the security adviser said to be in Room 101 of Broadcasting House, London. Paul went on to make a distinguished career for himself as an independent film-maker. It peaked with his iconic film *Hedd Wyn*, the bardic name of the Welsh soldier killed in action just weeks before being awarded the Chair, which was symbolically draped in black, at the Birkenhead National Eisteddfod of 1917.

During this whole period of building the radio services, I had hoped that Radio Cymru would have a blank daytime schedule to fill on its new VHF wavelength. Unfortunately, it was already occupied by schools programmes and I thought that moving them elsewhere would be relatively easy given reasonable notice. I was wrong. The Schools Broadcasting Council for Wales was the only sector of the BBC which was ring-fenced with statutory powers. We sat in on their quarterly meetings and could comment on programmes, but it was the Council's responsibility to approve programme series and, more critically for Radio Cymru, where they were placed in the schedule. We had no issue with the producers or their productions, and we had great respect for its Chairman, John Howard Davies. At the time he was the highly successful Director of Education for Clwyd and later became an equally effective Chairman of S4C at the end of the 1980s. We did, however, hope to reach a viable agreement on the schedule. The obvious solution lay in requiring schools to record their programmes off a late night schedule, but the Council argued that many schools either did not have the necessary recording equipment or the know-how to use it. A second proposal, that tapes should be sent to all the schools which wanted them, was partially implemented after years of discussion and delay during which John Howard Davies's diplomacy kept my thinly disguised frustration under control. Sixteen years after my first appearance at the Schools Broadcasting Council for Wales, I left the BBC with Welsh schools programmes still *in situ* in the afternoons, still preventing an uninterrupted daytime service for adults. The situation was only resolved in the mid 1990s.

There were other unexpected events on the road to the launch of the new national services. One evening, at a BBC public meeting in Wrexham, a member of the audience pleaded with London's Managing Director of radio, Aubrey Singer, for a BBC local radio station. To our surprise and completely off-the-cuff he said they could have one. Such a decision went against the policy in Wales of national rather than local services and could have had financial implications for Radio Wales and Radio Cymru. Thankfully, Aubrey Singer paid for what emerged as Radio Clwyd and we were then bounced into establishing Radio Gwent. Head of Programmes Geraint Stanley Jones was more sanguine about the possible knock-on costs than I was. He always had the feeling that Clwyd's large population required an extra incentive to listen to Cardiff-based Radio Wales, and initially decided to set up a temporary radio station for two months on Deeside which was suffering severe unemployment in 1980. It was so successful that Radio Wales news editor Gareth Bowen, who managed the exercise, was encouraged to extend it for a further two months. Radio Clwyd went on air in its place in 1981, using Radio Wales as a sustaining service when it had completed about two hours of early morning news and topics of local interest. It was manned by a small and hard-working team headed by former *Good Morning Wales* producer John Shone, aided by one other producer and a host of volunteers including John's wife. It was always a pleasure to visit Radio Clwyd and share a sandwich and the infectious enthusiasm of a great group of people.

The initial plan for Radio Gwent was pure comedy, occasioned by the seeming lack of an existing transmitter near Newport. The BBC Wales technical people had a map showing the location of every transmitter in Wales. It showed nothing in that area of Gwent. Geraint Stanley Jones thought he had seen one and disappeared for the day. He returned triumphant, showing where a transmitter should have been marked on the map. Profuse apologies from the technical information department. In the days before computers, the wall map in question showed all relevant masts by pinning each one to the map with tin tacks. The Gwent tin tack had fallen to the floor. The tiny Gwent station went ahead, run by managers Steve Taylor, who eventually left to present *HTV News*, and Chris Segar, the avuncular future 'Ferret' of HTV. Both services were closed down after my day.

By 1978 it was agreed that it was time to appoint dedicated editors for each of the services and expand them as soon as possible to a funded target of 65 hours a week each. In November of that year Teleri was appointed Editor, Radio Wales, and Meirion as Editor, Radio Cymru. The English service was launched in the same month. The relaunch of Radio Cymru could wait until November 1979 when Meirion had moved from Bangor to Cardiff and taken over the operation at both locations.

Radio Wales was only five months old and Radio Cymru not even relaunched when the March 1979 referendum result rejected democratic devolution decisively. The then Director-General, Ian Trethowan, pondering both a bad BBC licence fee settlement and that there was no longer any need to worry about Wales, froze further funding and a five-hour a week cut was imposed on both services in 1981, only two years after their launch. It was only the contrarian political agreement to launch S4C which saved the situation. By this time I was

Head of Programmes, and Geraint Stanley Jones had become Controller. I decided to ease the pressure on both channels by transferring part of the new seed monies being provided for the launch of S4C into the radio budgets. The figures were 'massaged' again. As a result, both Teleri and Meirion were able to disguise the situation, particularly since both services were already well ahead of their official targets.

As the channels grew I took a close look at the audience research figures but was never happy with the small random samples used to assess official listening figures for Radio Cymru or, in later years, S4C. I had robust arguments with one BBC Head of Audience Research who defended the results which were sound for the UK in general, and even for English-language programmes in Wales. I argued for a strategic sample of the Welsh-speaking population only – to little avail. BBC Wales's official historian, Dr John Davies, noted that by 1984, 'the Broadcasting Council for Wales was surprised to discover that, when interviews were conducted in homes rather than on the street, the listening figures for Radio Cymru increased by 50 per cent'. I never succeeded in making sense of the figures for Welsh-language radio or TV, which swung wildly from week to week. *Pobol y Cwm*, which should have been the most stable figure, could vary between 80,000 and 150,000. These figures demonstrated that the degree of error was much wider than the normal standard of five per cent either way, and would never hit a set of figures that made sense to me. In November 1985 I decided to hire the Wales-based company Beaufort to take a one-off in-depth 'photograph' of a statistically sound sample of 1,000 listeners in Wales which showed credible results. Radio Wales, then transmitting 12 hours a day, was reaching 400,000 listeners. Radio Cymru, with a daily output of 11 hours, attracted approximately 135,000 listeners a week, both figures subject to a five per cent degree of error either way. Radio 4 recorded a figure slightly above that of Radio Wales, while Radios 1 and 2 had the highest figures.

Audiences increased on both national channels as they

offered bigger and more balanced schedules. In 1974 the total radio output in both languages was a mere 1,600 hours. By 1981–2, both Radio Wales and Radio Cymru had passed the planned target of 65 hours a week with a total of 7,000 hours for the year. Radio Cymru and Radio Wales were on their way, each with their own very different stories to tell.

13

The People Own the Channel, 1977-90

THE STAR SALESMAN of Radio Cymru when it launched on VHF only on Monday morning, 3 January 1977, was Hywel Gwynfryn. Born to broadcast, equally at home on radio and TV, Anglesey-born Hywel was a child actor in the days of Sam Jones, the pioneer of broadcasting in Bangor. Following drama college, he joined Nan Davies's *Heddiw* team in the 1960s and was an active performer and songwriter for light entertainment before opening up a Saturday morning radio slot with the Welsh pop show, *Helo, Sut 'Dach Chi?* [Hello, How Are You?].

It was the first Welsh pop show on radio in the early 1970s when 'gigs' and recording studios such as Sain were flourishing, a scene which both radio and TV helped to promote. The ease with which Hywel interviewed people made him the obvious choice to present a distinctive sound for the new channel.

Senior producer Teleri Bevan selected Hywel Gwynfryn and production manager Gareth Lloyd Williams for the critical early morning schedule which started with Hywel's iconic greeting 'Helo Bobol' [Hello People] communicated to his audience with huge energy and enthusiasm. The letters BBC stood for 'Y Bobol Biau'r Cyfrwng' [The People Own the Channel], Hywel's second mantra, and the listeners responded.

Welsh speakers gradually bought new VHF radio sets,

justifying the heavy marketing exercises which preceded the launch.

Following that first extended coverage of the National Eisteddfod, Hywel has dominated radio broadcasting of the event ever since, in latter years in partnership with the multi-talented Caryl Parry Jones.

Gareth Lloyd Williams was given the young and versatile Gareth Rowlands as one of his two producers. Rowlands was always full of ideas, the first to try anything new, and within two years he moved on to launch the first lunchtime programme on Radio Wales, *Meet for Lunch*, before his restless nature gave him scope to develop his imagination on the new TV channel, S4C.

The second producer to be appointed was the long-serving and gregarious Ruth Parry, who eventually took charge of the Welsh equivalent of *Woman's Hour* – *Merched yn Bennaf* – as her landmark series.

Money was so tight that the first researcher, Lenna Pritchard-Jones, could only be afforded four days a week on a monthly contract. When the first month ended there was a party at the BBC Club to say goodbye and then it was announced that Lenna could carry on for a second month. She stayed for 12 years, succeeding Gareth Lloyd Williams as the radio production manager in charge of *Helo Bobol* when he decided to go independent.

The programme had already attracted erudite letters from highbrow critics condemning it. The St Fagans National Museum of History Director, Dr Iorwerth Peate, and my old Vice-Chancellor at Aberystwyth, Professor Thomas Parry, were two Establishment figures who regarded themselves as defenders of linguistic standards and wrote numerous letters expressing their concerns in no uncertain terms. Inventing shorthand terms, like 'hysbys' instead of the longer word for advertisements, was regarded by them as undermining standard Welsh. Moreover, mauling the gems of Welsh poetry by turning them into the lyrics of Welsh pop music and then playing them in between 'inconsequential' chat was anathema to them. It took seven months and a supportive speech by the emerging political heavyweight Dafydd Elis-Thomas at that year's National Eisteddfod to silence the critics.

Serious news was initially broadcast for 15 minutes each hour before 7 a.m., 8 a.m. and 9 a.m., but was later moved to traditional times on the hour. Those news bulletins were presented initially by Gwyn Llewelyn, one of the best journalists in Wales whom I had admired for his coverage of the Aberfan disaster while a member of HTV's *Y Dydd*. He had changed channels, first to join *Heddiw* on TV and then Radio Cymru. The team of Gwynfryn and Llewelyn excelled, before Gwyn left for the independent sector and Emyr Daniel teamed up with Hywel at their 'bwrdd brecwast' [breakfast table]. Emyr's knowledge of the political scene was second to none, and when he moved into management at HTV I often wondered whether he had made the right decision, such was his loss to the listener.

Hywel Gwynfryn's daily early morning commitment left us without a ready replacement for a pop programme on Saturday mornings. Fortunately, I found the very man while organising one of the first Welsh-language community radio stations in the run up to the 1977 launch. As noted, these three-day exercises were aimed at securing advance publicity for Radio Cymru. Having volunteered to organise Radio Llwynhendy, I wanted an all-local cast and heard about a young man who broadcast part-time on Swansea Sound. I had to trust people who told me he was good because when I met him for the first time it was impossible to ignore his pronounced stammer. In the event, Richard Rees's BBC career was kick-started when he anchored his home village's radio station. He took control of the self-operating mobile studio as to the manner born. Richard presented each of the day's events and played record requests for his neighbours. We identified three local characters who could reminisce all day and invited everybody else to join them with their individual stories. It was a community talking to itself. Richard's stammer never held him back from addressing a much wider audience on Radio Cymru when replacing Hywel Gwynfryn on Saturday mornings with his own show, *Sosban*. Saturday, 1 January 1977, saw a nervous Richard playing his own discs to a packed and excited gallery eager to hear the new recruit. I watched him closely for any sign of stress which could make him stammer. Mercifully, the occasional flutter in his breathing made for an attractive pause. There had always been a joke in circulation about a man with a bad stammer claiming to be a BBC announcer. Richard was the first to do so despite the objections of two appointment board chairmen from London who frankly disbelieved me about his ability to read a five-minute news bulletin when they were faced with him in a formal interview situation. Third time lucky.

Sosban not only lasted eight years but 20 years later Richard returned to the same slot. During that long interval he presented rock programmes for both radio channels, joined the agriculture unit as a TV director and studied for a science degree at the Open University.

The second half of Saturday mornings featured a man destined to show his eclectic interests on a range of programmes for Radio Cymru. Dei Tomos was working for Urdd Gobaith Cymru when Head of BBC Bangor Meirion Edwards selected him to present the late Saturday morning show. Dei has thrived with distinction on Radio Cymru, constantly reinventing himself in a variety of serious programmes, including current affairs, farming and now on his well-researched and highly respected Sunday evening magazine programme. He has served Radio Cymru for well over 30 years.

Sunday evenings have always been a good time to attract sizeable audiences to Radio Cymru despite competition from TV, including S4C. A major highlight each week was, and is, the continuing attraction of the popular poetry competition *Talwrn y Beirdd*, in which teams of bards still pit their skills in a clever war of words against each other. Chairman Gerallt Lloyd Owen guided this uniquely Welsh phenomenon for

32 years. He was one of the greatest exponents of the Welsh strict-metre 'cynghanedd', employing a wicked humour in his adjudications when rereading and analysing the double entendre hidden in some of the best compositions. Sitting beside him as his alter ego for many years was Dic Jones, member of an extraordinary circle of poets known throughout Welsh-speaking Wales as 'Bois y Cilie'. A farmer all his life, Dic spent hours on his tractor composing lines for his next 'englyn'. Both he and Gerallt had won the main competitions and were the great entertainers at every National Eisteddfod where the 'Babell Lên', the literary tent, was always too small to cope with the queuing crowds. More than any other programme on radio or TV in Wales, *Talwrn y Beirdd* is the ultimate expression of the very core of Welsh culture. It defines the greatest difference between broadcasting in Welsh and English, namely the continuity of an ancient tradition unique to the Welsh language.

The Dei Tomos series on Sunday evenings is in a long line of good-quality talk shows (as opposed to the two- or three-hour-long chat and record shows which necessarily fill up so much time on most radio channels nowadays). The series which preceded Dei's programme for many years appeared under the title *Rhwng Gŵyl a Gwaith* [Between Work and Play], featuring a large cast of characters with a natural gift for words and observations of the world around them. It was the brainchild of John Roberts Williams who had preceded Meirion as Head of BBC Bangor. John had been editor of *Y Cymro* before joining the BBC and Nan Davies's *Heddiw* unit, co-producing the show for years with Geraint Stanley Jones. Eventually, John moved back to his native north Wales, and launched the programme as a weekly miscellany for six weeks. It lasted 15 years. When he retired I asked him to present a five-minute homily on Friday evenings, *Dros fy Sbectol* [Over my Spectacles], a form of 'Letter from Bangor' which attracted a loyal following, his usually pessimistic commentary on the week's events in Wales and the wider world delivered in a downbeat voice, the content usually predicting doom and disaster, the glass always half empty.

John hired another outstanding wordsmith as the presenter of *Rhwng Gŵyl a Gwaith*. I.B. Griffith's glass was always half full. He became well known to a wider audience as the mayor of Caernarfon during the Investiture of 1969, somehow sailing through that divisive period with impunity. He was also popular on *Good Morning Wales* in English where, given even the most inconsequential item on which to talk, he could make it relevant with tongue firmly in his cheek.

The contributors to *Rhwng Gŵyl a Gwaith* were not all professors of Welsh, although two of them, Bedwyr Lewis Jones and Gwyn Thomas, were always seeking to be populist on the airwaves. I once asked Gwyn to write an original Welsh commentary to replace a prosaic English script on an expensive and beautifully shot network programme called *Wales from the Air*. He wrote it entirely in verse. Gruffydd Parry was another regular contributor, the senior English master at Botwnnog Secondary School who wrote drama scripts for Radio Cymru in his spare time. He was the very gentle brother of the more forbidding Establishment figure of Dr Thomas Parry but, unlike his brother, was a man anchored to his *Milltir Sgwâr* [Square Mile] on the Llŷn peninsula.

One very different character, with a pronounced south Wales accent, who stood out at BBC Bangor was the acerbic music producer Jimmy Williams, who could be guaranteed to welcome senior managers from Cardiff with some pointed remark about taking in the scenery, speaking loudly as he did so. Jimmy once referred in print to 'the divine right of capital cities', in a swipe at his Cardiff colleagues, and was only a touch more restrained in his hatred of the National Eisteddfod, despite years of having worked there. However, Jimmy did more than his share in cultivating the musical scene in north Wales in both languages: nurturing choirs throughout the region; creating the high-quality sound of the Gwynedd Singers; inventing the long-running network series *With Heart and Voice*; and cooperating with composer William Mathias and innumerable musicians in every corner of Gwynedd and Clwyd.

The much quieter musical presence of Gwyn L. Williams in the 1980s brought bright new musical ideas to the fore. He was awarded the Sam Jones Memorial Prize, enabling him to explore the music of Patagonia for Radio Cymru long before he eventually left to run the Llangollen International Eisteddfod and now Tŷ Cerdd – Centre for Welsh Music in Cardiff.

The gentle 'Poncs', Elwyn Jones from Ponciau near Wrexham, was an energetic and thoughtful religion producer who became a real force as Meirion Edwards's radio production manager for the whole Bangor operation. His flagship programme was *Canllaw* [Guideline], a social action series offering advice on a whole variety of subjects with a bias towards the aged and disabled. One of Elwyn Jones's stalwarts on the series was the blinded policeman Arthur Rowlands, who lost his sight when he was shot on Machynlleth bridge by a man on the run. Arthur continued in the police force as a telephonist and just carried on with his life. He could always be seen in Cardiff on international match days soaking up the atmosphere, with his son Gareth providing a running commentary on the rugby.

Elwyn and the then senior news assistant in Bangor, Ifan Roberts, combined to create the hilarious light entertainment series *Pupur a Halen* [Pepper and Salt]. It was so successful at satirising 'the great and the good' that the Broadcasting Council for Wales raised a concern that some prominent people might be targeted too often.

We were running out of space in Cardiff and reopened the Swansea studios to accommodate the new radio channels. Refurbishing the old studios gave Meirion Edwards the chance to appoint four radio production managers in three locations: Elwyn Jones in Bangor, Lenna Pritchard-Jones and Ceri Wyn Richards in Cardiff, and Lyn T. Jones in Swansea. Meirion Edwards was often a stern critic of the output he commissioned and jumped hard on production weaknesses and soft interviews. He ran Radio Cymru rather like a personal fiefdom, firm, fair and self-confident. He did not need to indulge in much collegiate thinking. Once he knew his financial parameters, Meirion Edwards got on with the job of expanding the schedule each weekday morning and throughout the day at weekends. By February 1982, barely two years after the relaunch in November 1979, Broadcasting Council for Wales's Chairman Alwyn Roberts remarked, 'it is now inconceivable to many people to imagine Wales without Radio Cymru'.

Meirion built the schedule to wrap around three fixed points in the period between 6.30 a.m. and 1.30 p.m. – the early morning Hywel Gwynfryn show, the mid-morning Sulwyn Thomas programme, *Stondin Sulwyn* [Sulwyn's Stand], and the lunchtime *Cyn Un* [Before One], presented by a variety of newsroom journalists. He commissioned a wide range of 25 shorter series for weekdays around these fixed points, a daily average of five very different programmes similar to the 'built' programmes normally associated with Radio 4. Meirion Edwards changed the schedule every quarter which allowed for variety as a key to serving so many different listener interests on the only radio channel in Welsh.

The important 9 a.m. junction featured strong, popular presenters – the ubiquitous Alun Williams, R. Alun Evans, Beti George and Gari Williams. All programmes would include a substantial element of talk. *Codi'r Ffôn* [Picking up the Phone], with R. Alun Evans, was particularly interesting as the first phone-in on Radio Cymru to depend entirely on interactivity with listeners in Welsh. Phone-ins later became a regular fixture in the post-11 a.m. Sulwyn Thomas show. Different series at 9.45 and often at 10.30 would allow for lighter music of different genre with announcers Menna Gwyn and Robin Jones, plus the long-running women's programme *Merched yn Bennaf* presented by Ruth Parry. Three programmes were placed before the religious thoughts at 11 a.m. delivered by Meurwyn Williams and Lloyd Walters (another fine presenter to die young), together with the statutory Welsh schools series. In the late mornings *Stondin Sulwyn* would be succeeded by a short serial drama one day, readings from a novel another, leaving room for comedy shows, quizzes or other entertaining series running up to the lunchtime news at 12.45. From 1 p.m., for half an hour, current affairs programmes or the long-running and knowledgeable *Byd Natur* [Nature World] mulled over timeless interests. In the late afternoons *Post Prynhawn* [Afternoon Post] caught listeners in their cars or returning home from work. It ended programmes for the day, unless important sporting events or orchestral concerts were relayed in the evenings. When Welsh programmes were unavailable, Meirion Edwards decided to use Radio 4 as the sustaining network. Night-time programmes for a younger generation during the week were introduced later when funds permitted.

Saturday was a time for pop and entertainment in the mornings and four hours of live sports coverage in the afternoon. Sundays were reserved for serious fare, with due attention to worship and hymn singing as well as the well-established Sunday night schedule. Most weekly programmes were repeated, judiciously placed at different times on different days.

Servicing this non-stop flow of seven hours each weekday and at least 20 hours at weekends meant that Meirion Edwards worked his small staff very hard to fill the shorter programmes. He gradually built the schedule to more than the targeted 65 hours a week.

As noted, the Swansea studios were reopened to cater for the expansion of output under radio production manager Lyn T. Jones. This offered a better balance of broadcasting from different Welsh-speaking areas. Meirion and Lyn had selected Sulwyn Thomas to develop the mid-morning show from Swansea. He, like north Walian Gwyn Llewelyn, had served his apprenticeship on *Y Dydd* before moving over to *Heddiw*. Sulwyn also had a healthy sense of humour which helped him develop a dominant presence as ringmaster of a programme which mixed serious issues of the day with plenty of laughs. It started life for half an hour but gradually stretched to 75 minutes a day as its popularity grew. One hilarious April Fool's Day, Sulwyn 'discovered', with the help of the Reverend I.D.E. Thomas, the experienced Welsh correspondent based in Los Angeles, that the National Eisteddfod had been quietly chosen to be held in California, much to the consternation of the audience. Sulwyn and senior Eisteddfod organisers teased protesting listeners to great effect.

Sulwyn's producer Lyn T. Jones was a former manager of the Welsh National Theatre company and was now the de facto head of administration of the small Swansea operation, helped by two loyal and welcoming Swansea secretaries, Thelma Jones and Diane Thomas. Thelma had kept the studios open for freelancers and contributors for many lonely years. The reopening of the Alexandra Road studios launched a new chapter in Swansea's broadcasting history. New blood brought in by Meirion and Lyn included Aled Samuel, whose development as a cheeky entertainer with scant regard for political correctness has been a refreshing presence on the airwaves for many years; Jon Gower went on to become a first-class writer and commentator on the arts; Gary Slaymaker, the doyen of Welsh film critics; and Geraint Davies, the producer who was a member of numerous leading pop groups. He strengthened the youth scene with series such as *Bambw* and a wide range of entertainment productions. Swansea produced drama, quiz shows, comedy series *Deffro! Mae'n Ddydd* [Wake Up! Dawn Has Broken] and *Atodiad Lliw* [Colour Supplement] in association with the West Glamorgan Youth Theatre. One young researcher, Arthur Emyr, was playing on the wing for Wales when he was appointed.

My old mentor T. Glynne Davies brought his Welsh wanderlust to a close in Swansea with his last series, *Ddoe yn Ôl* [Bringing Back Yesterday], celebrating a career spanning well over 30 years covering news and commentary on current affairs with some of the best writing in both languages, testimony to the most sensitive of poets and novelists. He once told me that he had lived and worked all over Wales, moving house 13 times and had made a loss on each one of them. T. Glynne Davies was a born pessimist who managed to prove he was a loser in material terms but never understood how much he was loved and appreciated by those who worked with him.

In Cardiff all producers were expected to work in support of the Hywel Gwynfryn show as well as make other feature programmes. Female researchers and producers multiplied, leading to one appointments board when Lenna Pritchard-Jones voiced her private concern that Hywel Gwynfryn was the only man in the unit! The outcome was exactly the same. Another woman was appointed!

The post of researcher displaced the entry point into production traditionally associated with studio managers. Their numbers declined as self-operating studios allowed more presenters to multitask. It was a skill with which old stagers like Alun Williams could not cope, but he was excused the need to adopt new working methods.

Ceri Wyn Richards was first a researcher, then a producer and finally the second radio production manager in Cardiff. Ceri was always full of ideas. She needed to be. Her workload concentrated on the innumerable short series required to fill Meirion Edwards's demanding schedule. Ceri Wyn was queen of the quiz shows and several light entertainment series before becoming one of the earliest and most successful independent producers working in radio.

There were, however, many early losses as the launch of S4C attracted many young people to TV within three years of the Radio Cymru expansion. Gwenan Gallagher was well known to Meirion Edwards as one of his brightest university recruits, and she zoomed through Radio Cymru into TV light entertainment, earning attachments to the prestigious situation comedy department in London and never returned to radio. She continued to pursue a highly valued freelance existence for drama series on the networks and in Wales.

Similarly, Lowri Morgan, the quiet and serious-minded producer who cut her teeth on Radio Cymru, moved on to make fly-on-the-wall TV documentaries. They were but two of many bright young things who were deflected from a longer career in radio. On the other hand, there were fewer people who stayed too long in radio than in the TV service which was already 15 years old, and where some producers were already reaching their sell-by date.

The nine general producers allocated to Meirion Edwards were limited in number because of the need to create the first dedicated Radio Cymru newsroom. The voices of Handel Jones, Allan Pickard, Gwyndaf Owen, Geraint Lewis Jones and Aled Gwyn were already well known. Handel was the newsroom's leading practical joker, always creating a new spoof for April Fool's Day. On one such morning he informed the nation that Snowdon was sinking and the Brecon Beacons were rising. It was a Handel classic. Many years later Handel was joined by another prankster. Aled Gwyn was adept at never answering questions directly and instead making mysterious remarks which left people unsure as to whether he was joking or not. When he was serious, Aled specialised in establishing 'insider' contacts on long-running stories, most memorably during the miners' strikes and the Tiananmen Square protests in Beijing. This was a long-running international story with network reporters, including the formidable Kate Adie, trying to find out what plans the Chinese student protesters had in mind daily. Aled knew of a Welsh speaker, enrolled at Beijing University, who lived inside the student campus, totally cut off from the outside world. Nobody suspected that contact was constantly being made with her in Welsh. Not only did Aled break the stories first on Radio Cymru, he informed the London newsroom of the content but not his source, much to the astonishment of reporters based in Beijing who saw the students' strategy unfold in front of their eyes, just as Aled had predicted.

As Radio Cymru grew in size, an eclectic group of

journalists joined and eventually moved on, some quite quickly. Ifan Wyn Williams was one who was never sure whether he wanted to be in broadcasting or education. He was headmaster of two Welsh secondary schools and joined the BBC three times, once as a journalist and twice as an announcer. He was a highly intelligent, very able and popular character who just did not settle anywhere long enough to fulfil his massive potential. Ifan Wyn died while working for Radio Cymru news at the age of just 55.

William H. Owen was Ifan Wyn's total opposite, a quiet man who was highly respected both for his journalistic skills and a gentle way with people. When Wil finally retired from the post of editor of Radio Cymru news, he was persuaded to take on the editorship of *Y Cymro*.

As the years rolled on, the young recruits of the late 1970s and the early 1980s became the next generation of senior journalists. Garffild Lloyd Lewis worked in Bangor before moving to Cardiff as editor of Radio Cymru news and then the staff of S4C; Tomos Morgan moved the other way to become senior producer of *Post Cyntaf* [First Post] in Bangor, responsible for an even younger presenter who only joined the newsroom in 1989 – Dylan Jones.

The demands on the newsroom increased even further with the launch of S4C, but this benefited Radio Cymru as well. S4C was allocated a Lobby ticket for the House of Commons by virtue of its existence as a separate organisation, but the new Lobby correspondents worked for both channels. First Dylan Iorwerth, and then Huw Edwards, took advantage of it and were based in London as political correspondents, while Bethan Kilfoil moved fairly rapidly from being based in London, then Brussels as Europe correspondent, before retiring to Dublin all too soon. Dylan Iorwerth left the staff in order to launch the highly successful weekly news magazine *Golwg* [View], and continues to use his razor-like mind when presenting one of Radio Cymru's current affairs programmes to this day.

Huw Edwards remained in London to become the most

prominent Welsh presence on BBC TV, anchor of the most watched UK news programme and presenter of prestigious documentary series' for Green Bay and BBC Wales on subjects as varied as *The Story of Wales*, *Lloyd George* and *Patagonia*. When I first met Huw as a sixth former at the family's Llangennech home, I did not notice the growing resemblance to his father Hywel Teifi. As time passed, I observed a similarly large, energetic and dominant presence emerging, admittedly more cautious by virtue of his vocation, although at times, and particularly when speaking in public events, I now feel Huw restraining himself when faced with remarks his father would have called 'bloody nonsense!'

When the Radio Cymru news editor post was vacated at one stage in the early 1980s, I thought of one neglected journalist to fill it at short notice. Gwilym Owen was a controversial former HTV news editor turned independent producer, who had faced accusations of overspending in a film he was making for S4C called *Madam Wen*. I persuaded Geraint Stanley Jones, who was about to visit north Wales, to invite Gwilym in person to take over Radio Cymru news for a trial period. The output of news on the channel was so much greater than on S4C – it was important to hire a heavyweight. Gwilym accepted immediately and brought his huge experience as a journalist to bear in the BBC newsroom. He was so successful that I promoted him to the top job of editor of news and current affairs in Wales when David Morris Jones left for ITV in 1989. At the BBC I found Gwilym to be editorially sound and managerially tough to the point of being feared and even disliked by many on his staff but credited for the appointment or promotion of several young journalists who cut their teeth on Radio Cymru and *Newyddion Saith* on S4C.

Guto Harri was one of them, following Huw Edwards not only as Welsh Lobby correspondent in London but also to the BBC's political unit and a period presenting Radio 4's *World at One*. He suddenly left a promising career path in mainstream journalism to become communications director for his old college friend and then London mayor, Boris Johnson. He then joined Rupert Murdoch's empire, with the tricky task of repairing the reputation of News International (now News UK) following the organisation's infamous phone-hacking scandal. Having now exited News UK, he now works for Liberty Global, a media company based in London. Guto also sits on the board of S4C Authority.

In the 1980s four women graduated from the newsroom into managerial positions both within and outside BBC Wales. Iona Jones was regarded as a highly competent Radio Cymru news producer by Gwilym Owen and her staff but left for ITV Wales and ended up following Huw Jones as Chief Executive of S4C. Unfortunately, Iona became embroiled in the Authority's messy public row which led to her resignation and that of Chairman John Walter Jones. She retired while at the height of her abilities.

Angharad Mair developed into a first-class TV presenter both on *Newyddion Saith* and, with a lighter touch, demonstrated her ability during her days on the children's series *Bilidowcar* [Cormorant]. She now heads up the largest provider of independent productions to S4C – Tinopolis in Llanelli – combining both presentation and managerial responsibilities.

Bethan Williams moved from Cardiff when promoted to run the Bangor newsroom and is now Head of BBC North Wales, and responsible for about 100 staff in Bangor and a modern complex serving Clwyd.

One could tell from her nickname that Elin 'Rwsia' Roberts was a free spirit. She joined the newsroom as part of the 1982 intake and was regarded highly enough by Controller Menna Richards at the beginning of the Millennium to be one of her aides in management. The free spirit won in the end and Elin Wyn went into media training and production.

Then there were another three men and one outstanding woman who continued as presenters. Sian Pari Huws was, from the start, a really serious and thoughtful broadcaster. She was one of only a handful of people who were equally at home presenting *Good Morning Wales*, or even classical music on Radio 3, while also working at Radio Cymru. Sian was an exceptional person, as engaging in private as she was on air. Even in the early 1980s she seemed to have a wisdom way beyond her years. Sian had a caring nature and was sensitive to other people's feelings which showed up clearly in some outstanding interviews down the years. Her all-round personal and professional gifts could well have taken her in any direction she wished, but all such speculation came to a sad end with the tragic death of her huge talent in 2015 when Sian was only 55 years of age.

The breezy Garry Owen seems to have read more news bulletins on both radio and TV, in both Welsh and English, than anybody else on most days of the week for the best part of 30 years – a certain candidate for inclusion in the *Guinness Book of Records*.

Two other personalities came to the fore when Hywel Gwynfryn moved from the early morning to a more sociable mid-morning slot. He was replaced by the dual early morning act of former HTV journalist Vaughan Hughes and the young Russell Isaac, a blend of two very good journalists. It also signalled a change of direction towards a more serious early morning output, now that the channel was well and truly established.

Radio Cymru depended on the 'supply' departments to provide it with regular programmes on religion, music and sport. One particularly brilliant development was the Saturday afternoon sporting coverage. Editor Tom Davies created a parallel channel with Radio Wales which was incredibly efficient. His Radio Cymru producer was the pipe smoking and jazz-loving Emyr Williams. Each channel had their own presenters but Welsh-speaking reporters had to supply the inserts for both channels on a very fast merry-go-round, using cheap fixed radio points from all the major rugby and football grounds. Tom listened back to both outputs on Saturday nights and expected all contributors to listen to the output on Monday and undergo constructive criticism. 'Tomos,' as he was known, once wrote to me as follows: 'A good producer always knows what is best for his viewers and listeners. The customer is never right.' [*sic*!]

Despite his quirky views and stubborn nature, he was nevertheless one of the hardest workers and most loyal colleagues ever to work at BBC Wales.

It was not merely female researchers, reporters and producers who were prominent on the channel. Slowly but surely, new female presenters now came to the fore on Radio Cymru. Beti George had started as a Swansea reporter working for Wyre Thomas on T. Glynne Davies's *Bore Da* in the mid 1970s. I had known Beti since her first week as a student at University College, Cardiff, where she befriended my future wife, Mari. A native of Coed-y-bryn near Llandysul in deepest rural Cardiganshire, her mother was the village school's cook and the headmaster was T. Llew Jones, Wales's best-known author of children's books. There was no doubting the quality of her spoken Welsh and the clarity of her speech, born of competing at local eisteddfods. Beti held strong opinions on several subjects in private, but was wise enough to keep them under wraps while on air. She started broadcasting for *Bore Da* as a reporter without any experience of journalism, and instinctively concentrated on the harsh realities of strikes and disasters from the perspective of the family. She interviewed women who were unused to microphones by getting to know them and putting them at their ease. She became an expert on interviewing people in the street for vox pops – the instant reactive response. Beti co-presented TV's *Newyddion Saith* on the first night of S4C with Gwyn Llewelyn, and stayed on the programme for several years while branching out into music programmes on both media, a genre which completely suited her personal interests. For many years she has also hosted *Tocyn Wythnos* [Weekly Ticket] at the National Eisteddfod, a well-rounded summary and serious analysis of each day's cultural events. Beti's longest lasting contribution by far, however, has been *Beti a'i Phobol* [Beti and her People], the popular Welsh-language version of *Desert Island Discs*. Her natural interaction with her guests, combined with her enjoyment of other people's musical tastes, has always struck a chord with listeners to this longest lasting of formats. She is now a member of the elite 40-year club and still going strong. In recent times she has also fulfilled her determination to publicise dementia far and wide, with the making of a bold film on the decline – if difficult to watch in detail – of her partner, former rugby commentator, the late David Parry-Jones.

Beti George's one-time producer, Menna Gwyn, was originally an actress who had played the part of a nurse in the very first run of *Pobol y Cwm*. She switched to the presentation department where she became senior announcer on Radio Cymru and presented her own middle-of-the-road music she deemed 'suitable for housewives tied to the ironing board'. Menna felt strongly about lowering the voices of younger female presenters.

Unfortunately, voice training seems a lost craft in some sectors of broadcasting today! Menna led a team of Radio Cymru announcers, including the dependable and loyal Wyndham Richards and the duo of John Evans and Geraint Jones, whose voices became synonymous with snooker commentaries on S4C during its popular period throughout the 1980s. They are still involved in reporting and reading news bulletins and sports results on Saturday afternoons, following a lifetime's service to both Radio Cymru and the sports unit.

When Meirion Edwards moved on to become the first holder of the new post of Head of Radio, he was followed as editor of Radio Cymru by Lyn T. Jones, one of his four production managers. Lyn deserves the credit for having restored the fortunes of the Swansea studio.

After my time he was succeeded as editor of Radio Cymru by Aled Glynne Davies, the son of T. Glynne, who followed in his father's footsteps, entering journalism first at Swansea

Sound, then moving to the BBC newsroom before becoming editor of Radio Cymru news and finally the third editor of the channel. His brother, Gareth Glynne Davies, divided his time between composing music in the mornings and hosting the news magazine *Post Prynhawn* for no less than 34 years. Gareth stood out as arguably the fastest speaker I ever heard on air in Welsh, surely more rapid than the broadcaster's norm of three words a second.

The current editor of Radio Cymru, Betsan Powys, is another in that mould, the daughter of outstanding broadcaster R. Alun Evans. She has gone from being a diffident cub reporter in the very late 1980s, through a highly successful period as BBC Wales's political editor to emerge as the fourth holder of her present post with the added challenge of developing the service on the web. Her slight frame disguises a steely determination to be her own woman, a person with eclectic interests while thoroughly steeped in the Welsh cultural scene.

The team effort which led to the initial growth of Radio Cymru certainly started when Teleri Bevan, as always, put her head above the parapet during the initial launch, but Meirion Edwards must take the credit for developing a success story hailed by the Broadcasting Council for Wales less than five years after Hywel Gwynfryn first greeted his audience with the words, 'Helo Bobol'.

14

Radio 'Two and a Half', 1978-90

THE BIRTH OF Radio Wales was difficult. In November 1978, the new early morning schedule caused huge controversy. Teleri Bevan, the editor appointed to launch the new service on the channel, was caught in the headlights on two counts. She had dared to challenge the powerful opposition in the newsroom to the dropping of *Good Morning Wales*, particularly its influential editor Gareth Bowen. Teleri had also handed the dissenters extra ammunition by replacing it with a new early morning programme, *AM*, and a presenter, Anita Morgan, who, although an excellent and experienced broadcaster, turned out to be the wrong choice for that time of the morning. Teleri reserved the right to lose the battle as long as she won the war. Listeners who were comfortable with Vincent Kane's *Good Morning Wales* and all-talk radio complained in droves, while the newsroom journalists declaimed, 'We told you so!'

In fact, Teleri, Controller Geraint Stanley Jones and I wanted to attract a larger audience which had never been tapped before, one attracted to a combination of music, chat and snappy news packages. *Good Morning Wales* had been a great programme for serious listeners but, in the days before the arrival of the Senedd, a potentially larger audience existed for a different sound from that of the previous sustaining network of Radio 4. Teleri wanted nothing less than to forge a distinctive identity for English-speaking listeners in Wales. We deliberately dubbed the project 'Radio Two and a Half'. Vincent Kane sarcastically claimed himself to be 'the half', although he was quite happy to move to the more sociable working hours with his new programme, *Meet for Lunch*. The Broadcasting Council for Wales were worried, many even hostile to the early morning revolution, but they gave time for the channel to settle down. The start of Radio Scotland had a similarly difficult time, and the first radio management team there was sacked. In Wales, Teleri was in the front line but in no such danger. Although hurt, she never showed her true feelings and faced the flak with courage and conviction. It took some six months before we received the first audience research figures. It showed a slight increase in the audience. Relief all round, despite the initial loss of many opinion formers who preferred Radio 4. Changes were made, compromises brokered, and it took nearly a year for her inexperienced production teams to bed down. The policy itself, however, was never negotiable.

Chris Stuart replaced Anita as the early morning presenter and peace broke out with the Radio Wales newsroom and the growing audience. Anita was commissioned to record and edit feature programmes from Swansea which were her real *métier*. Chris was a former *Western Mail* journalist with a friendly, easygoing and cheerful personality and a vast knowledge of light music combined with the ability to change gear when serious interviews were needed. Audiences were gradually built up not only through interviews with ordinary people relating extraordinary stories, but also with the introduction of regular slots which included a hugely popular 'Mystery Voice' competition and a humorous weekly 'Letter from Aberdare' written by a newcomer to broadcasting, Roy Noble.

Chris presented *AM* for nearly a decade and was so successful that he went on to present early morning programmes for Radio 2 for a further three years. He was also leader of a sophisticated music band which specialised in contemporary and original humorous songs. 'Baby Grand' had several airings on radio and TV for some five years before it split up. He also had his own TV chat show on BBC Wales. Chris was the ideal answer to the *AM* situation. He married a Radio Wales producer, Megan Stuart. Teleri regarded Megan so highly that she eventually became the third editor of Radio Wales, unusually promoted to the position immediately on her return from maternity leave. Megan only stayed for a couple more years before deciding to spend more time with the family. Chris and Megan later set up a production company, Presentable, which took on a wide range of commissions, including an innovative late night TV series on poker. They were an important part of Teleri's team which made Radio Wales a success.

The news editor of Radio Wales was Gareth Bowen, a highly experienced journalist from Merthyr. He could be a demanding boss but was respected by staff and management alike. The long-term stars of his eclectic staff were Geoff Williams, a future successor to Gareth and nowadays Head of Sport at BBC Wales, as well as Peter Johnson from Pontypridd, who reported and presented daily current affairs programmes with a variety of titles – including *AM*, *Good Morning Wales*, *Good Evening Wales* and *Home Run* as required – with great panache and enthusiasm. Peter's background knowledge of events is second to none but he wears a priceless memory lightly when interviewing in a deceptively genial manner.

An equally friendly but totally different character who also worked for Gareth Bowen was the more vulnerable Herbert Williams, a fine writer and published poet who wrote the most moving account of his wasted youth spent at Talgarth's TB hospital. Yet another long-term reporter, Swansea-based Gilbert John, has been interviewing people in west Wales for as long as Peter Johnson.

The news team expanded to meet the increased number of news bulletins, but Gareth Bowen had been deeply disappointed by the loss of the editorship of Radio Wales to Teleri Bevan. It was the first senior production post in BBC

Wales advertised without the requirement to speak Welsh. He was an all-rounder, a member of the Cardiff Polyphonic Choir with a genuine love of classical music. He failed to get the job because his serious-minded philosophy of broadcasting clashed with the new management policy for Radio Wales. He was appointed news editor for Radio Wales with the added challenge of integrating international stories into the news packages for the first time. Gareth was a true professional who served the BBC very successfully and knew his Wales as well as his son Jeremy knows the Middle East.

As editor of *Good Morning Wales*, Gareth Bowen had the best presenter in English-speaking Wales. Vincent Kane had been Wales's most accomplished broadcaster on TV current affairs since the early 1960s, but he always claimed that radio was his real love. The Swansea broadcaster Peter Stead said of him that in the days before a Welsh Assembly, Vincent took its place as arch-inquisitor. When presenting *Good Morning Wales* he had been known to complete the *The Times* crossword before the end of the programme. Vincent was essentially a private person, self-sufficient, courteous off-air but never 'one of the boys'. He possessed a highly sophisticated sense of humour despite his usually serious demeanour on air. When he presented *Meet for Lunch* for the new Radio Wales, he enjoyed the phone-ins and the Friday quiz programmes. The knowledgeable regular guests – Jenny Randerson, Ian Skidmore and Peter Stead – had great chemistry and always provided pleasant listening.

Vincent found a new freedom in *Meet for Lunch*, away from the straitjacket of news and the constant political confrontations of *Week In Week Out*. The programme explored issues both light and serious, often at angles tangential to the news with a regular group of good talkers. One morning the irrepressible Ray Gravell, who presented the mid-morning show which preceded *Meet for Lunch*, ended his programme with, 'Over to you, Vincie Baby!' Both production galleries froze.

How would the great man reply? Quick as a flash Vincent responded with an appropriate laugh and an empathetic reply to Wales's most lovable broadcaster. His *Meet for Lunch* senior producer was multi-talented Gareth Rowlands who had already served his apprenticeship as a producer on Radio Cymru's *Helo Bobol* in January 1977. He moved to Vincent's new series in November 1978 and on again to TV when S4C launched in 1982.

Teleri may have made enemies in the newsroom but she had the total loyalty of her nine new production staff. By the time I joined the management team in 1974, Teleri had massive experience outside news and current affairs and had already forged ahead with ideas for the future.

The first step in English had been the series called *Nine Five on Mondays* in the autumn of 1974. It grew slowly over the years into a mix of talk shows with live studio audiences at an improbable time of the morning. In order to attract studio audiences at the beginning, Teleri's secretary, Madeline Hopkins, even dragooned the cleaners to make up the numbers as they finished their shifts. Wyn Calvin, the only Welshman to become 'King Rat', was able to attract to his own show all the entertaining 'Rats' of his era, such as Ken Dodd and Swansea's Stan Stennett. Actor Rupert Davies of *Maigret* fame drew a full house at the Penrhyn Hall in Bangor.

Nine Five gradually appeared on other weekdays. *Sixth Sense* featured sixth formers grilling VIPs, with the reliable Gerry Monte in the chair. A highlight of the series was the day Prime Minister James Callaghan came out of the studio muttering, 'Never again!' He admitted that he had forgotten the old adage of never appearing with animals or children. These eclectic programmes also featured the famous and bubbly fortune-teller Russell Grant, and Dan Damon, the first Englishman to learn Welsh live on air, taught by expert Cennard Davies. Although Dan decided to further his career on Radio 4's *You and Yours*, many more took up the challenge of learning the language on *Catchphrase* in successive years.

By 1981 it expanded into a *Sunday Catchphrase Colour Supplement* when consumer champion Sylvia Horn took it over. The young researcher first appointed to look after Dan's language learning skills was Vaughan Roderick, who developed into the leading Welsh political analyst of the new Millennium. Vaughan was appointed despite a complaint from a member of the Broadcasting Council for Wales that he was a Welsh Language Society activist. Vaughan was followed into the BBC and ITV by a number of former members of the Society who were considered to have completed their radical rites of passage.

Teleri built a blend of experience and youth during the early years of Radio Wales, best illustrated by the willingness of four of the most distinguished radio broadcasters in Wales to put their stamp on the channel – namely Cliff Morgan, Alun Williams, G.V. Wynne-Jones and Wynford Vaughan-Thomas – all of whom had spent their best years in Teleri's favourite milieu of live outside broadcasting. There was the excitement of launching *Morning of the Match* on international rugby match days from Westgate Street, with Cliff Morgan talking to the fans as well as his old rugby friends, building the atmosphere on the streets for hours before handing over to the commentary team in the stadium. This was live broadcasting at its best, full of hope and expectation, of laughter and good storytelling. It deserved its nomination for a Sony Award. Despite his commitments as Head of TV Outside Broadcasts in London, Cliff was happy to record a Sunday record request programme with a choice of music which demonstrated his knowledge of Welsh hymns, of which the tune 'Berwyn' was his personal favourite.

Wynford Vaughan-Thomas, then a Director of Harlech TV, continued to work for Radio Wales. To celebrate the new channel, the 70 year old walked over Welsh mountains for a remarkable and strenuous week.

The third of the quartet was the ubiquitous Alun Williams. He had been a household name since 1946 and took it for granted he would be on the *Radio Wales Roadshow*, interacting with the audience wherever he happened to be in Wales.

One pleasant surprise was the return to the microphone of G.V. Wynne-Jones ('Geevers'), the great Welsh rugby commentator whose gruff and gravelly voice had conveyed exactly the right balance between excitement and disappointment for a generation of committed listeners in a pre-TV era. He had opted out of commentating after a row with the Wales Rugby Union and had semi-retired, maintaining a bon viveur lifestyle as secretary of the controversial Cardiff & County Club in the days before women were allowed membership. It took a little time to persuade Geevers to return to the microphone and present a selection of the week's programmes, and it completed a quartet of characters which gave class to the new channel.

Teleri selected a journalist, David Nicholas, to edit the contentious early morning sequence, but he was kept out of the managerial politics surrounding the launch and got on with the job of appealing to its new audience with the help of producer Dave Simmonds. Thoughtful, pipe smoking David was one of those loyal colleagues who were the bedrock of BBC Wales, stubborn when asked to compromise with the pressures of the early days. He always needed convincing that any change constituted evolution rather than capitulation. When he retired he was often called back to help out TV's *Wales Today* and *Newyddion Saith* as a freelance producer.

Dewi Smith was totally different; an extrovert appointed as senior producer in charge of the lighter daytime schedule, he was one of many people recruited by BBC Wales with a sound musical background. He was acutely aware of the problems associated with the choice of music on a hybrid channel. I remember him declaring 'all music is disruptive to somebody', an aphorism which coloured his attitude. All BBC radio channels, bar Radios 1 and 2, still appealed to an older generation but the boundaries of the word 'older' still had to be tested. Dewi was certainly in no doubt that the Welsh choral tradition still resonated in the memories of a generation that had lost the daily use of the Welsh language. He mounted annual competitions for both Welsh brass bands and choirs. Both genres had been an integral part of the Welsh cultural scene in the industrial villages of both north and south Wales for over a century. The grand final of the *Radio Wales Band of the Year* was often held in a packed Parc & Dare Theatre in Treorchy, the judges traditionally hidden behind curtains, as if they could not recognise the tone of each of these well-known bands within seconds!

During his time at Radio Wales, Dewi nurtured the talents of several inexperienced broadcasters, two of whom were John Geraint and Phil George. John had barely taken his degree before Teleri signed him up to help Dewi Griffiths on the local community exercise in their native Rhondda which preceded the launch of Radio Wales. Phil spent ten years as a teacher before joining Dewi Smith as a researcher. Both eventually moved to TV in the mid 1980s. They always remembered the emphasis Dewi laid on parity for north and south Wales, particularly for his native Clwyd.

Dewi was a close friend of the radio planning manager, the equally musical Cedric Jones, who successfully exploited his position as a planner to record the outside broadcast programmes he enjoyed for both Radio Wales and Radio Cymru. Cedric made everything seem possible, with a sense of humour, a wicked memory for funny incidents and as one who knew where all the bodies were buried.

One interesting researcher and producer who appeared on the scene was very different from her distinguished father, Alun Williams. Eli Williams was not immediately noticeable because her quiet nature was in stark contrast to her father but, in the tradition of the best producers, she allowed presenters and their subjects to do the talking and was particularly good at editing the material into a polished end product. Like her father she has lasted the pace, continuing to contribute radio documentaries to this day.

Some people who moved into radio in 1978 had already worked in TV as freelancers. The continuity team was headed by Italian-speaking opera buff Frank Lincoln, who had launched his career as an actor in many popular Welsh drama series and was always in demand as stage presenter for all the early *BBC Cardiff Singer of the World* series at St David's Hall. He was supported by a number of staff announcers, notably fun-loving Mari Griffith who had previously taken part in a host of light entertainment series from *Ryan and Ronnie* to *Poems and Pints*. She was often seen singing with her guitar, as one of a gifted earlier generation of all-round entertainers, but when Radio Wales began she became an announcer because 'I was looking for a proper job'.

Gifted people also emerged and stayed in radio. Mark Owen, also young when appointed, was totally immersed in the opera scene and had many friends and contacts among professional singers. Teleri and Mark recorded a series for Radio 4 which featured interviews and music with the finest voices in the land – Janet Baker, Gwyneth Jones and others – who had reached the operatic heights. Unfortunately, Mark retired early for medical reasons and was a great loss. Equally distressing was the early death in service of the inventive Richard Thomas who produced the best comedy of Radio Wales's earliest years, the hilarious *Aunty Nellie's Handbag*.

There were so many other noteworthy contributions, whether from high-output producers like Eifion Evans, or sensitively made documentaries from researcher Kate Fenton whose programmes won high praise on Radio 4.

If Chris Stuart led the first wave of presenters, Roy Noble replaced him in the early mornings as the biggest name on the channel. He was everything Radio Wales ultimately required as its defining Welsh voice. Clever, humorous, well prepared, approachable to the man in the street, he was the natural heir to his more senior colleague Alun Williams as Mr BBC Wales. Roy was a primary school headmaster in Llwydcoed, Aberdare, when Radio Wales launched. He began writing 'Letter from

Aberdare', sending them to Teleri's office with appropriate cartoons attached. They were opened by Madeline Hopkins whose voice could not be ignored. She told Teleri she had better see Roy. He was asked to broadcast his letters. A year later he took the plunge, left teaching and became a household name. Roy helped build the Radio Wales audience to new peaks when he was given a daily outlet for his talents. He emerged as one of the most in demand after dinner speakers, not only in clubs all over Wales but also at St David's Welsh societies throughout the world.

Several Radio Wales presenters were invited to open new stores and restaurants and became popular after dinner speakers. Vincent Kane was much in demand; Ray Gravell was a regular in Dublin and at Welsh rugby club events.

Teleri's love of live broadcasting came to the fore again with *Snow Specials* during the occasional heavy winter when all programmes included running commentaries from listeners turned reporters of the situation on the roads, the farms, from cut-off villages, with local emergency services trying to help them out of their difficulties. There was considerable competition from local commercial radio stations who could go one better than Radio Wales in the cities. They could interact with people at a street by street level but only had local coverage. The advent of the blanket coverage of *Snow Specials* marked another milestone in the evolution of radio. The phone-in was no longer a one programme a day phenomenon. Interacting with the listeners had come to stay. Slowly but surely, a modern radio service evolved with more news bulletins, better weather forecasting, road reports and much more trailing of upcoming programmes.

One day I received a phone call from a London radio Controller asking about the high listening figures for Radio Wales at 4.30 on Sunday afternoons. He was speechless when I told him we had kept the long-running Welsh-language programme *Caniadaeth y Cysegr* [Sacred Songs] on an English channel. I explained that an older generation still sat down for afternoon tea to listen to the great hymns of Wales, even though they now had only the memory of the language. Obviously mystified, he merely said, appropriately enough, 'Good God', and rang off.

Sundays still featured more serious material with *All Things Considered*, an outstanding series which has stood the test of time. Head of Religion John Stuart Roberts took responsibility for the whole of the Sunday schedule and appointed medically trained Barry Lynch to produce it while continuing to work part-time as a doctor. He then recruited another talent from St Andrews University, David Peat, who started as both presenter and producer and went on to become a strong departmental head at Radio Wales. David eventually decided to join his partner Ruth Jones in writing and co-producing situation comedy, which included the iconic *Gavin & Stacey*. *All Things Considered* also featured the diminutive, cheerful and engaging Reverend Roy Jenkins as its reporter and presenter; he also made regular contributions to 'Thought for the Day' on Radio 4 for many years. *All Things Considered* has featured consistently thoughtful discussions, as well as personal testimony in a modern era full of moral dilemmas which resonate in a post-Christian society.

Worship dominated the first and the longest running of all radio outside broadcasts. *Morning Service* was the first series to be considered important enough to bolster the people's faith at the beginning of the Second World War in 1939, following the most unusual of the BBC's internal debates. (See Appendix)

Music, both popular and classical, has always been a mainstay of Radio Wales. Beverley Humphreys was a chorus member of the Welsh National Opera before being asked to present a series of six programmes based on her own eclectic musical interests in the late 1980s. That was over 25 years ago and she is still on air waiting for her first contract! Beverley's enthusiasm in encouraging young musical talent is legendary, and she follows their careers with interest and acclaim. She continues to sit on the Ryan Davies Memorial Fund committee founded by Geraint Stanley Jones, which also benefits from additional funding from the Pendyrus Male Choir fund in memory of its great character, musical director Glynne Jones, himself a lively and humorous contributor to Radio Wales in the past. Another member of that same committee, Alun John, was a former teacher of chemistry and music who was recruited originally as a studio manager through a chance encounter at a bus stop in the 1960s with Rae Jenkins, then the ageing conductor of the BBC Welsh Orchestra. Alun provided years of musical pleasure, both instrumental and choral, on the channel and, like Beverley, was particularly interested in nurturing young talent. Alun claimed to have been the first to feature schoolboy Bryn Terfel on his early series *Shop Window*. He and the younger Huw Tregelles Williams were producers of the BBC Welsh Orchestra which relayed many concerts in halls unsuitable for classical music. They were much happier with the standards of sound in the cathedrals or Swansea's Brangwyn Hall. When the St David's Hall opened in Cardiff in 1983, it replaced the cramped Music Studio in Llandaff where music devotees used to bring their sandwiches to the lunchtime concerts on Radio 3. By now, the upgraded and renamed BBC Welsh Symphony Orchestra's regular classical concerts attract a larger audience to its new home and they enjoy good sound at last.

The BBC Welsh Symphony Orchestra has received funding second only to the Welsh National Opera from the Welsh Arts Council, particularly since 1973 when it benefited from the financial support for 22 extra players. Since then the Council has spread its patronage over a wide spectrum of the arts in Wales. For many years Nicola Heywood-Thomas covered the whole gamut of that scene in her own weekly series. Originally a researcher on *Wales Today*, Nicola worked for HTV before returning to pursue her real interests on Radio Wales.

On Saturday mornings there has always been plenty of humour, music and chat on Radio Wales, with another long-serving presenter, popular Merthyr personality Owen Money, at the helm. But the laughs stopped when the sports unit took over after the lunchtime news in the 1980s.

Sports editor Thomas Davies was the most dedicated producer I ever knew, but he refused to accept that one could have a laugh during his four hours of fast-moving sports news, commentary and analysis. I pleaded with him to include some humour to lighten the atmosphere just occasionally. Tom got to the point before I had finished the sentence. 'If you are telling me to interview Billy Mainwaring's mother, I resign now.' Period. Mrs Mainwaring usually sat next to another hardcore Aberavon fan, Lord Heycock of Taibach, and was the most vocal supporter of Aberavon RFC; indeed the loudest female supporter in Welsh rugby, particularly when her Welsh international son Billy was on the field of play. She was one of the great characters of Welsh rugby.

If that were not enough, Tom banned horse racing because it encouraged gambling. He demanded total dedication from his numerous contributors each Saturday, launching sports services on both Radio Wales and Radio Cymru simultaneously from neighbouring studios while sharing the same permanent outside microphone points from each of the grounds in order to maintain good quality sound. It was a non-stop sportsfest, unique in the efficient use of resources. After attending chapel on Sundays, Tom would listen back to all the Saturday tapes and on Monday morning expected even freelancers to attend feedback sessions in his 'No Smoking' office in the days before a corporate ban was imposed on the weed.

Geraint Evans was the first of several presenters of Saturday's highly successful *Sportstime* on Radio Wales, while Brian McCann fronted it for far longer, his rapid but calm demeanour disguising the frantic pace with which channels were switching reporters behind the scenes.

There was an unfortunate parting of the ways between Tom and Peter Walker, one of his best presenters. Peter was an extremely busy freelancer – making up for lost time, he used to say, as a poorly paid Glamorgan and England cricketer. Peter never gave the time Tom Davies required in the build-up to or the aftermath of the Saturday show. I tried to mediate but Tom was not one for compromise. Peter soon found work elsewhere in the building and took the change in his circumstances so much better than others who failed to understand that they were paid more than the staff partly because they had no security of tenure.

On one occasion Tom and I interviewed a young Aberystwyth Town manager for a job as soccer commentator. Tom asked him how his last game had ended. When he admitted his team had lost 6–0, we decided he would make a better broadcaster than a football manager and gave Ron Jones the job. He was an extremely fluent voice on Radio Wales and then Radio 5 for many years.

Some of Tom's Saturday people were ex-rugby internationals, such as perceptive analyst Brian Price, or schoolteachers just passionate about their sport. They included a couple of eccentrics among them. One was a primary school headmaster in Cardiff who led his school's morning service each Friday with the same prayer, 'Please God, make Cardiff City win tomorrow', and would follow it up on the following Monday morning with thanks to God if the result was to his liking!

Another, a first-class commentator, never admitted to his mother he was working for the BBC. She would refer callers to his law firm in total ignorance of his whereabouts.

No longer does Radio Wales have to prove its tone is different from Radio 4. It has long since forged its own identity as a mixed music and talk channel, even if today the music doesn't start until 9 a.m. Events have also moved on. One year after the birth of the channel the Welsh people rejected devolution in the 1979 referendum. The change of heart in 1997 brought an added level of responsibility to Radio Wales. It now has to act as a pillar of democracy monitoring the successes and failures of a Senedd with the greater gravitas that that demands. The original policy evolved with time and is now distinctively Welsh in tone. It has long since passed the original target of 65 hours a week. It is much more than the original target of a 'dawn to dusk' service and it reached and sustained a weekly audience of up to 450,000, give or take a degree of error of five per cent either way, by 1990. Radio 'Two and a Half' is here to stay thanks to risk-taker Teleri Bevan who endured the first battle but finally won the war.

15

TV's Tragedies and Challenges, 1974–80

THE TRAGIC DEATH of Derek Boote was a terrible loss to Welsh broadcasting as well as to his family. He was smoking a cigarette during a break while rehearsing a children's programme. Ash dropped on his costume and it went up in flames with Derek trapped inside. He was rushed to the burns unit of a Chepstow hospital where he died a few weeks later. It was a traumatic time for us all and emotions ran deep. His close friend Hywel Gwynfryn, producer Brynmor Williams, and the production teams of the children's and light entertainment departments were deeply affected.

Having joined the management team as deputy Head of Programmes only a few weeks before, I barely knew Derek. However, his enormous screen presence on a variety of programmes had marked him out as a multi-talented comedy actor and musician, a highly regarded entertainer in constant demand by two major departments. He had been cut down in his prime. Nor was Derek's death the only personal and professional tragedy to befall BBC Wales in the years ahead.

In 1974, in the pre-S4C days, BBC Wales still had a bilingual schedule. From the start new Head of Programmes Geraint Stanley Jones was keen to bring a new dynamic to the creative departments through increasing our presence on the networks. He targeted light entertainment, drama and music, knowing full well it was going to be an uphill struggle.

The Head of Light Entertainment was his former *Heddiw* colleague Jack Williams, following on from the retirement of Meredydd Evans. In the 1970s he produced the Max Boyce shows which were wowing Welsh viewers and rousing audiences in halls to a fever pitch with his grand entrances, bedecked in Welsh colours and carrying a massive leek, demanding an immediate response from his adoring fans with his war cry of 'Oggie Oggie Oggie!' He exalted our Welsh rugby heroes with great humour, laced with appropriate pathos when they lost. He followed the centuries-old tradition of the Welsh bards praising their princes in victory and courage in defeat but in a modern idiom and a different language.

Geraint Stanley Jones also wanted to develop the different talents of Ryan Davies in English. Ryan was already starring in the hilarious Welsh-language sitcom *Fo a Fe*, and as the lead partner in the comic duo of Ryan and Ronnie in both languages. An attempt was made to write an English version of *Fo a Fe*, but the script of 'George and The Dragon' lacked credibility.

Ryan and Ronnie did earn a network placing on late Sunday afternoons. The series was only fairly successful but could not hope to compete with the massive budgets, the number of scriptwriters or the preparation time given to *The Two Ronnies* or *Morecambe & Wise*. In truth, Ryan and Ronnie had to earn their living in the clubs and halls all over Wales, as well as on any other Welsh programmes which offered them extra income. Unfortunately, they worked in a different universe to their more illustrious counterparts. Ronnie never recovered properly from the break-up of the partnership and found some solace in drink. He never had Ryan's self-discipline or self-confidence. Ronnie once said to me, 'Was I ever an announcer?'

It was all bravado. He continued to work as an actor but the good days were over. Amazingly, he survived for many years before committing suicide by walking into the sea. Ronnie's talent as a sketchwriter – and essential foil to Ryan – in the duo's success was not always fully appreciated by the Welsh audience. He was destined to live in Ryan's shadow.

Ryan was already planning his future when the partnership ended. Talks were held with London's Head of Comedy, Jimmy Gilbert, as to how best to use Ryan's talents, but tragedy struck with the entertainer's sudden death in New York State at the age of only 40. The news of his death came through during a Broadcasting Council for Wales meeting in Bangor which came to a sudden halt. Geraint Stanley Jones said that his passing had cut short the development of light entertainment in Wales for a generation, and so it proved.

Geraint liked planning major events, mounting a series of Welsh-content programmes in English around St David's Day or any other suitable anniversary. In 1978 the National Eisteddfod was held in Cardiff, years before the opening of St David's Hall or the Wales Millennium Centre. Geraint and Jack Williams hired the massive old wooden pavilion for the week before the event itself, and produced a series of popular showstoppers for five nights to packed audiences. One night was dedicated to the music of Ivor Novello; another to local music hall star Tessie O'Shea; a third night featured rock bands; a fourth to massed Welsh male voice choirs, and the final evening ended with a bang with the augmented BBC Welsh Symphony Orchestra's rendering of Tchaikovsky's *1812 Overture*, complete with earth shuddering cannon. The residents of Pentwyn were warned in advance!

In drama, one production talent stood out. John Hefin had launched *Pobol y Cwm* in 1974 and his partnership with scriptwriter Gwenlyn Parry was to prove critical in both languages. John had great interpersonal skills and an ambition to produce network drama, hence his membership of the Chelsea Arts Club where he could network with London colleagues. It helped with network Controllers who reacted to so many TV directors from Wales with the question, 'Who's he?', when we tried to sell programmes to them.

Geraint's very first piece of luck was with BBC1 Controller Bryan 'Ginger' Cowgill, who commissioned the story of the Welsh Robin Hood, Twm Siôn Cati, for late Sunday afternoon viewing. It proved to be a tough learning curve for a production team unused to the rigour and professional disciplines of network drama.

John Hefin's productions flowed through in the following decade but he was no departmental manager. He tired of *Pobol y Cwm*, the costs of which he believed stifled other creative ideas. His personal portfolio of productions, however, remains second to none in the annals of BBC Wales. John will always be remembered for several wonderful programmes in English. First there was his association with Gwenlyn Parry in the writing of the peerless comedy *Grand Slam*, which has been repeated more often than any other drama in Wales and was the first production from Wales to be placed on a video cassette for general distribution. The story of the trip to Paris from one Welsh village for the biennial France–Wales international was written on the assumption that Wales were there to achieve another clean sweep of the Five Nations championship. Shock! Horror! Wales lost the match and the script had to be rewritten overnight. The added sense of pathos made the film even funnier, helped by the superb acting of undertaker Hugh Griffith, who had won an Oscar for his role in *Ben-Hur*; French jailbird Windsor Davies; the only gay in the village, Siôn Probert; the drunk Dillwyn Owen; lover boy Dewi 'Pws' Morris and his sex kitten, a semi-naked Sharon Morgan. It was the perfect troupe of actors for a brilliantly revised script.

When I accompanied Geraint Stanley Jones to the next BBC1 offers meeting with Controller Bill Cotton Jr, the extremely experienced former Head of BBC Light Entertainment said, 'Why should I be interested in a comedy about Welsh rugby?'

'It's very funny, has a strong cast and lots of pathos because Wales lost,' said Geraint.

'I'll look at it,' said Bill.

'It's worth a good placing,' said Geraint.

'The subject is not worth 9.25. Perhaps 11.15,' came the reply.

'I'll take it to BBC2 rather than throw it away at midnight,' said a determined Geraint.

'Alright,' said Cotton wearily, '10.15 but it had better not bomb.'

It certainly did not bomb.

The story illustrates the difficulties of selling even the best programmes to London and, even then, Cotton only paid a pittance for it. On the rare occasion a network Controller took an interest in something Welsh they never covered total costs. The idea for making *The Life and Times of David Lloyd George* came from a chance meeting Geraint had with Cotton's successor, Aubrey Singer, who happened to be reading a biography on Lloyd George. Aubrey commissioned it and paid enough to make us squeeze all the resources of BBC Wales way beyond our normal production capacity. We managed to bury the overspend. A BBC research report estimated that 87 per cent of the UK audience rated the series A or A+ or 'Very interesting', while almost half the respondents said they were not familiar with the story. The audience peaked at four million over the nine episodes and only seven per cent stopped watching it because they thought it was boring. Philip Madoc's personal rating of 88 per cent is one of the highest ever recorded. His performance was thought 'convincing, sensitive, and for many the outstanding feature of the whole series'. The production received similarly lavish praise, with a 96 per cent rating 'for an excellent production. The period atmosphere, the clothes, furniture, settings and decor just right.'

The scripts were written by Elaine Morgan who was pre-eminent in the craft of adapting novels for TV, demonstrated earlier in John Hefin's highly successful production *Off to Philadelphia in the Morning* from the novel by Jack Jones. It focused on the extraordinary life of composer Joseph Parry and his travails in the ironworks of Merthyr and America before returning to Aberystwyth as a professor of music. I have a particularly fond memory of the casting of the late opera singer Delme Bryn-Jones in the series, another talent who died before his time. All Elaine's drama scripts were written from her home in Mountain Ash where her husband Morien typed them out meticulously despite an eyepatch said to be a memento from time spent in the Spanish Civil War.

John Hefin's next work, *Bus to Bosworth*, was a minor classic: the tale of a teacher taking a busload of children to visit the site of the famous battle. Kenneth Griffith played the headmaster and, as always, was more of a problem to the production team than the children were, but his was still a great performance.

His appearance in that role led to his playing the revolutionary Thomas Paine in *The Most Valuable Englishman Ever*, perhaps the best of many passionate polemics he brought to the screen. I was not totally persuaded by Ken's performance, partly because I thought he overegged the fury in his acting. His perfectly valid advocacy of Thomas Paine merely made me think of several others who had a leading role to play in support of the French and American revolutions, such as the forgotten Welsh genius Richard Price of Llangeinor near Bridgend. However, Griffith was as attractive to the networks as he was difficult to work with, and it made for lively TV. I preferred his film *Black As Hell and Thick As Grass*, which explored the arguments on both sides of the Zulu War, somewhat glamourised in Stanley Baker's film *Zulu* in 1964. Moreover, Ken Griffith was at the forefront of a contemporary documentary genre which was built around the personal views of selected personalities who were 'naturals' at challenging conventional wisdom.

Gwyn 'Alf' Williams was the greatest and most popular of Welsh polemicists; a short, fiery professor who had returned to Cardiff from the University of York. His stammer could be as engaging as that of Nye Bevan's, the hiatus in the phrasing giving added emphasis to the *coup de grâce* which followed. His diatribe on behalf of Dic Penderyn, martyr of the Merthyr Riots, made for great TV but annoyed an element of the Broadcasting Council for Wales which thought it too one-sided. Gwyn had a commanding personality and was certainly one of a group of Welsh historians who made a long-neglected subject highly attractive to audiences from the 1970s onwards. This, despite Gwyn's notorious temper, capable of exploding when his Marxist opinions were queried, after which he would suffer a bout of asthma and coughing which was terrifying to behold. I was sorry to lose him to the independent producer Colin Thomas. Together they made more fine documentaries together.

Richard Lewis emerged from early days as a director of *Wales Today* into a drama-documentary scene which was also in vogue in the late 1970s. He had directed my first TV film profile of the Christian Communist T.E. Nicholas in 1966. Richard developed the taste for individual portraiture in dramatic form. He was a loner who did not fit in with the drama department. 'Dick' entered the network scene with journalist and biographer Paul Ferris as his scriptwriter. They worked together on five productions. These included three particularly effective portraits. One was the remarkable story of the 'Revivalist' Evan Roberts who shot to fame like a comet during the short-lived Welsh religious Revival of 1904, and fell just as quickly into anonymity; the other two were major biopics on the lives of very different internationally acclaimed Welshmen. The film *Dylan*, on the poet Dylan Thomas, made a major impact on BBC2 in 1978 and led to the commissioning of a similar treatment on Nye Bevan for transmission in 1981. The casting of both characters was always going to be difficult, given that most viewers remembered the looks and voices of both men, but their portrayal on screen was totally convincing. Between them, John Hefin and Richard Lewis continued to dominate network drama from BBC Wales for a decade.

Shaking up the music department led to one of Geraint Stanley Jones's best appointments. The BBC Welsh Orchestra spent most of its time playing for Radio 3. The music department in London tended to think of our 'Works Band' as part of their empire, but Geraint wanted the orchestra to appear more on TV. As noted, the orchestra had grown to symphonic strength and its name changed to the BBC Welsh Symphony Orchestra in 1976. This allowed it to play larger classical works for the first time. The young, talented musician Huw Tregelles Williams had arrived in 1973 and had used this development to improve orchestral standards. The appointment of Mervyn Williams as Head of Music infuriated the musical mafia in London, since Mervyn was a 'mere' geographer by training. Moreover, he and the BBC Welsh Symphony Orchestra now had regular exposure to TV which the other BBC orchestras lacked. This enabled Mervyn and Huw Tregelles to hire high-class conductors such as Paavo Berglund and Andrew Davis in the first instance, all of which made the orchestral players very happy. I recall the somewhat eccentric Berglund causing a stir with the health and safety people when insisting on sleeping overnight in his dressing room.

Mervyn emerged as one of the great characters of BBC Wales. Despite his educational background, his sense of direction on the road was so bad that he was known to drive right around roundabouts and return from whence he came! He and I had joined forces on several overseas filming trips in order to share facilities, but he was scared stiff of flying. When he tried hypnosis to cure the problem, he succeeded in making the hypnotist afraid of flying. However, Mervyn was never afraid of airing his strongly-held views in his favourite restaurant where he would settle down for the afternoon and where waiters would serve his regular diet of steak and chips washed down by bottles of red wine without even bothering to take his order. He and Geraint Stanley Jones came together and brought a new dimension to music-making in Wales. One of his first ideas for BBC2 after 1980 was to have the BBC Welsh Symphony Orchestra perform two series, one of Haydn symphonies, the other of Mozart symphonies, both presented by the leading musicologist and world authority on the composers, H.C. Robbins Landon.

Both Geraint and I were keen on exploring co-productions in order to boost our English output. Geraint landed the biggest one for Mervyn's growing music portfolio in 1979 when he negotiated a recording of Benjamin Britten's *War Requiem* at Dresden's Roman Catholic Cathedral, some 35 years after the devastation of the city by Allied bombers in February 1945. It was a moving occasion involving the BBC Welsh Symphony Orchestra and East German choirs. It was produced by Mervyn but organised by Geraint under the most difficult of circumstances a decade before the Berlin Wall was torn down. The East German government was notorious for being the most obstructive in the whole Communist bloc. Overcoming those problems required diplomacy, patience and determination. The success of that production was, according to Geraint, the proudest moment of his career. The return visit of the East Germans to perform Handel's *Messiah* at Chester Cathedral was less successful however, since several Germans defected from the group and requested political asylum. That made future co-operation impossible.

As noted, I had already negotiated the first co-production for BBC Wales in 1975, a 50-minute documentary called *Come Out, Come Out Wherever You Are!* in association with NDR Hamburg and broadcast at peak time on BBC1. It told the humorous story of the biggest escape by German POWs in Britain during the Second World War, although the authorities did not find it funny at the time. Sixty-seven Germans tunnelled their way to freedom from Island Farm Camp No. 198 near Bridgend on a moonless Saturday night in March 1945, but they were all recaptured within seven days following a massive manhunt. Four escapees stole a doctor's car with a flat battery and were given help to restart it by a group of drunk off-duty camp guards. They got as far as a wood near Birmingham Airport where they hoped that one of their number, a Luftwaffe pilot, would fly them home. Spotter planes helped police and farmers to capture them. Two women living on their own in a remote cottage near Merthyr Mawr were so scared they decided to put milk and sandwiches outside the front door to prevent intruders from breaking in! One farmer was left wondering who had milked his cows in the early morning after the escape. Tiredness, lack of food, and a poor command of English led to the recapture of all the escapees.

We re-dug the escape tunnel and brought four of the escapees back from Germany to recall their stories of life in the camp and laugh over the paintings of the thinly-clad girls still clearly discernable on the Nissen hut walls. The programme was directed by Piers Jessop, the first independent co-producer BBC Wales ever employed and whose experience in the fast-moving advertising industry showed up well in the finished product. Researcher Herbert Williams wrote a book on the story. It was well received in the UK but an element of the NDR Hamburg audience complained that the ex-prisoners in the programme enjoyed their reunion too much!

I also kept an eye on the camera lens when George Thomas was elevated to the ultimate job in what he constantly called 'The Mother of Parliaments', namely Speaker of the House of Commons in 1976. I reminded him that BBC Wales had made the first ever programme on the Welsh Office when he was Secretary of State for Wales and asked him to do the same as Speaker. We were allowed unprecedented access to Speaker's House and the corridors leading to the House of Commons. We only had one brush with the security, the bouncers of Israeli Prime Minister Menachem Begin during a courtesy call to see Speaker Thomas. There was one much repeated shot in the programme, a 45-second slow 'dolly' camera movement on rails which kept pace with 'Mr Speaker, Sir!', dressed in full regalia, marching purposefully to open proceedings in the House. He celebrated St David's Day in style with a dinner party, paid out of the Speaker's budget, in his chandeliered state dining room. It was in contrast to his usual practice of eating a fry-up prepared by a maid alone in his own quarters, a bottle of HP Sauce on the tiny table, the scene reflecting a sense of isolation which came with the job. As with the earlier film on the Welsh Office, it was the first attempt to peek behind the traditional veil of secrecy surrounding the workings of the House of

Commons. George could not resist a last anti-Welsh shot as we left the St David's Day dinner. When my wife thanked him for inviting her he said, 'A pleasure, my dear. I don't invite many Welsh Nationalists here.' Then, the famous cackle.

Documentaries still flowed from Selwyn Roderick. *The Colliers' Crusade* was a telling series relating Welsh involvement in the Spanish Civil War of the 1930s. Miners, untrained for armed battle, volunteered for the campaign to rid Spain of General Franco's fascist government. Several Welshmen died or were injured while living and fighting in terrible conditions. Communications with family and friends back home in Wales were so bad that a memorial meeting was held for Tom Jones, a leading north Wales trade unionist, several months before he suddenly arrived home unscathed.

Throughout the years from 1974 until the launch of S4C in November 1982, the BBC Wales TV schedule carried a total of 12 hours a week of programmes in both languages. Regular Sunday afternoon rugby highlights had begun in 1969 in black and white. From 1971 the combination of a golden age of Welsh rugby, aided by the advent of glorious colour, attracted massive audiences which contributed to a tremendous growth in national pride. Gareth, Gerald, J.P.R. et al. were toasted as heroes in song by Max Boyce and through drama in *Grand Slam*.

That sense of nationhood, however, did not transfer into nationalism. Monoglot viewers still had a choice of only three channels. Only BBC2 did not show Welsh-language programmes. The two bilingual channels inflamed viewers' attitudes towards the Welsh language and was undoubtedly one of many major factors in the rejection of devolution in the 1979 referendum. The number of telephone complaints made to the Llandaff switchboard signalled the fact that BBC Wales was a pawn in the battle between two opposing camps.

BBC Wales and HTV Wales planners phoned each other regularly to ensure that there were never two Welsh programmes scheduled at the same time, but the complaints continued. Secretary of State for Wales Nicholas Edwards told me he was still receiving letters from constituents fed up with two Welsh programmes clashing. On examining the problem again, we suddenly realised that the beginning and end of the junctions between the programmes sometimes produced an overlap of up to 30 seconds. That was remedied, but there was no hope of social harmony until the launch of S4C and Channel 4 England which increased the choice of channels overnight from three to five for many viewers in Wales. After November 1982 I felt a gradual improvement in both the tolerance and empathy levels towards the Welsh language everywhere in Wales – except in the BBC corridors of power in London during my time.

My role in developing the radio services brought me into constant contact with the four departments supplying programmes to both radio and TV. The BBC Wales schedule in English was dominated by *Wales Today*, *Week In Week Out* and *Sports Line-Up*. *Wales Today* was the anchor of the schedule and had a very strong presentation team spearheaded by David Parrry-Jones and the evergreen John Darren. Vincent Kane asked the hard questions on fiery editions of *Week In Week Out*. It was undoubtedly one of the strongest on-screen teams I can remember, despite the morale problem behind the scenes over the Clive Clissold affair, as noted earlier.

David Parry-Jones was a constant presence on the screen as both presenter of *Wales Today* and lead rugby commentator on *Sports Line-Up* which often delivered the highest audiences, even for each weekend's Welsh club rugby played between 16 teams for which BBC Wales had an exclusive broadcasting contract. Neath, Newport, Pontypridd, Pontypool, Llanelli, Cardiff, Swansea and Bridgend were the clubs which attracted the largest crowds on Saturday afternoons – the selected main match being edited for Sunday afternoon's analysis.

The programmes in Welsh which irritated English viewers so much, nevertheless, had a very strong following in the pre-S4C years. The long-running daily series *Heddiw* continued to provide not only a varied picture of Welsh life but also the most valuable film archive of Welsh contemporary history from 1961 until 1982. It roamed far and wide as a news magazine, featured ordinary and extraordinary characters and events in both Wales and a wider world. Its presentation and production teams changed every few years. In its last year before *Newyddion Saith* replaced it on S4C, the polished professional Gwyn Llewelyn was the main anchorman, with Richard Morris 'Moy' Jones, Alun Lenny and all-rounder Dei Tomos contributing film items from all around the country.

Light entertainment department's *Fo a Fe* continued to dominate the viewing figures in 1974 when *Pobol y Cwm* was launched. It was arguably a time when Welsh viewing figures for individual series reached their peak since audiences had such limited choice.

Summer in Wales is the time when the broadcasters go out to the people, as young and old compete in poetry, dance and song. The tradition of taking part in an eisteddfod has given generations of children the opportunity to develop their ability and self-confidence on stage. The old cliché of Wales being the 'Land of Song' is actually a truism. The choral societies and brass bands of the older industrial communities still exist; children still engage in literally hundreds of eisteddfods in chapels and schools, in villages and towns, wherever there is even a memory of the Welsh language. Eisteddfods encourage people of all ages and of all ability to join in the competitive spirit. A pyramid of eisteddfods allows the best performers to move up the different levels of competence, reaching a pinnacle at the three festivals – the Urdd National, National and Llangollen International Eisteddfods – where music of all genres dominates and where massive coverage has been, for BBC Wales, a *sine qua non*. It is the National Eisteddfod which has given a platform for many to hone their skills before turning professional. It is undoubtedly responsible for the high proportion of Welsh men and women who have graced the stage of La Scala opera house in Milan, the theatres of the West

End, the film sets of Hollywood, to say nothing of the hordes of actors and musicians who became professional broadcasters.

The annual Urdd National Eisteddfod is the first step for young hopefuls to display their potential before moving on to the National Eisteddfod. Although it is conducted entirely in Welsh, there are no linguistic barriers to the success of the massive musical talent which has emerged over the years on both stages.

The hard core of Welsh-speaking Wales moves to wherever the peripatetic National is held every year, and it expects to attract over 20,000 visitors a day. It has expanded into a temporary city of well over 200 tents of which the main Pavilion is merely the largest. Coverage of the the National Eisteddfod literary tent, 'Y Babell Lên', is as important for recording future programmes as is news coverage of political protests outside the Welsh Office tent. Businesses, even marginally dependent on making money from the Welsh language, increasingly set out their stalls for the week – large tents for the likes of BT, medium size for the universities, small ones for booksellers. Many people turn up year after year just to promenade around the 'Maes', finding old friends by chance, avoiding the bores, staring at the several outings of the Gorsedd of Bards in the hope of spotting a famous face half-hidden by green, blue or white headwear. White used to be the colour of the Eisteddfod elite-bards who had earned their right to be there or the film, opera and rugby stars who had served their nation with distinction. Today the white robe is reserved for winners of the literary honours only. The lower orders, wearing blue and green, were formerly given for those with degrees in music or Welsh or emerging talent.

In the evenings professional musicians and actors gradually displaced the talented amateurs who once graced the popular 'Noson Lawen', which was dominated in the early 1960s by the London Welsh when Ryan Davies and Rhydderch Jones were teaching there. The BBC Welsh Symphony Orchestra considers the Eisteddfod a regular venue, often with chorus and top professional soloists – Sir Geraint Evans, Stuart Burrows, Dennis O'Neill, Dame Gwyneth Jones, Dame Margaret Price and Rebecca Evans – to name but a few. I recall the night Sir Geraint Evans was visibly distressed in the first half of one such concert and fainted into the arms of a nurse backstage at the interval. She calmly asked him, 'How long have you been suffering from diabetes, Sir Geraint?' It was the first he knew of it. Geraint seemed larger than life on the operatic stage, his singing and acting totally co-ordinated as always. Was there ever a greater event in Welsh opera than the night at the New Theatre, Cardiff, when he appeared as Falstaff together with Margaret Price as Nannetta? Sir Geraint was the life and soul of the *Cardiff Singer of the World* parties, although initially angered by one London executive who queried the need for the word 'Cardiff' in the title of the competition. It was a privilege to attend his last appearance at Covent Garden in a performance of *L'elisir d'amore* before he finally retired to his splendid house overlooking Aberaeron harbour and his yacht *Caradog*.

Stuart Burrows was brought up in the same street as Sir Geraint in Cilfynydd. He had the purest of tenor voices which motivated his schoolfriend Geraint Stanley to produce several series of *Stuart Burrows Sings* for BBC2 audiences. Although Sir Geraint, Stuart and Dennis O'Neill played in the great opera houses of the world, they would always return to the old songs and hymns of Wales as their first love. Stuart once told me his ambition was to emulate the portfolio of a much earlier favourite, David Lloyd.

Before the Millennium, modernity at the National Eisteddfod was only delayed by the quaint ban on alcohol on the Maes by the 'Old Wales' governing body. Prohibition naturally encouraged lawbreaking. Since BBC Wales had the largest site on the field and it was one of the best weeks of the year to indulge in public relations, a caravan was hidden away with enough alcohol to slake the thirst of many a VIP who broke the rule he or she helped to create. When senior journalist

Gwilym Owen joined BBC Wales in the 1980s, I remember taking some 'liquid' refreshment with him before announcing his intention of filing a report on the alcohol smugglers. The ban was the last gasp of an amusing hypocrisy which outlived even the increasingly bizarre referenda on Sunday opening times for public houses in north and west Wales. The only embarrassment we had at the Eisteddfod was when the Celt-loving Director-General Alasdair Milne came visiting. Since he regularly drank a whole bottle of Glenmorangie malt whisky most days, it was necessary to depute Iwan Thomas, the good natured PR officer, to look after Alasdair with a bottle of the hard stuff concealed in his overlarge mackintosh in order to satisfy the boss's urge for 'a wee dram, boy!' in a suitably discreet location on the Maes!

There were no such restrictions on alcohol at the two other great summer events. The Llangollen International Eisteddfod has always been the most colourful of festivals and continues to attract choirs and dancers from all over the world. It was a magnet for both the young and older Luciano Pavarotti who paid homage to an event where 'nation shall speak peace unto nation', the motto of the BBC World Service, even on the streets of the town. In 2017 the lead singer of the Manic Street Preachers, James Dean Bradfield, made a similar reappearance – this time with his Welsh world-renowned band – since singing in a choir from the Monmouthshire valleys as a youngster. Llangollen was the only event that the BBC lost its broadcasting rights in the late 1980s when Mervyn Williams, by now an independent producer, sold a new sponsorship idea to organisers who always needed to look for greater investment opportunities.

The most popular event of the summer, however, continues to be the Royal Welsh Agricultural Show on its permanent site in Llanelwedd. It is the rural community's annual holiday week, when farmhands still bed down with their animals in their lorries. It has grown into a festival, for up to 70,000 people a day flock to watch the entertainments in the main ring; the sheep shearing and the tree felling; admire the manicured animals and buy from the huge variety of Welsh foods on display. The radio and TV outside broadcast units cover all four festivals in a period of eight weeks, an exhausting time for the technical and production teams who work on them.

November 1982 saw the end of bilingual scheduling. A more peaceful era of social harmony dawned when S4C was launched. When the new channel appointed BBC Controller Owen Edwards as its first Chief Executive, Geraint Stanley Jones succeeded him as Controller in April 1981 having been Head of Programmes for seven years. I replaced him in the hot seat and Teleri Bevan was appointed Deputy Head of Programmes. We were now required to plan a seismic shift in the TV landscape of Wales.

16

S4C's Shotgun Marriage, 1980–90

IT WAS JOHN Elfed Jones, the straight-talking member of the Broadcasting Council for Wales, who dubbed the relationship between the BBC and the newly constituted S4C a 'Shotgun Marriage'. In fact, as one royal personage once remarked about her own situation, there were three partners with very different personalities in this marriage as well. The third partner, HTV, had to be dragged screaming to the altar pending difficult prenuptial negotiations. BBC Wales tied the knot Indian-style, the ceremony arranged in advance with the BBC paying a dowry of ten hours a week in the hope that one day the betrothed would fall in love with each other. No provision was made for a divorce, and love would be a very long time coming, if ever. It would be more accurate to call it a marriage of convenience.

In 1980 Radio Cymru and Radio Wales had only just got into full swing when Gwynfor Evans announced his intention of fasting to death unless the Conservative Government's broken promise of establishing the Welsh Fourth Channel was reversed. I was already spending much more time supporting Geraint Stanley Jones on TV during the days of increasingly intense and bitter public debate over the future of TV in Wales in both languages. The problem was best summarised in one sentence by the Cardiff branch of the Association of Broadcasting and Allied Staffs Union: 'There are two arguments for a Welsh

Fourth Channel: the need for Welsh programmes and the need to offload Welsh.'

My first intervention was not particularly helpful. Having been frustrated by the stop-start nature of the radio developments during the previous five years, I became so worried about the woeful political rhetoric surrounding the Welsh channel I feared it was heading for a disastrous outcome. As late as May 1980, Wyn Roberts, Parliamentary Under-Secretary of State at the Welsh Office, was still talking of a Welsh-language ghetto ending at 7 p.m. at weekends on the existing channels. Director-General Ian Trethowan was making no secret of the fact that the negative result of the devolution referendum on St David's Day 1979 meant that extra funding for Welsh broadcasting was unnecessary. ITV and HTV were against a fourth channel in Wales. Strong supporters of the Welsh language, such as Jennie Eirian Davies and Professor Jac L. Williams, were adamant that mixed language households would not watch a dedicated channel in Welsh. Crucially, nobody talked about money, structure or anything I recognised as pragmatic. This critical division of opinion was a genuine concern. There was an inbuilt irony to the situation. In one survey, 88 per cent of non-Welsh speakers were in favour of the channel, more than the 77 per cent of Welsh speakers. In another poll over 60 per cent of the Welsh-speaking audience regularly watched *Y Dydd* on HTV as well as both *Heddiw* and *Pobol y Cwm* on BBC Wales. No separate fourth channel could match those figures. It is true viewers still only had a choice of three channels and a restricted number of programmes until 1982, but at the time we had no idea what form the new channel would take. I came out against it in an interview with Emyr Daniel on Radio Cymru, and this was relayed to the *Guardian* newspaper. I was duly carpeted by the BBC Welsh Governor and Chairman of the Broadcasting Council of Wales, Glyn Tegai Hughes, who had led the Council in giving total backing to the channel. He told me in no uncertain terms that if I could not take the heat like the rest of the management team, I should get out of the proverbial kitchen. I chose to stay in the kitchen.

The steadfastness and determination shown by the Broadcasting Council for Wales paid off. The battles over S4C had swung from one side to the other. The situation became confusing with so many different fingers in the pie. Two very different reports appeared on the same day in July 1978. The Trevelyan Report, written by a civil servant, indicated that there was no money for the channel. The other, a Government White Paper, stated that the Welsh language should be given priority in the use of the new fourth channel network. Trevelyan suggested extra funding for children's programmes as soon as possible, and the then Labour Home Secretary Merlyn Rees, under pressure from the three Plaid Cymru MPs who were keeping the Labour Government afloat, offered a £1 million grant for the children's idea. The BBC Governors were against taking state funding for programme budgets, but gave in to Glyn Tegai when he threatened to resign unless the offer was accepted.

In November 1979 *Yr Awr Fawr* was launched on BBC2 on Sunday mornings. This gave us the opportunity to expand the department and appoint several bright young producers under the innovative head of department, Dyfed Glyn Jones. There was no better training ground for young producers than the varied skills required to keep the attention of children. We set about helping Dyfed Glyn to appoint his new staff. He had followed Evelyn Williams as head of department in 1974. He was both eccentric and efficient, quirky and comical, determined and decisive. He had once worked for the BBC flagship programme *Tonight* in London, edited at the time by future Director-General Alasdair Milne. Before that he had worked in the advertising industry, thinking up new catchphrases and slogans. It was said that he was one of the team which created the famous Dulux dog advert. Dyfed once explained to me the commercial difference between a Mars bar, marketed to people who do not share, and Kit Kat's four-fingered bars, better suited to chocolate lovers who shared.

Having returned to Wales as a member of the *Heddiw* team, Dyfed now brought in fresh ideas and provided an attractive and encyclopaedic mix of entertaining items under the umbrella of a single hour. It prospered with the appointment of young and creative producers: Alan Cook, Rhys Ifans, Delwyn Siôn, Iwan Griffiths and Brynmor Williams, plus a large cast of researchers and presenters. Several, such as Alan Cook and Dewi Wyn Williams, later joined *Pobol y Cwm*; others made documentaries for the new S4C. Delwyn Siôn and Rhys Evans, Gwynfor's youngest son, were already popular members of leading Welsh pop and rock groups. S4C's first Director of Programmes, Euryn Ogwen Williams, also worked on the series for a time. These were the advance troops of BBC Wales's new army in the event of a political decision in favour of a Welsh Fourth Channel.

Yr Awr Fawr was a fast-moving show which included jokes, cartoons, slapstick sketches and quizzes. Significant individual contributions were made by versatile actors Emyr Wyn and Marged Esli who co-presented the series.

As one who was never attracted to farce, the one exception was the long-running double act of Syr Wynff (Wynford Ellis Owen) and Plwmsan (Mici Plwm), a clever ongoing verbal row between Syr Wynff, the boss, and the extremely stupid Plwmsan which attracted children of all ages. Both were great comedy actors who were flexible enough to succeed in straight parts in a range of other drama series.

Geraint Stanley Jones took Dyfed Glyn to Eastern Europe and a year later I accompanied him to the Cannes TV market in order to view and buy cartoons which could be dubbed into Welsh. We rejected Japanese products because of their violence, although their technology was state of the art. We were then accused of hypocrisy, given the popularity of *Tom and Jerry* in Britain. The big difference was that the Japanese cartoons lacked humour.

By the time *Yr Awr Fawr* went on air in November 1979, however, the Labour Party had lost the May 1979 General Election. On 12 July, Home Secretary Willie Whitelaw, quoting the support of Secretary of State for Wales Nicholas Edwards and Parliamentary Under-Secretary of State Wyn Roberts, stated that the Welsh Fourth Channel would not go ahead. There was uproar in public and the reaction inside BBC Wales became heated. At a meeting of the Broadcasting Council for Wales, held during the unfortunate hiatus between the retirement of Glyn Tegai Hughes and the appointment of new BBC Welsh Governor Alwyn Roberts, the acting Chair, Paul Flynn, was so incensed at the decision to scrap the fourth channel idea that he announced his resignation at the start of the meeting and walked out. It was a surreal moment, reminding me of that famous dictum by Oscar Wilde. To have lost Glyn Tegai was bad enough. To lose the highly popular senior member of the Broadcasting Council for Wales and future Labour MP as well was unsettling. By this time the debate over the channel seemed like the tower of Babel. When new Broadcasting Council for Wales Chairman and BBC Governor Alwyn Roberts was appointed, he called for coordinated action among all stakeholders.

Gwynfor Evans's sudden threat to fast to death, unless the Welsh Fourth Channel was given the go-ahead, stopped everybody in their tracks. Plaid Cymru had been in the doldrums since the voters showed little enthusiasm for devolution in the referendum of 1979. Gwynfor was looking for a cause to restore morale and found it in the Welsh Fourth Channel. Gwynfor's threat was a controversial decision, even within the party. There were those who were appalled at the idea that a religious pacifist should commit suicide. The wider political community was staggered that anybody would wish to die for the sake of a TV channel. Those who knew Gwynfor realised he would go through with it. He had dedicated his life to the party, had marched on doggedly despite having many more downs than ups – and he was stubborn. I remembered that trait when failing to change his mind over the timing of his first Party Political Broadcast. A worried Secretary of State for Wales Nicholas Edwards took the same view and once asked me for possible solutions over lunch in August 1980. I trotted out the current BBC party line of adding 18 pence to the licence fee. The gruff but well-meaning Cabinet minister exploded, 'How do you expect a blind old lady in Winchester to pay for a channel she could neither see nor understand?'

A delegation of three 'Wise Men', led by former Welsh Secretary Cledwyn Hughes, told Home Secretary Whitelaw that Gwynfor's action could lead to civil disorder in Wales. Whitelaw envisaged another Northern Ireland situation. By this time all but one of Wales's Conservative MPs wanted to return to the manifesto promise. One unsung hero was the respected Welsh Conservative, Lord David Gibson-Watt, who told Nicholas Edwards he could not back the Government's position in the House of Lords. It was enough. Mrs Thatcher made her first U-turn. S4C was agreed in principle. Gwynfor insisted on a good funding settlement before calling off his threat. There were exactly two years remaining to get S4C on air at the same time as Channel 4 England.

One room at Cardiff's Angel Hotel has a famous balcony from which victorious Welsh rugby teams used to wave to their devoted fans below. In early 1981 it was the location for a more prosaic, even bizarre event. The first Chairman of S4C, Sir Goronwy Daniel, was attending his first briefing on how to run the channel. At that moment he had no staff. Eirion Lewis of the Independent Broadcasting Authority had asked the BBC and HTV to attend as programme providers to the new channel. HTV's Huw Davies and I agreed to join Sir Goronwy, whom I remembered as the lofty and reserved Permanent Under-Secretary when I produced the first film on the Welsh Office over a decade earlier. In his new position he reminded me of Lord John Reith, founder of the BBC, in both build and viewing tastes. Sir Goronwy told us that if he had his way S4C's schedule would consist entirely of religious and philosophical programmes, and we were there to persuade him otherwise. He did not watch TV, he said, but now he had to do so. We told him what to watch. He wrote the times of *Y Dydd* and *Heddiw* slowly in his diary, as if he had never heard of them, and then accepted my invitation to visit the set of *Pobol y Cwm* in Llandaff. He entered the large studio, looked up at the dozens of lights, and asked me why we needed so many cameras. I had wondered whether he was 'having me on', but realised that he genuinely knew nothing about the medium. When chairing S4C Authority meetings he was always interested in finance and audience research as a trained mathematician, but was known to walk out of programme discussions. However bizarre his interests – he once enquired of a dinner guest what she knew about earthworms in South America – this most eccentric but engaging of chairmen turned out to be well respected by politicians and broadcast managers alike for launching, defending and steadying S4C during its early years.

Astonishingly, the funding for the new channel was more generous than anybody had dared hope. It had already been decided to launch S4C in the same week as Channel 4 England. The project costs, whereby both new channels shared Treasury taxes levied on ITV and transferred directly to the broadcasters in the ratio of C4's 83 per cent to S4C's 17 per cent, was said to have been dreamt up by a senior female civil servant in the Home Office. It was a neat solution but, crucially, did not include the cost of BBC Wales's contribution of ten hours a week which had to come from the licence fee.

The backing of the Broadcasting Council for Wales was a necessary element in pressing for the funding required to provide an extra and much richer mix of two and a half hours a week in Welsh. Its unanimous support for the channel was crucial to the backing given by the BBC Board of Governors in London.

The situation was helped by two totally supportive successive Director-Generals in London. One was the arrogant and impatient Scot, Alasdair Milne, who called everybody

'Boy!' but who understood 'the Celtic fringe' as a former Controller, Scotland. The second was Michael Checkland, the more humble and pragmatic former Director of Resources, an accountant from Birmingham who knew where all the BBC bodies were buried and where to find money when the chips were down. We had always enjoyed a good working relationship with Michael and had no doubt that when Geraint Stanley attended the critically important meeting of the BBC's TV development committee, the £10 million announced from the chair by Managing Director Bill Cotton had actually been calculated by a silent Checkland sitting alongside him. Cotton justified the cost to some of the dumbfounded executives sitting around the table by stating that, since the launch of S4C was inevitable, the BBC, as the UK's public broadcaster, had to set the necessary professional standards. We were all pleased by the outcome. However much I wished for even more money, it could well have been much worse.

There was one amusing sideshow that day. Train lover Owen Edwards missed the meeting because his train had broken down while he was riding the footplate. He did not enjoy being teased about it, particularly since it was his last journey to London on behalf of the BBC before joining S4C.

As Head of Programmes for the BBC's output on S4C, my simple strategy was to dominate its viewing figures with a mix of popular and serious programmes at a lower cost than anyone else. It was essential to prove that the world's most expensive minority channel could attract the punters. From a BBC point of view, it was also a safeguard against Welsh-speaking sceptics who would always regard the 'British' public broadcaster as less than fulsome in its support for S4C. The in-house costs of an integrated BBC Wales were much lower than those of HTV which spent months haggling over its contract with S4C. The independents included good quality producers like William Aaron, eagerly waiting for a chance to make their contribution, but the channel would take time to build an audience. Moreover, the Government had said it would review the success of the channel three years after the launch. We knew that audience figures would be uppermost in the minds of the judges come that time, and forever in its future.

Geraint Stanley and drama chief John Hefin were saddened by the chase for audience ratings which limited the money available for the more expensive single plays, but agreed that the audience would prefer more episodes of *Pobol y Cwm*, so much so that S4C paid for the initial repeats.

A competition was arranged between HTV Wales and BBC Wales as to which channel provided S4C with its news output. This was critical because we already had one Welsh language news outlet for Radio Cymru and it was good for morale to offer our existing journalists the flexibility of working in both media over time. BBC Wales could also provide such a service at a much lower cost than HTV. The BBC's salary levels were lower, and an integrated newsroom with its common input desk offered economies of scale. Probably the crucial factor was that the BBC provided the news service free of charge to the new channel. The S4C Authority duly set up interviews at Gregynog Hall near Newtown. Although we were confident that S4C did not wish to pay HTV for the service, we produced one more ace. The director of BBC News & Current Affairs, Richard Francis, came to the meeting and offered a desk in the London newsroom for a Welsh sub-editor who could select any international footage required for *Newyddion Saith*. He also gave permission to re-edit the material as necessary. HTV were not allowed the same flexibility or access by the great Tregaron-born editor of ITN in London, Sir David Nicholas. It was with great relief that we won the argument because it constituted almost 20 per cent of the BBC's ten hours a week for S4C.

The provision of the 520 hours a year developed into a nightmare in the planning stage. The hours were fixed by statute but the budgets didn't match. Inflation had overtaken the original costings calculated 14 months before we launched, and I reported a projected shortfall of £150,000 in the first year. Every time I tried to align the money available to programme costs I was always half an hour short. I counted the hours by day, and recounted them to sleep at night with no obvious solution in sight. Salvation came from an unlikely quarter. Rugby guru Carwyn James quietly suggested snooker as the answer, and invited me to accompany him to the World Snooker Championships in Sheffield to meet the 1979 World Champion Terry Griffiths. We arrived to find Terry, by now the Chairman of the World Professional Billiards and Snooker Association. He cut a lonely figure, having been knocked out in the first round. I asked him for Welsh-language coverage of snooker for S4C given that the BBC networks had the basic contract. To my relief Terry said, 'Why not? It's for Wales, isn't it?'

It cost nothing in extra money for 26 hours a year in contracts or cameras, merely the relatively small expense of commentators. The ten hours had been achieved – in theory at least.

Working out a schedule for the first ten hours was the easy bit. The only grumble I recall hearing about content in the first year's plan was the inclusion of popular hymn singing programme *Dechrau Canu, Dechrau Canmol*. S4C wanted it for the new independent sector. HTV's Gwyn Erfyl wanted to take it over himself and change the format. I told him that if he came over from HTV he could. It was my last tongue-in-cheek attempt to get him to join us. I saw no reason to lose a top-five audience series which had originated and flourished as a BBC production. The Welsh love their hymns even if they no longer listen to sermons. We had the outside broadcast vehicles moving around Wales, sharing their time with our rugby coverage. The series had constantly changing and attractive venues, while making the most efficient use of expensive resources. If the programme fell into the hands of independent producers who were trying to make a profit, sooner or later they would end up cutting down on locations and filling time with compilations as budgets tightened. More importantly, there would be a problem keeping the BBC's big vans working at full capacity, which in turn would make the rugby coverage more expensive.

I was confident that our experienced production teams could deliver quality programmes for S4C. At the time we had all the current heavyweights in Welsh drama available to us, limited only by the ten hours and money!

Dechrau Canu, Dechrau Canmol was under the control of religion department head John Stuart Roberts who had appointed Huw Brian Williams to look after the series and could always be relied on to accept extra commitments.

Mervyn Williams, Head of Music, always had strong choral and orchestral ideas for the Easter and Christmas schedules which were hugely enriched during Aled Jones's brilliant period when he was the greatest of boy sopranos.

We had no peer in the coverage of rugby. BBC Wales had the contracts and everybody agreed each weekend's edited highlights should be shown on S4C's Saturday nights before Sunday afternoon's *Sports Line-Up*. A new TV commentary team took the form of Huw Llywelyn Davies, who had already served his apprenticeship on Radio Cymru, assisted by the irrepressible rookie Ray Gravell. The duo would dominate the rugby scene in Welsh for many years to come with their unique mix of authority and entertainment. Head of Sport Onllwyn Brace directed their first rugby international on S4C in February 1983. He was initially angry at the late appearance of Ray ten minutes before transmission. Threats of the sack for 'Grav' before he had even started his new career stopped when Onllwyn suddenly realised 'Grav' was being interviewed on BBC1. He had called in on the *Grandstand* team, was invited for a live interview and immediately publicised his new job on S4C. That interview attracted many new viewers to S4C immediately!

The 21-year run of *Heddiw* was brought to an end. It was replaced by *Newyddion Saith* which was in the safe editorial hands of former HTV journalist and *Heddiw* producer Deryk

Williams. Former *Heddiw* editor Arwel Ellis Owen had been promoted and was overall editor of news and current affairs. Deryk would later become Director of Programmes for S4C and much later Arwel became interim Chief Executive of S4C.

The presentation team of *Newyddion Saith* was both strong and experienced. All had already worked on *Heddiw* and Radio Cymru. Gwyn Llewelyn, Beti George, Huw Llywelyn Davies, Bethan Jones Parry and Rod Richards had strong backing from a raft of political and roving overseas correspondents. The newsroom was further strengthened with S4C being allocated a Lobby ticket, the first time BBC Wales journalists were allowed to enter that inner sanctum in Westminster for *Newyddion Saith* and double up for the three-year-old Radio Cymru news. One presenter with a distinctive personality was Rod Richards, a former Royal Marine whose real ambition was to enter politics. He took time off from *Heddiw* to fight an election for the Conservatives and then returned to present *Newyddion Saith*. Eventually Rod not only won a parliamentary seat, he became a junior minister in the Welsh Office where he is credited with launching a successful project which involves sending a regular number of teachers to promote the Welsh language in Patagonia.

The very first political correspondent in Westminster, albeit without a Lobby ticket at the time, was Dewi Llwyd who joined the BBC in 1980 and became the best known and credible face on Welsh TV after taking over the chair of *Newyddion Saith* in 1986. He left the programme over 25 years later in 2012 to present Radio Cymru's afternoon *Post Prynhawn*, a Sunday morning magazine programme, and a weekly *Any Questions?* type programme in Welsh on TV, all of which he presents to this day. During the past 38 years he has covered seven general elections and both devolution referenda, as well as innumerous forays abroad to Washington DC and elsewhere, particularly to South Africa when Nelson Mandela was released.

In light entertainment, head of department Ruth Price

and producer Ieuan Lewis continued a lengthy run of the *Hywel Gwynfryn* chat show which was transferred to S4C. The highly innovative and versatile Gareth Rowlands, who had moved on from both Radio Cymru and Radio Wales, was lined up to produce S4C's first ambitious musical dance show, *Hapnod*, with music director Cefin Roberts's troupe of young performers based at his Bangor school. Gareth proved to be the most flexible of TV producers, offering a number of series ranging from motoring to drama. He has since directed a huge variety of drama productions through to the present day, from *Pobol y Cwm* to *Teulu* [Family] and *Byw Celwydd* [Living Lies], interspersed with several years spent as an independent producer advising and producing programmes for the Gaelic-speaking TV services in both Scotland and Ireland.

In all, exactly 57 young production staff and over 200 technical and support personnel were appointed in advance of the launch.

Some of this talent was poached by HTV and the independent sector from Radio Cymru and several TV departments at this the most difficult of times. They were being attracted to the higher salaries paid by HTV and the 'sweetheart' deals offered by S4C to several independents. We lost two good, recently promoted studio directors to HTV from *Wales Today* alone. John Roberts, later HTV's Head of Sport, remembers turning back in the corridor with his fellow escapee Phil Lewis rather than face a friendly chat with me when I was in total ignorance of their impending departure. We were losing experienced people by the week. It is true that *Heddiw*, and ultimately Radio Cymru, benefited from the haemorrhaging of HTV staff on *Y Dydd* before 1978, but that was when we were competing on two different channels.

The biggest challenge of all was the inevitable problem arising from a new and unique situation in British TV. The BBC commissioned and retained full editorial control over its contribution of ten hours to S4C, but lost its scheduling power to the new publisher, the S4C Authority. Because I wanted to maximise the audiences for the BBC shows, tensions arose with S4C over programme placings, particularly *Newyddion Saith* and *Pobol y Cwm*.

S4C's Director of Programmes Euryn Ogwen Williams was a wily operator and knew full well that the ten hours a week from the BBC and about six hours from HTV were totally inadequate for the new channel. He needed the freedom to commission many more hours from the new independent sector over which he had carte blanche. Since all these productions at the 1982 launch were new, Euryn naturally wanted to give them time to build audiences. It involved creating a schedule which meant using the 'inheritance factor' of *Pobol y Cwm* and the other established BBC programmes to give an impetus to the unknown pulling power of some new 'indies' series. Euryn had the upper hand on the schedule by statute. The BBC was only the programme provider.

Tensions were not confined to poaching and scheduling. The BBC was very unpopular when it came to S4C's advertising strategy. Until 1982 no BBC programme had ever appeared on any channel in the UK which carried advertising. The one and only instruction I received from Director-General Alasdair Milne before planning the BBC's ten hours was, 'Don't create a precedent which would compromise the BBC in the future.'

As a result, I could not possibly allow advertising within BBC programmes and insisted on a buffer of promotional material for 30 seconds before and after the BBC Wales logo. Since *Pobol y Cwm* and rugby had the highest audience of the week, this restricted advertising income potential.

The more we examined our mutual positions, the more John Elfed Jones's remark seemed trumped by one BBC executive who thought the situation was more like 'a dog's dinner'. It was inevitable that, with three stakeholders involved, S4C was a battleground of the brands. S4C had to develop its own, and BBC Wales had to protect its own. Hundreds more people worked on the BBC's ten hours than in S4C's offices. BBC technical and support staff were uneasy about working for a different channel and needed reassurance that their work was recognised as a BBC product commissioned by BBC Wales. We agreed with the unions that it raised an issue of morale, and it became necessary to confine all professional discussions between the BBC and S4C to named senior managers which excluded even heads of programme departments. Otherwise, S4C could be seen to be interfering with the BBC's editorial control. Producers had to be made accountable to the organisation which paid their salaries and pensions. It also prevented production teams playing one management decision against another.

As a result of all these limitations, S4C managers never gave credit to BBC productions for several years in public meetings with stakeholders. I turned grumpy enough to remonstrate directly with my own friend and former colleague, S4C Chief Executive Owen Edwards, in the middle of a Cardiff street after one public meeting of S4C's programme providers. It was not even Owen's fault. I was not S4C's favourite person. Nor was HTV its favourite institution for that matter.

Once the difficult initial negotiations with S4C were settled, Deputy Head of Programmes Teleri Bevan played 'good cop' to my 'bad cop' and established a good ongoing relationship with Euryn. Throughout this period Euryn and I worked to the same end and I had nothing but growing respect for his huge success in building the channel and have often wondered why he never took the helm at HTV or S4C. Euryn had all the qualities – a vast experience of the industry, good judgement and a quiet determination to get what he wanted. Our differences in those early planning days brought us closer together as friends in the long run. We had been placed in a unique broadcasting arena, yet were expected to deliver the same results from totally different perspectives. We both found the experiment exciting and stimulating, even if Euryn sometimes pitted his deviousness against my bloody-mindedness.

Only in retrospect did I realise how peaceful the relationships between the two institutions were above our respective pay grades. Controller Geraint Stanley Jones allowed me free rein while keeping cool with his counterpart Owen Edwards. The S4C Authority, chaired by Sir Goronwy Daniel and which included BBC Welsh Governor Alwyn Roberts, were too wise to raise their heads above the parapet.

After the two years of planning, everybody settled down to concentrate on programme transmissions. S4C's independents, HTV and BBC Wales had much to celebrate. The opening week in November 1982 produced the praise S4C deserved and the audiences the BBC had hoped for. Way over 100,000 watched *Pobol y Cwm* and *Newyddion Saith* in the first week. Six of the top-ten shows came from the BBC. S4C was on its way.

The initially high audience figures for S4C decreased dramatically by mid 1984 with the result that any figure above 100,000 either reflected a particularly important rugby match or a large degree of error on the upside. *Pobol y Cwm* varied betwen 65,000 and 86,000 for individual episodes by the end of the 1980s. The figures suffered wild swings between successive episodes and different weeks. They told us which programmes were more popular than others on average, but the size of the swings pointed to large degrees of error. Unfortunately, publicity is always given to headline figures without any such caveats. This leads to highly misleading conclusions. To quote one example, zero audiences are often declared for children's programmes on S4C. 'Scarcely believe,' as actor Stewart Jones used to say!

Nobody can escape the possible consequences if a channel is solely judged on dodgy statistics. Yet audiences are bound to fall year on year. The choice of channels has increased dramatically, and the younger generation is moving away from the TV monitor to the internet and new digital technology. Cuts to the BBC licence fee may impact on S4C and lead to more political controversy. If it does, the problem may yet involve another interested partner in the very long run – Y Senedd.

17

BBC Wales TV goes Monoglot, 1982–90

'WHAT THE HELL do you think you are doing? You have cameras shooting hundreds of striking miners picketing in the Rhymney Valley and only two policemen trying to keep control. I'm coming to see you now!'

It was the angry voice of fiery Viv Brookes, the Deputy Chief Constable responsible for policing the year-long miners' strike in 1984. Before he arrived to give me hell, I guessed that *Ms Rhymney Valley 1985*, directed by Karl Francis, was causing the mayhem. Karl was a law unto himself, a leading freelance film-maker who was aggressively anti-Welsh when it came to what he termed the 'jobs for the boys' policy in BBC Wales. Karl was an all-or-nothing personality. He once brought me the idea of following and filming a poet he was convinced would win the Eisteddfod Chair or Crown, on condition the adjudicators would agree to be filmed selecting the winner. When that condition proved impossible a good idea died. Karl left me a letter naming the poet. He was correct. It was Siôn Eirian.

It was easier to face Karl than the Deputy Chief Constable. I was forced to grovel to Viv Brookes over a placatory sandwich, but he grudgingly accepted that the newsroom's daily coverage of the strike was causing few problems. Karl's film was a contemporary story, full of humour and pathos, of miners organising a beauty contest while on strike. He explored the serious issue of the sexual stereotyping of women with a light touch, at a time when the Miss World beauty contest was about to disappear from the screens for being politically incorrect.

The 1984–5 miners' strike was a tragic event which echoed George Orwell's nightmare scenario in his futuristic novel. The conflict was given blanket coverage daily on the British media. There were several Welsh angles, not the least of which was the loyalty of Welsh miners to a strike which had not gone to a ballot and only a minority ever wanted. The battle between Big Brother Mrs Thatcher (often regarded as 'the only man in the Cabinet') and the equally stubborn miners' leader, Arthur Scargill, could only end one way. The Government had prepared for the fight by ensuring coal stocks were large enough to cope with a lengthy war with the National Union of Mineworkers. As a grandson of two miners, my heart was entirely with the mining communities and families who all suffered increasing deprivation from lack of money and food. My head feared the worst.

Wales Today covered the strike with greater sensitivity than was sometimes acknowledged, particularly when a sense of hopelessness followed the tragic death of David Wilkie – a taxi driver taking a miner to work – killed when a brick was thrown from a bridge. The culprits, both striking miners, were given an eight-year sentence for manslaughter.

In the south Wales coalfield the strike was remarkable for the degree of tacit collusion between the strike committee, the media and the police. Picketing had to be restricted to a few pits in order that sufficient numbers made an impact for the cameras. Both the broadcasters and the police were obviously helped by a strategy which suited everybody's limited resources. Nearly a year passed by before Scargill admitted defeat, but not before the miners spent a sparse Christmas with their families, trying their best to give the children the best possible time in the worst possible circumstances.

When the strike ended in March 1985, I felt a lump in my throat as I watched news coverage of 'Red' Maerdy's 753 miners marching back to work, the band blaring defiantly in front, women and children behind, viewers watching a community which had lost so much – and yet had kept its pride. Five years later Maerdy was the last pit in the Rhondda to close. It brought a sad end to over 200 years of a tumultuous chapter in Welsh industrial history.

*

We had to relaunch the channel without extra resources while still attracting the largest viewing audiences for programmes made in Wales. Geraint Stanley had warned me that with only 18 months to go S4C had to be the first priority. Of my 57 new production recruits for the S4C development, none could be allocated for the relaunch of BBC Wales TV. Nevertheless, the massive expansion of technical personnel and equipment for S4C meant that we now had greater capacity than before, enough to make more network programmes at a marginal cost. Fortunately, the BBC TV networks were still open to persuasion on that basis and, in 1982, Alun Richards was given the opportunity he always dreamt about – to write a drama series located around his beloved Mumbles lifeboat crew. *Ennal's Point* starred Philip Madoc, following on from his outstanding success as Lloyd George. By 1984, the great duo of 'soap operas', Julia Smith and Tony Holland, were brought in to create *The District Nurse* with a team of writers headed by William Ingram. Thirty-six episodes were shown over a period of three years, starring *The Liver Birds*'s Nerys Hughes with great support from John Ogwen and Margaret John, whose cameo performances in *Gavin & Stacey* 20 years down the line would remind younger audiences of her great ability to deliver double entendre with an innocent face. I remember discussing with Teleri and Julia Smith the possibility of a network soap opera grounded in a modern Welsh setting. Julia showed a genuine interest in the idea. Within months BBC1 asked her to develop a new ongoing series based in London. It was called

EastEnders. London would never have countenanced the idea of a daily diet of Welsh accents.

As noted, we were particularly fortunate in having three heads of department who had the ambition to think outside the box. One was Head of Children's Department Dyfed Glyn Jones who was driving *Yr Awr Fawr*. The second was the equally well-established and forceful Head of Music Mervyn Williams. The third was an emerging empire builder, Head of Religion John Stuart Roberts.

Cardiff Singer of the World was one of Mervyn's many 'simple' ideas which became a large and complex biennial event from its very start. Convincing the musical establishment that there was room for another international competition was always going to be a problem as we all sought the support of sponsors, network placings and resources. Geraint Stanley had noted the wonderful potential offered by the opening of Cardiff's St David's Hall in 1983, and spent hours with Mervyn thinking of different BBC events to fill it. Cardiff City Council was happy to provide the hall free of charge for the BBC Welsh Symphony Orchestra's regular concerts, and keen to sponsor an international festival which would attract visitors to Cardiff. Fortunately, Director-General Alasdair Milne used his influence to ensure the backing of BBC2 for a broadcasting slot on five consecutive nights. Singers were invited from 18 countries for the first competition in 1983.

We involved the publicity and presentation departments, headed by the enthusiastic John Watkin, which provided organisational back-up.

John had been Evelyn Williams's first TV producer in 1970. He had been inventive in the use of the young *Heddiw* presenter Hywel Gwynfryn, making popular travelogues for children of all ages in countries such as Tunisia and Malaysia at a time when films showing Hywel eating snakes or snails were either wondrous to behold or disgusted viewers. John had launched the 13-year run of the magazine *Bilidowcar* with Hywel and Marged Esli as presenters, but he was a rolling stone who returned to bury the series having joined and left the BBC on a total of three separate occasions. First he was seconded to the wealthiest country in the world – Brunei – as Head of Programmes for three years, and returned to Cardiff for several more as Head of Presentation, Publicity and PR when he became critical as management's 'fixer' for overstretched large outside broadcasts, such as *Cardiff Singer of the World* and religious programmes. John left again to work for the Welsh entrepreneur Alfred Gooding in China. They went into Asia too early, and John returned once more to the BBC, this time as Head or Children's Programmes when Dyfed Glyn Jones fell ill. Unfortunately, HTV spirited him away within months, after which he went on to become a successful independent producer.

All went well with the first *Cardiff Singer of the World* until the week before the opening night. Suddenly we realised that the event was not attracting an audience in the hall. John Watkin and his cohorts, including Iwan Thomas, 'papered' the hall with invitations to all and sundry free of charge. The first night arrived. The hall was full. We held our breath. Announcer Frank Lincoln opened the proceedings. Within five seconds of listening to the first singer on stage, we knew that in Karita Matilla from Finland we had a true 'Singer of the World' who quickly developed into a great international diva. The competition was here to stay.

During the first 30 years of what Cardiff taxi drivers called 'the Cardiff Sing-Song', it was the music department's PA turned manager, Anna Williams, who held the organisation together. Anna was a perfectionist who literally went the extra mile during the first year when she called taxis to take the singers from their hotels to St David's Hall and ran to meet them as they arrived. Every singer who came from far and wide loved Anna. She was eventually given a rolling contract to work half-time on the biennial event while the first Chairman of Judges, Welsh National Opera Managing Director Brian McMaster, hired her to work for him when he became Director of the

Edinburgh International Festival. Anna organised both events from her Clynderwen home in Pembrokeshire.

The *Cardiff Singer of the World* competitors usually arrived with a small entourage of teachers or voice trainers. Particularly interesting entries came from the Central Conservatory of Music in Beijing, always accompanied by its director Professor Chen. Over lunch at home one Sunday, Chen related the story of how his 'bourgeois Western academy' was closed down by the Red Guards during Mao's Cultural Revolution. Chen was sent to a labour camp in a distant province for three years before being allowed to return and reopen the Conservatory, his delicate hands so damaged that he was no longer capable of playing any instrument in public again. Chen was a remarkable man dedicated to the promotion of classical music in a once-hostile environment and was merely pleased that he had at least survived to tell the tale.

If the opening of the St David's Hall offered BBC music-makers new opportunities, the second event was the fortuitous emergence of the God-given treble voice of Aled Jones. Senior producer Huw Tregelles Williams, who accompanied him often on the organ, recalls 'the happy and quite unreal period of Aled Jones which had to come to a natural end'.

When Mervyn Williams first heard Aled in rehearsal, performing Handel's *Jephtha* with the BBC Welsh Chorus in April 1984, he thought that Aled was using a microphone, such was the power of his voice. The young boy's performances gave a huge impetus to the newly-reformed BBC Welsh Chorus under regular conductor John Huw Thomas. When both soloist and chorus combined with the BBC Welsh Symphony Orchestra, capacity crowds booked seats weeks in advance. Aled starred in many programmes on the networks and S4C, often directed by the young Hefin Owen who seized his opportunities to hone his directing skills with large casts of choir and orchestra. Mervyn Williams and I planned a series of Christmas music from Israel with Aled and the BBC Welsh Chorus, although neither Mervyn nor I actually went there.

It could be as difficult to work in Israel as Geraint Stanley had discovered earlier in Communist East Germany. Having filmed in Israel 15 years previously, I had befriended a local co-producer who was totally trusted by his Government's security services. David Goldstein organised the visit brilliantly. He cleared the most aggressive customs authority in the world without a problem, and travelled with a van containing signs which closed down the busy street outside the Garden of Gethsemane in order to record perfect sound. The stunning visuals added up to a series which wowed UK audiences that Christmas, particularly Aled's unforgettable clarity and range in a moving rendering of 'Pie Jesu'. He really did have the voice of an angel.

When his voice broke it was the end of an 'unreal' era for us all, but his huge experiences as a child helped him forge a new and highly successful career in both speech and song on stage, radio and TV.

Our Israeli 'fixer' David Goldstein reappeared in later years to help the religion department make a series on the New Testament in both languages. By that time John Stuart Roberts had expanded his department through manipulating budgets between different channels. As noted, he had initially recruited three graduates in quick succession from the unlikely source of the University of St Andrews for the development of Radio Wales in November 1978. One of them was Dr Barry Lynch who had been the first presenter of the long-lasting radio series *All Things Considered*. Barry took the first opportunity to branch out into TV and quickly targeted the network religious series *Everyman*.

He was one of several non-Welsh speakers to take up the part-time Wlpan Welsh learning course made available to all BBC Wales staff. Barry learnt the language well enough to produce a documentary for *Everyman* on the prominent Welsh hymn writer and mystic, Ann Griffiths. It was presented by the Reverend Donald Allchin, whose researches into spirituality outside the orthodox Christian tradition brought a wider audience to an extraordinary woman hidden in the hills of Llanfihangel-yng-Ngwynfa in Powys.

Two such documentaries were usually regarded in London as a year's work. Another of his *Everyman* documentaries had its origin in John Stuart Roberts's rubbish bin. Barry had spotted an important anniversary for St Benedict which had been thrown away. Further research revealed the extent which the Benedictine Revival owed to Welsh Catholic priests, such as the martyr John Roberts. The programme was one of several major documentaries for the series in subsequent years.

Meanwhile, John Stuart Roberts had been asked to present the network series *Songs of Praise* which allowed him scope to appoint Huw Brian Williams to look after religious outside broadcasts in Wales. Despite having a prominent stammer, Huw became one of the most respected directors in the TV gallery.

One day I received a call from the Head of Religion in London who needed help. His TV producers were not versed in religious matters and he needed someone to oversee the two series *Everyman* and *Heart of the Matter*. Would I release John Stuart Roberts who was well known to him? John agreed to a year's attachment while continuing to run the department in Wales in the hope that he could return full-time with more network commissions. His involvement in London gave him the opportunity to mix and match his budgets between network TV, BBC Wales TV and S4C. In the middle of all this, two massive outside broadcasts had to be planned. One was the Queen's Silver Jubilee visit to Llandaff Cathedral in 1977, and the other the Pope's visit to Cardiff in June 1982. Producer Huw Brian Williams now came into his own. These two large events were the biggest challenges of his career. Together, John Stuart and Huw Brian collected cameras from all over the BBC for the Pope's visit and, with the co-operation of the Association of Broadcasting and Allied Staffs Union, even shared HTV cameras for the occasion. Attachments and directors were provided from other departments, including management 'fixer' John Watkin.

Barry Lynch presented the day's events. It was the biggest outside broadcast ever mounted by BBC Wales. The Popemobile was in the sight of over 40 cameras throughout a hugely exciting day, with more than 100,000 people attending Mass in Pontcanna Fields, and a rally with 33,000 young people packed into Ninian Park football ground.

One who stayed in the religion department was John Geraint, a Radio Wales producer who badgered John Stuart into an idea for a series about his native Rhondda valley. Having been appointed as the youngest producer on Radio Wales when it launched in 1978, John Geraint felt strongly that the working-class voices which had come to the fore during his years in radio should be heard more often on TV. The series was certainly different in style from Gethyn Stoodley Thomas's elegantly written film *The Long Street* in 1965. It kick-started a distinguished TV career for John Geraint, including two documentaries for *Everyman*. One, a profile of 'Nantymoel', led to a heated debate at the Broadcasting Council for Wales on the balance between the depressing and optimistic views of people living in a once-thriving industrial community. The other was the extremely difficult and sensitive 1988 documentary, *A Place like Hungerford*, following the terrible massacre in the small town by a lone gunman. I also remember with affection his partnership with the poet Dannie Abse in *Return to Cardiff* in 1984, a warm and lyrical evocation of a non-sentimental journey from his Jewish childhood through to his undying loyalty to Cardiff City Football Club. John Geraint would eventually succeed Barry Lynch as Head of Features and Documentaries before being appointed BBC Wales Head of Production in the 1990s and then leaving the BBC to become the Creative Director of Green Bay.

John Stuart Roberts did not do well at school but was eventually ordained at Carmarthen Theological College. Unlike others without degrees I had known at the BBC however, he was not afraid of appointing university graduates. He claimed he bought the brains of others – and he certainly did that – but his troops were not fooled. They all knew he was well read, extremely self-confident, although a person so private he was often unpredictable. His technique was to expand his department by accepting every new request for management help on any project. It gave him easier access to subject areas where God did not normally tread – and led to the relentless extension of his empire.

The seven hours of English-language programmes which remained on BBC Wales following the launch of S4C could still be challenging. Scheduling opt-out programmes still caused complaints every time a popular BBC1 series was delayed.

On Sunday afternoons, for example, sporting coverage of all kinds had a large and passionate following. On one such occasion I totally misjudged the situation. We dropped an international women's doubles match at a tennis tournament in order to cater for a Welsh golf tournament. The telephone lines went berserk. We promised the irate female viewers that the tennis would follow the golf and dropped a boxing tournament. The boxing fraternity shouted blue murder down the lines. It was a no-win situation.

As Head of Programmes I decided to keep all BBC Wales programmes on BBC1, since it would automatically attract a higher audience than the BBC2 channel. I wanted a range of popular and minority programmes, but still attracted flak for displacing a popular network programme in order to run a serious documentary on BBC1.

I bought a series of Tom Jones concerts at the Cannes TV Festival for a fraction of what it would have cost to make them, and Teleri Bevan flew to Los Angeles to interview him as a background to the shows. She chatted with him by his swimming pool, complete with a background shot of a brightly painted British telephone booth.

I had never subscribed to the pessimistic view of the 1970s that huge numbers were watching *Points West* instead of

Wales Today. Tens of thousands did have their aerials pointing towards Bristol while also being able to watch BBC Wales.

When Wales were playing Ireland during one of several Triple Crown deciders during that great decade of rugby successes, audiences of up to 45 per cent of the nation were watching BBC Wales. On such days weddings were missing male guests taken ill at the last minute. The M4 motorway was empty for two hours. We could only wonder what the other 55 per cent were doing!

The real problem was that *Wales Today* and *Sports Line-Up* filled 50 per cent of our Wales schedule and left us with only enough money for three and a half hours of all other programming.

One landmark historical series, *Wales! Wales?*, was presented by the personable and provocative Dr Dai Smith and repeated on BBC2. It was produced by the experienced Selwyn Roderick, together with Patrick Hannan who had moved into 'docs' after retiring from the front line of political reporting. A major retrospective season of John Ormond's programmes marked the end of his pioneering career.

Celebrating the centenary of the Wales Rugby Union required a well-written documentary. *A Touch of Glory* was given over to the experienced TV scriptwriter Alun Richards, aided by the advice of rugby guru Carwyn James. Alun, who had already made his mark in network drama through his long association writing the seafaring *The Onedin Line*, developed a close friendship with Carwyn which cured him of strong anti-Welsh prejudices.

On one occasion Alun arrived at my house on his powerful motorbike, swearing loudly at Carwyn who had nodded off to sleep while riding pillion. Alun was delivering freshly caught mackerel as a peace offering and as an excuse to discuss progress on the programme.

As the years rolled by, sponsorship and co-productions became more important. The trick in landing co-productions was to match BBC resources to a partner's money. As a production house, the BBC had limited cash, but if carefully planned we could offer camera crews and film editing as our contribution.

For a time Max Boyce's own written material, based on Welsh rugby success and schoolmate Billy Williams for the televised shows, continued to be popular with new BBC1 Controller Alan Hart. I took him to see Max take an audience by storm at Croydon's Fairfield Hall, engaging with them from the moment of his entry on stage. Backstage, before the event, he was a bundle of nerves, psyching himself up, pacing up and down like a caged animal waiting to be let loose. The larger the hall, the greater the outpouring of energy and sweat while driving the noise levels of the audience ever higher. Alan Hart was duly impressed and wanted more for his schedule but there was a limit to the new material Max could write.

Two new co-production agents from a company called OPIX had noted Max's boundless energy and superb fitness, derived from his earlier days working down the pit. They came up with the idea of *Boyce Goes West* in which he tried his luck riding bucking broncos in a Texas rodeo. It was physically dangerous, but Max was game and he pulled off a brilliant piece of entertainment. He repeated the exercise by inviting Billy Connolly and Ringo Starr to join him in *To the North of Katmandu*, the World Elephant Polo Championships in Nepal – a very different form of comedy! For Max world travel was a break from writing his own stories and songs.

The same co-producers had the idea of exploiting Wales's position at the heart of world rugby and took the rights of *Focus on Rugby*, a coaching series and a book presented and written by Carwyn James, with illuminating insights from another great teacher, former Secretary of the Wales Rugby Union, Ray Williams. The series was sold all around the rugby world.

Meanwhile, both John Hefin and Richard Lewis had continued success on the networks. The Falklands War gave John the idea of *The Mimosa Boys*, exploring the mindset of Welsh soldiers on board a ship sailing to fight 'the Argies'. Some of the enemy were Welsh-speaking Patagonians descended from the settlers who had made the difficult crossing from Liverpool in 1865, arriving in Porth Madryn on *The Mimosa*. John had found it easy to work with the quiet Welsh-speaking Ewart Alexander twice before in the early 1970s, when Ewart was making his name writing for a variety of network series, including the hugely popular *Softly, Softly*. His script of *The Mimosa Boys* contained 98 four-letter words. In 1985, a general BBC edict demanded that all F-words be referred up to Managing Director Bill Cotton. He decided that only two F-words be broadcast. It was an age still living in fear of Mrs Mary Whitehouse.

Much more shocking than bad language, however, was the suffering on both sides of the conflict. The aftermath of the war concentrated more than usual in revealing the stories of those who were badly injured, particularly after the bombing of the troopship *Sir Galahad* tragically killed and injured so many Welsh troops as they waited to land on the shores of the Falklands. One of those severely burnt was Simon Weston, who underwent several painful operations and cosmetic surgery on his face and body, all of it sensitively filmed by a London production team. Simon has since become a talisman for all those who have survived the Falklands and other wars, a national hero who is regularly called upon to broadcast.

Both John Hefin and Richard Lewis produced two stories of totally different bombing incidents which had one theme in common – the English 'colonisation' of Wales.

John's production of *Penyberth* re-enacted the burning of a RAF bombing school on the Llŷn peninsula in 1936 by three leading Welsh Nationalists – Plaid Cymru's first president Lewis Valentine, its second Saunders Lewis, and the writer D.J. Williams. The three gave themselves up to the police and were put on trial in Caernarfon where a mainly Welsh jury failed to agree on the verdict. A re-trial at the Old Bailey found them guilty and they were sentenced to nine months imprisonment in Wormwood Scrubs. It was the first *cause célèbre* to bring both publicity and notoriety to the party. The production was significant for being the first to be repeated with English subtitles on BBC2. Equally notable was that during his time in jail, Saunders Lewis's play *Buchedd Garmon* [The Life of Garmon], written in *vers libre*, was transmitted on radio in Welsh on 2 March 1937. Its nationalist sentiments contained some of the most memorable lines in the Welsh language. There would have been considerable debate inside the BBC's regional management in Wales regarding the sensitivity of its message before the play was transmitted. Likewise, Saunders Lewis's lecture, *Tynged yr Iaith* [Fate of the Language], in 1962.

Richard Lewis's 1984 film, *The Extremist*, was a totally different character study of former British soldier John Jenkins, a loner intent on disrupting life for the English Establishment around the time of the 1969 Caernarfon Investiture. It was a chilling portrayal of a man driven by hate and lacking a positive agenda.

It was now becoming obvious that the networks had lost interest in investing in drama from Cardiff. The only way forward was to look for co-production funds, but they were difficult to find and often fell through before contracts were exchanged.

John Hefin and I wanted to film a four-part series on the extraordinary life of famous American architect Frank Lloyd Wright, whose Welsh mother inspired his career. Our travels to Wright's architecture school in 'Taliesin East', Wisconsin, found little favour with Wright's widow who then refused to meet us at her home in 'Taliesin West', Arizona. The project died.

I found £250,000 of co-production money for Richard Lewis from French TV which liked his treatment of the world-renowned missionary and organist Albert Schweitzer. Unfortunately, Richard refused to make three cuts to the French version of the script which was considered libellous under French law. A time-consuming and expensive co-production collapsed. A second exercise in co-production failed, this time on Mounmouth-raised Charles Rolls of Rolls-Royce fame, when Richard contradicted me on a detail during my sales talk at the final network offers meeting with Controller Alan Hart. We were not singing from the same hymn sheet. Alan merely said, 'When you two agree we can come back to it.' The project was killed off in that sentence. Richard did not understand the difference between the editorial discussions conducted earlier in the year and offers meetings in which the decisions were finally agreed and financial approval given. There was no other big English-language drama already on the table to replace it. I was furious. Dick subsequently suffered a growing disillusionment with BBC Wales management. He eventually left to join Mervyn Williams's fledgling independent drama unit. Nevertheless, his contribution to TV drama in Wales and the respect with which he was held by writers such as Meic Povey, his production teams and actors, all confirmed his status as a major contributor to the BBC Wales drama-documentary scene in both languages.

Help on co-productions came through the sudden appearance of a short, energetic man who had wild curly hair, half-hidden by a hat more suited to the Australian outback, bohemian-style clothing and very extravagant expletives. Ian Bodenham's looks ensured that he would always be stopped by customs officers. He had worked in Germany for nine years and wanted to return to live in his Llangennith farmhouse on Gower, the only one of its kind outside St Fagans, complete with an old 'bed in a cupboard' by the downstairs hearth. It so happened that I needed help for the most unpopular and meticulous producer on the staff who was due to work on a BBC2 film of a family enjoying their Christmas lunch. Other staff directors used good excuses to take leave, but Ian accepted the challenge. The resulting film may have pleased viewers but ruined the family's lunch. At least it proved that Ian was capable of coping with an impossible boss. His linguistic skills helped find co-producers in Europe and further afield as he infiltrated the London co-productions department on our behalf.

The long-serving Head of Planning and Resources Owen Thomas had retired and his deputy, Ken Hawkins, succeeded him. Ken was expert at holding a comprehensive knowledge of technical and financial information in his head, which justified the old adage 'Information is Power'. He gave answers to most queries about the availability of resources so quickly that I sometimes wondered 'that one small head could carry all he knew'. He was very helpful when we were moving TV monies around in order to maintain the weekly hours of Radio Cymru and Radio Wales during a period of cuts. The TV planning department worked overtime when fitting together a huge jigsaw puzzle to cope with two separate channels from 1982 onwards, solving the problems of clashing schedules and the forward planning of productions over periods ranging from a year on documentaries to three years on drama.

We managed to maintain a respectable presence on the networks, particularly with music and documentaries on BBC2, through stretching all available resources. BBC2 Controller Brian Wenham, always desperate for an annual opera, would guarantee a placing for a Welsh National Opera production – for which he had no money anyway! I travelled with the cheerful, creative and highly-respected Welsh National Opera Managing Director, Brian McMaster, in search of sponsorship. On one occasion a letter of interest arrived from a London agent purporting to be acting on behalf of one of the princes of Saudi Arabia. McMaster and I arrived at a massive and beautifully appointed office off Regent Street to meet him and discussed sponsorship for a series of TV operas – and then nothing. It emerged that the man was a fraudster, interviewing a variety of business people in the hope of accruing upfront money. His London office and his secretary had been hired for the day. However, the Welsh National Opera did succeed in delivering two brilliant productions of *Othello* and *Aida*, both directed by Peter Stein, a famous

East German theatre director. Stein had never worked in TV before and exhausted both our technical resources and our patience, albeit to great effect. Both productions received stunning reviews.

There was one documentary idea Wenham could not refuse. I had access to the Prime Minister of India, Mrs Indira Gandhi, through a Cardiff City councillor who was a regular presenter of the Asian radio programme *Hum Tum* on Radio Wales. Shaam Verma had married into a powerful industrial family in India. His brother-in-law, D.N. Sinha, arranged a meeting with Mrs Gandhi who by this time had fallen out with the BBC's most famous foreign correspondent, Mark Tully. As we entered her office, passing a group of cabinet ministers in their white dhotis who would wait for hours in the hope of getting an audience, she looked at us with cold, unwelcoming eyes and a stony silence. The three of us took it in turns to talk to the most powerful woman in the world for no less than 13 increasingly desperate minutes, her tiny figure dressed in a beautiful sari, seated behind a massive desk, not even acknowledging our presence. It was when I mentioned our wish to film her grandchildren that she cracked.

'Where?' she asked quietly. They were her Achilles heel. She changed her attitude completely and agreed to be interviewed for a 50-minute programme. We joined her on the daily morning Durbar on the large lawn where she always met a selection of her vast electorate. It was January 1984 and Mrs Gandhi had warmed enough towards us to invite me to sit alongside her at the magnificent annual Delhi Republic Day parade. It is one of the greatest regrets of my life that I put duty before pleasure and flew home as planned. Teleri Bevan travelled out later to record the interview with John Watkin and a film crew – just six weeks before her death on 31 October. The day before Mrs Gandhi died I had taken the completed programme to London. While staying overnight at the Kensington Hilton, the early TV news reported Mrs Gandhi's assassination at the hands of her bodyguards as she walked in her garden where I had been with her only months earlier. I rushed into BBC TV Centre. The film was suitably re-edited and transmitted the very same evening on BBC2.

The broadcasting scene within Wales had undergone a total revolution, first in radio between 1977 and 1980, and then in TV between November 1980 and November 1982 – a period of only six years.

In 1985 Geraint Stanley Jones was asked to join an efficiency savings committee called 'Black Spot' under the chairmanship of BBC Director of Resources Michael Checkland. The BBC needed to come to terms with a bad licence fee settlement. Later in the year, Geraint Stanley was persuaded to work in London, first as Director of Public Affairs and subsequently as the BBC's first Director of Nations and Regions. As a result, I became Acting Controller before being appointed to the post permanently in January 1986.

The proposals of 'Black Spot' heralded tougher financial times. During the past 12 years of working alongside Geraint, we had been privileged to lead BBC Wales at a time of constant growth. He had shown great leadership throughout a decade of constant change. We had often agreed to disagree in private, but never in anger. In public and in front of the Broadcasting Council for Wales we maintained a watertight partnership based on mutual loyalty. We had enjoyed working and watching as the tide came in. As the senior member of Geraint Stanley Jones's team for the whole of that time, I was now expected to manage the turn of the tide.

18

The Turn of the Tide, 1986-90

As I PREPARED to present my first report as Controller to the BBC's Welsh National Governor Alwyn Roberts and the Broadcasting Council for Wales in January 1986, there were increasing signs that the good days of growth were over. In Wales the BBC had enjoyed a decade of investment and launched three different channels, Radio Wales, Radio Cymru and the weekly ten hours for S4C. Now belts had to be tightened. The suffering of the wider Welsh economy put BBC Wales's frustrations over the slow growth of its services into perspective. The dismal winter of discontent under Callaghan's Labour Government in 1979 preceded the depressing failure of the referendum on devolution to increase democratic accountability. The Welsh economy crumbled under a Thatcher Government which was unwanted and unloved. These were dark days for an increasingly social and economic divide during the de-industrialisation of Welsh working-class communities; a divide between the 'haves' who still had jobs and the 'have nots'; where women often became the only breadwinner in the family; where thriving communities turned into Cardiff commuter belts. In the countryside, rural life was suffering dramatic social change as small farms became uneconomic; the young drifted away to the cities, leading to a decline in school numbers; village houses were sold off as second homes; an ageing generation was left with fewer services and dying chapels. Even the Wales rugby team lost its lustre in the 1980s.

Mrs Thatcher's hatred of the unions was only a touch greater than her hatred of the BBC. After our monthly meetings in London, the three national Controllers – the self-styled 'Brothers' – always invited a guest to lunch. The combative Brother Scotland, Pat Chalmers, asked Scottish-born Cabinet Minister Malcolm Rifkind to one such event. The venom with which Rifkind attacked us took us all aback. One could feel the icicles forming on the sides of his chair. The threat to disband the BBC was obviously on the lady's agenda, and her disciples were more than enthusiastic in delivering the message. I came away thinking how much more direct the Scots are than the Welsh in dealing with each other. Fortunately, Mrs Thatcher, who had made one U-turn over S4C, had appointed Tory 'Wet' Peter Walker as Secretary of State for Wales in June 1987 as a means of keeping him quiet 'inside the tent'. On the only occasion that we talked, he asked how many members of the Broadcasting Council for Wales were under 55 years of age. I had to admit – none. He had a perfectly valid campaign encouraging companies to appoint younger people on the quangos, but I left the BBC before the problem was addressed.

It was, however, time to consolidate the four broadcasting services. It hadn't taken me long to decide that Teleri Bevan should take over from me as Head of Programmes. This, despite the opposition of a couple of senior TV producers, including one who still believed a woman's place was in the kitchen, and another who told her to her face not to apply. They had forgotten that she had played an inspirational role in the radio developments, followed by five years as Deputy Head of Programmes. She knew about the strengths and weaknesses of the TV operation and had sat on all the appointment boards for the up-and-coming TV production staff. As Head of Programmes it was Teleri, risk-taker to the last, who would force through the increase of *Pobol y Cwm* to a five-day-a-week operation in 1988.

Together, we decided to create separate posts of Head of Radio and Head of TV instead of a Deputy Head of Programmes across all channels. The growth in radio broadcasting hours and staff during the previous decade had stretched our ability to monitor them. BBC Wales had the largest staff outside London, but we had resisted an expansion in the programme management team in order to maximise the number of producers.

As a result, Meirion Edwards was appointed head of both national radio channels. He had produced and presented radio programmes both on staff and as a freeelancer. As noted, Meirion had been Head of BBC Bangor before being appointed the first editor of Radio Cymru in November 1978. He had established the channel as a highly successful and respected service from the moment he relaunched it in November 1979. Meirion was a fast and robust decision-taker. His experience of handling tight budgets was exemplary. His staff at Radio Cymru respected him for his firmness and fairness. He had swatted away public concerns over acceptable standards of Welsh on air with great authority. Most importantly, Meirion had constructed a daytime schedule for Radio Cymru which included a rich mix of programmes to suit a variety of audience demands within the confines of the one channel.

He was now responsible for the output on both Radio Wales and Radio Cymru which had crept up to around 7,500 hours a year – nobody knew quite how much because both channels had exceeded their official targets. He had a choice of experienced radio production managers from which to appoint his successor, and selected Lyn T. Jones who had been running the Radio Cymru output from the Alexandra Road studios in Swansea. Lyn's background, however, was in the theatre and he had produced several dramas on Radio Cymru, including the whole canon of Gwenlyn Parry's single plays. By 1987, such was the stability of the Radio Cymru schedule that Hywel Gwynfryn had already been saying 'Helo Bobol' for over ten years since exhorting people to buy VHF sets. Allan

Pickard could still be heard presenting the lunchtime news *Cyn Un*, and Gareth Glyn was well on his way to 34 years at the helm of *Post Prynhawn*. The young Aled Samuel broadcast his own inimitable brand of humour the same week as his father Alwyn, the long-serving and quieter expert on folk songs, was discussing the finer points with Meredydd Evans, now an academic authority on the subject. Sunday night audiences were still attracted to *Talwrn y Beirdd* as the bards not only competed with each other but also the counter-attractions of S4C.

When Meirion took over both channels he was fully conversant with the way Radio Wales had developed. In November 1988 Megan Stuart was already its third editor. Teleri had given way to Bob Atkins as the channel's second editor but there seemed to be very little meeting of minds between Bob and some of his senior staff. I felt his approach was more academic than pragmatic, and he eventually moved on to head the postgraduate Diploma in Broadcast Journalism at Cardiff University. Ten years on from its launch however, Radio Wales had bedded down well. Professor Dai Smith said of it in the *Radio Times* of 5 November 1988, 'Radio Wales has never been pompous. Nor has it been parochial. It's a sound that is experienced, authoritative and relaxed.'

The schedule had a settled look about it; the mornings beginning with Maldwyn Pope, then Peter Johnson's *Weekday Wales* at 7 a.m. followed by Roy Noble at 8.30 a.m. for two hours, and *Streetlife* with the ubiquitous Alun Williams, Frank Hennessy or Ray Gravell until midday. That left 30 minutes for individual features before Vincent Kane's *Meet for Lunch* at 12.30 p.m. It was personality-led listening with plenty of other times given to documentaries, as well as a rich vein of humour produced by Richard Thomas.

The appointment of John Stuart Roberts as Head of TV was more controversial, since some older producers had failed to notice that John had quietly built the religion department into a small empire. He and Head of Children's Department

Dyfed Glyn Jones were the only senior TV producers who had nurtured new talent in the late 1970s; Dyfed Glyn in Welsh programmes, but John was growing an output on all channels and was manipulating his various budgets to expand further. He was now challenged by Teleri to find six new TV producers who would be a force on either channel in the future. One wag dubbed them 'the Red Arrows'. They included Phil George, bright, cheerful and talkative, possessed of a high intelligence. Having joined the BBC as a Radio Wales producer, in TV he contributed extensively to the series edited by Barry Lynch, *Between Ourselves*, which included two of Phil's most memorable documentaries. One was the fascinating story of the greatest of all Welsh love songs, 'Myfanwy', which is still shown around the world today; the second, on Swansea binmen, was a hilarious portrait of a close-knit male working-class community. Phil George would later become Head of Arts, Music and Features before joining his close friend and colleague John Geraint in establishing the hugely successful independent company, Green Bay. The company specialises in documentary and drama-documentary series on Welsh historical themes for BBC Wales and BBC4 in the main, currently an area of prime importance for English-language TV programmes made in Wales. In 2016 Phil stepped down from the front line of broadcasting when appointed Chairman of Arts Council Wales.

All the new 'Red Arrows' were expected to contribute to *Between Ourselves*, an ambiguous title designed for a long-running series which could build an audience. The serious-minded Lowri Gwilym joined the same stable and made significant contributions both with her series *Women in Politics* and a classy fly-on-the-wall documentary series, *Aber! Aber!*, which was a highly realistic reflection of student life in Aberystwyth in the late 1980s. Lowri's early death while working as content editor for factual programmes at S4C was yet another tragic loss to Welsh broadcasting.

Paul Islwyn Thomas was still a student when he phoned

257

Barry Lynch in search of an opening, and eventually emerged as one of Wales's leading documentary producers. Following several years as an independent producer, Paul was the one leading broadcaster to return as Head of Arts, Music and Features – and then leave again to pursue new directions.

The young Jonathan Davies, nephew of Hywel Davies who had first launched BBC Wales in 1964, became a highly skilled long-serving studio and outside broadcast director of major events.

The equally enthusiastic Linda Mitchell's early series on youth unemployment highlighted the issue in Wales knowledgeably for the first time as one would expect from her ethnic background in Tiger Bay. She then branched out into other areas of broadcasting. No institution could contain Linda's wide-ranging interests for long.

Series editor Barry Lynch was now a major driving force in TV. He launched two series on cooking and three important series on health, all of which created considerable interest from the networks as well as massive book sales. One was *The Big C & Me* which broke the silence on the greatest taboo subject of the day. Another, *Don't Break Your Heart*, impelled BBC1 Controller Michael Grade to launch it in Cardiff. The third series concerned itself with *The BBC Diet Programme* which topped the charts of the BBC Books department for a whole year.

John Stuart's appointment as Head of BBC Wales TV was a no-brainer given this track record. A footnote to one chapter in John Geraint's draft Ph.D. thesis reads, 'John Stuart's influence on me was profound and inspirational. An autodidact and something of a maverick at work, his management style and determination could be divisive, but he had a real commitment to making programmes in Wales for Wales, as well as making a mark for Wales on the networks.'

The word 'divisive' in that plaudit refers to the split in the camp between the waves of younger people the highly ambitious John Stuart had appointed, as opposed to a few more experienced senior programme people whom he tended to ignore because, he told me, 'they did not fit in with my requirements'. These included a couple of producers on the staff whom we had 'carried' for years because Geraint Stanley and I found that sacking people had always been difficult and time-consuming. John Stuart took advantage of the first availability of voluntary redundancies to remedy that situation. Instead, he wanted a younger generation who were expected to work flexibly according to his programme schedule.

From the mid 1980s onwards there were several major changes at head of department level as the first major intake of 1964 reached retirement age. Ruth Price was one who completed a distinguished career as a founding member of Meredydd Evans's groundbreaking light entertainment department in 1964. Ruth's name will always be associated with a generation of young folk and rock groups as well as individuals who were given a voice on air in the 1960s and 1970s – many from non-Welsh-speaking backgrounds – whose songs have stood the test of time. Onllwyn Brace had started at the same time as Ruth, and had developed the high reputation of the sports department over a similar period of time. He retired in 1988 and was replaced by Gareth Davies as Head of Sport, making him the third consecutive former Wales rugby international in the post, with a mandate to maintain our monopoly of the rugby contracts. Editor, Wales News & Current Affairs, David Morris Jones was very reluctant to leave his beloved newsroom in 1989 where he had been its anchor for over 25 years, but gave in to the financial package offered by commercial TV in the south of England. Losing David was a big blow. He had always been the enforcer of the newsroom's independence. If he referred up for a management opinion, one knew it involved a serious matter. I was fortunate in having a ready replacement in Gwilym Owen who had vast experience of journalism and was currently in charge of Radio Cymru news.

I was particularly sorry to lose Mervyn Williams, a family friend and the hugely successful Head of Music who had done so much for the TV musical scene in BBC Wales. Mervyn had decided on a new life as an independent producer, although I suspect the timing of his departure was not unrelated to the appointment of the new TV management team. I replaced him immediately with Huw Tregelles Williams who had done all the spadework in creating the highest standards of musicianship with the orchestra as well as the selection of its top conductors for more than a decade. One of the leading organists in Wales, Huw's self-confidence and air of natural authority made him highly respected in the corridors of London where he might well have become a Controller of Music had he taken an interest in such an idea.

I encountered two London Music Controllers during my years working with Huw. Both were insufferable snobs who had the power to select or exclude conductors for the annual Albert Hall Proms. The BBC Welsh Symphony Orchestra was guaranteed three concerts every year, but Huw had to fight to retain the conductors he wanted for each Prom. Both of these controllers appeared at St David's Hall concerts in their time. One, the extremely tall ex-Scots Guards officer Robert Ponsonby, looked down from his great height at my wife during the interval of one such event and boomed, 'Have you read 3?' – a reference to an esoteric and short-lived publication of a very highbrow magazine dedicated to Radio 3. I had difficulty in keeping a straight face as I watched her struggle to understand what he was talking about. The other Music Controller, John Drummond, accepted an invitation to an open discussion on BBC music policy with interested Welsh music lovers one evening. From the chair I called a young and hopeful composer who asked Drummond for more Welsh composers to be given airtime on Radio 3. Back came the reply, 'There are two mountains in Wales: Mount Hoddinott and Mount Mathias. Both have been climbed.'

Huw could cope with that form of arrogance better than

I could. He had the musical background to combat their airs and graces.

The greatest perk for a Controller in Wales was to follow the 'BBC Welsh' wherever they went on tours around Wales, the three annual Albert Hall Proms, and their overseas venues. Travelling with Huw for the next few years to some of the world's great concert venues, such as the Concertgebouw in Amsterdam and the Shostakovich Philharmonic Hall in the then Leningrad, was both a privilege and a priceless personal education in classical music. The tour of Holland included a concert in the city of 's-Hertogenbosch which had been freed from Nazi occupation by Welsh army units in 1945. I was humbled to be asked to lay a wreath on the local war memorial which proudly displays the gratitude of the Dutch people to the Welsh soldiers.

The tour of Russia encompassed Kiev, Leningrad and Novosibirsk, the scientific research city in southern Siberia. Our guest conductor, Mariss Jansons, was not allowed to conduct a foreign orchestra in his own country but played host to Principal Conductor Tadaaki Otaka, who was also permanent conductor of the Tokyo Philharmonic Orchestra. Both the Latvian and Japanese conductors were equally popular with the 88 permanent players. The concert in Leningrad's famous Shostakovich Philharmonic Hall was the most prestigious in the orchestra's history. I shall never forget waiting for the reaction of the knowledgeable Russian audience to the performance of Brahms's Symphony No. 1. As the last chord faded, an agonising silence was broken by slow, quiet applause which built steadily into a crescendo of Russian-style handclapping, the complete reverse of Western audiences. The BBC Welsh Symphony Orchestra received its seal of approval as a truly international-class orchestra that night. Mariss drove Otaka and I around the rough roads of Leningrad, swearing loudly at the potholes but excited when he and Otaka discovered that they had both been taught their conducting skills by the same maestro in Vienna. Our hosts at the tour's last concert in Novosibirsk was the friendly local symphony orchestra. The Welsh orchestral players suspected that the small group of 'hangers-on' were staying at the better of the city's two hotels until Iwan Thomas and I were spotted waiting in different queues for whatever food, if any, we could find at queue's end to go with the unlimited vodka. It was an eye-opener on life in the most modern scientific city in Communist Russia.

A month earlier the orchestra had celebrated its 60th birthday with a Diamond Jubilee concert in a packed St David's Hall with a programme of Mozart and Mahler. It had been 60 years of struggle and eventual success. The turning point had been the support of the Welsh Arts Council in 1973, a partnership which made the orchestra less vulnerable to BBC cuts and had boosted the number of players to full symphonic strength. In 1976 it was renamed the BBC Welsh Symphony Orchestra, a national orchestra in all but name and even that small campaign of mine was remedied eventually in 1993. In its early days it had only 20 players and died not once but twice, rising like a phoenix from the ashes of the Second World War to play the compositions of Grace Williams and Daniel Jones; with conductors Mansel Thomas and Rae Jenkins, as well as father and son Arwel and Owain Arwel Hughes.

Meanwhile, Mervyn Williams's first talks with Teleri Bevan as an independent producer led to a fundamental disagreement over the 'ownership' of the third *Cardiff Singer of the World*. Teleri invited Mervyn to produce the June 1987 event for the BBC. He wanted it organised by his own independent company. We were not in the business of 'selling the family silver'. Given that Mervyn's sums were always worked out on the back of an envelope, I also doubted that he realised how much more expensive his proposal was compared with the flexibility we had of using existing BBC staff from different departments as support for a complex exercise, rather than hire in expensive freelancers. The talks with Mervyn broke down, but another highly experienced executive producer, Humphrey Burton, a former member of Huw Wheldon's *Monitor* team, was more than willing to run the show. It was Humphrey, Huw Tregelles and the indefatigable Anna Williams who oversaw what surely was the greatest night of *Cardiff Singer of the World*, the fourth final in June 1989 when the young Bryn Terfel, winner of the Lieder Prize, narrowly lost the main event to the Russian Dmitri Hvorostovsky in a truly world-class 'Eisteddfod'. It led to the launch of two glittering international careers and Bryn donning the operatic mantle of the Welsh judge on the night, Sir Geraint Evans.

Changes in the staff were easier to handle than the loss of Alwyn Roberts who had been the heavyweight Chairman of the Broadcasting Council for Wales and BBC National Governor for Wales for seven years. Alwyn was a tower of strength during a period of constant change, not only as our Chairman but also as a BBC Governor in London and an ex-officio member of the S4C Authority. A former missionary in India and Pro Vice-Chancellor of Bangor University until 1997, he had a brilliant mind and could summarise a situation quicker than anybody else I ever met. His farewell dinner in the council chamber of Broadcasting House in London was held on the eve of a dramatic meeting of the BBC Governors on 30 January 1987. Following the farewell speeches in his honour, the Welsh contingent retired to Geraint Stanley Jones's office to wonder why there was such a strange atmosphere throughout the evening. We were joined by Director-General Alasdair Milne and Assistant Director-General Alan Protheroe. Next day all was revealed. At the Governors' lunch Chairman Marmaduke Hussey had tapped his wine glass and informed them that Director-General Alasdair Milne had 'resigned'. Protheroe left in the same putsch. Hussey had waited for Alwyn Roberts to have his farewell dinner before sacking Milne, since Alwyn was known to be his only ally on the Board of Governors. I had lost Director-General Alasdair Milne and Broadcasting Council for Wales Chairman Alwyn Roberts, both of whom had appointed me Controller, within the space of 24 hours. It would result in unfortunate ramifications for Wales.

The selection of the new Broadcasting Council for Wales Chairman and Welsh BBC Governor proved both difficult and disastrous. Sir Richard Lloyd-Jones, the diminutive Permanent Secretary at the Welsh Office, had a wonderfully dry sense of humour and was the height of discretion. He was the civil servant initially responsible for 'taking soundings' on who should replace Alwyn Roberts on behalf of the Government. During our telephone conversations I became very unhappy about one name being touted and, thankfully, following some straight talking, the name disappeared. Two weeks later, at a party in the house of Dr Jennifer Lloyd, a member of both the Broadcasting Council for Wales and the Liberal Party, the well-known lawyer and former Montgomeryshire MP Emlyn Hooson was noticed asking rather pointed questions as to how BBC Wales was run. We immediately suspected that he was about to be made our Chairman and Governor and looked forward to his appointment – but it never happened. Instead, we were informed that a veterinary surgeon based in Brecon, John Parry, President of the Royal College of Veterinary Surgeons, was to be our Broadcasting Council for Wales Chairman and BBC National Governor for Wales. I subsequently discovered that Emlyn Hooson's name had been rejected by Prime Minister Margaret Thatcher, who would 'entertain nobody from a third party' on the BBC's Board of Governors.

Several crises struck in the first week of January 1987. I had joined Teleri and new Chairman John Parry for a quiet sandwich on his first day in office. My initial concern at that meeting was the potentially life-threatening situation arising from Teleri having to undergo the removal of a kidney the following week. A message then came through that my loyal former TV PA, Brenda Thomas, who had worked with me as my only member of staff for my eight years in TV, had died on the first day of her retirement. At the end of the same week John Parry's position as the new Chairman was totally undermined by an article in the *Observer* reporting his failure to pay for a car he had bought over a month before his appointment. I was faced with a lame Chairman/Governor, a Head of Programmes waiting on a life-threatening operation, as well as the sad task of having to speak at the funeral of the most loyal of colleagues. Fortunately, Teleri returned to health and work within three months, but I worried as to whether she would be fit enough to hold down the most stressful job in BBC Wales. In the event she never faltered and showed yet again a toughness of both character and constitution.

Chairman John Parry was anything but tough. He survived as a BBC Governor but only because the Chairman of the BBC Governors Marmaduke Hussey kept him on as a 'puppet' for all his major votes. We now had nobody at the top table we could rely on to fight our cause, and certainly nobody that London could respect. In the past we had benefited from the strength of character of two consecutive chairmen in Wales, Glyn Tegai Hughes and Alwyn Roberts. Their loss marked a major turning point in the balance of influence between BBC Wales and London.

19

The Admiral
Takes his Leave

IN *BROADCASTING AND the BBC in Wales* historian John Davies described the Corporation's attitude towards Wales as 'benign'. Having experienced the highs and lows of relationships at all levels of the organisation over a period of 16 years, I found this to be true only of the Board of Governors despite their number including only three members representing Wales, Scotland and Northern Ireland. Taking note of their views was a political necessity, unless they were very weak individuals. At all executive levels attitudes varied considerably. BBC Wales received outstanding support from two Directors-General, namely Alasdair Milne and Michael Checkland, but none whatsoever from Ian Trethowan or deputy and future Director-General John Birt. Below that high level I would describe HQ's feeling about Wales – with honourable exceptions – that at best we were a nuisance and at worst a waste of time and money. Some senior managers in London were arrogant, patronising, dismissive and even ignorant in their attitudes. Others wanted good ideas from whatever quarter and were good listeners, supportive, courteous and caring – as long as we didn't expect to be paid in full for our programmes – if at all! One Managing Director, Will Wyatt, was totally dismissive of our output, except for Welsh National Opera productions. Although the evergreen Bill Cotton Jr had handed over £10 million for the ten hours of S4C in 1981, even his jokey demeanour turned cold and crystal clear when I hosted a dinner for him in Cardiff as Managing Director, TV. When coffee was served I broached the vexed question of network drama with him. He looked at me straight in the eye and said, 'Here's the deal. You take over the network rugby programmes each Sunday and don't make any other offers.'

'No deal, Bill.'

It was obvious that the £10 million had stuck in the gullets of network controllers, and when financial cutbacks cut deeper from 1986 onwards the attitudes changed for the worse. As Head of Programmes I had good relations with BBC1 Controller Alan Hart, as well as a lot of fun bargaining over pennies with Brian Wenham, the BBC2 Controller. He would always say, 'You want to make the programme for BBC Wales. I can repeat it.'

When they made way for three successors, two of whom were former Heads of Drama, commissions dried up. The issue came to a head in November 1988. Teleri Bevan, now in her third year as Head of Programmes, was told by BBC1 Controller Jonathan Powell, 'No drama from Wales next year.' Full stop. No discussion. The following day the Broadcasting Council for Wales happened to be holding its monthly meeting at Bush House in London as the guests of the BBC World Service. Teleri, who had informed the previous meeting that the new five-day-a-week *Pobol y Cwm* had settled down well, now reported that there would be no network drama from Wales for the first time in 14 years. The Broadcasting Council for Wales took it up immediately with Director-General Michael Checkland who happened to join the meeting. He promised to discuss the matter with me.

Later the same week current BBC2 Controller – the clever but arrogant Alan Yentob, nicknamed 'Botney' by *Private Eye* – kept Teleri and John Stuart waiting on their own long enough for Teleri to phone me and say she would not tolerate such rude behaviour any longer and was coming home. While on her way, Yentob phoned me, shouting, 'Where the hell is

Teleri?' The offers meeting was hurriedly rearranged. Yentob survived in management as the BBC's Creative Director until December 2015.

At the next monthly meeting of the three nations' 'Brothers' with Director-General Michael Checkland, he gave up enough contingency money from his official 'back pocket' to enable us to produce more drama. At lower levels we were immediately dubbed 'the Welsh whingers'. The funds were sufficient for new drama producer Ruth Caleb to oversee a short series of single plays which included works by Alice Thomas Ellis and Bernice Rubens. John Stuart had befriended Ruth Caleb during his attachment to London and she was appointed acting Head of Drama for BBC Wales before her situation was made permanent after my time.

A producer from John Stuart's *Everyman* days, David M. Thompson developed drama ideas with religious themes in Wales. One was the voyage of the *Mayflower* in *New World*, starring James Fox and Bernard Hill. The second dramatised the poignant story of religious academic C.S. Lewis in *Shadowlands*, with Joss Ackland in the leading role. It won a BAFTA for Best Play in 1986 and an International Emmy for Outstanding Achievement in Drama.

I continued the search for co-productions and flew to Banff's emerging TV festival to find new partners. Pat Ferns was a Canadian entrepreneur who offered good ideas tying Canada to Wales. I was very pleased to co-produce his first film in Wales, *Going Home*, the strange story of the mysterious deaths of Canadian soldiers stationed at Kinmel Park army camp in March 1919. Rows of military graves mark their burial place in Bodelwyddan. The Canadian and relevant British authorities had always been reluctant to talk about it. Was it really a flu epidemic or had there been a mutiny by soldiers keen to go home, as rumoured locally?

Much nearer home John Hefin and Gwenlyn Parry had teamed up again, this time in association with director Ken Howard of London-based Landseer Productions to make *A*

Penny For Your Dreams in both languages. The creative input of film editor Chris Lawrence, as well as leading actors Dafydd Hywel and Sue Roderick, added up to an outstanding re-creation of Wales's first film-maker, William Haggar, and the magic of his travelling cinema.

All these productions made their way to the networks and S4C which stretched our technical resources to the limit, particularly given that the Welsh productions for S4C: *Pobol y Cwm*, Richard Lewis and Meic Povey's *Sul y Blodau* and Rhydderch Jones's *Lliwiau* were already embedded in the schedule. Drama managers Geraint Wyn Davies and Brian Roberts worked wonders to fit the resource jigsaw together.

In 1989 a partnership called the Wales Film Agency was set up between BBC Wales, S4C and the Welsh Arts Council to which John Hefin was seconded as its first director. A stuttering start would eventually lead to a more successful merger with Ffilm Cymru Wales.

In all, BBC Wales was working to full capacity without any help from network controllers. We still had friends at the programme series level. Welshman Keith Williams was London's drama script editor before becoming Head of Single Plays. He took a direct interest in ideas from Wales. Likewise, Ashley Hill, the Cardiff-born Head of Planning for BBC2, knew where and when his Controller had gaps in the schedule. Head of Comedy John Howard Davies, arguably the genius who originated many of the best situation comedy ideas of the 1970s and early 1980s, only thought he might be Welsh, but supported us – and the Welsh rugby team – anyway.

Our efforts in the search for sponsors and co-productions compensated and disguised the situation, but it took a great deal of management time.

Solving the acute accommodation problems in Wales was much easier. High on my agenda was bringing the staff together on one site in Cardiff. Ever since BBC Wales had been launched in 1964 it had been forced, by sheer growth of numbers, to locate people in four different buildings in

Cardiff. In the 1960s the radio operation was still based in Park Place and around the corner in Museum Place. The TV staff were housed in the General Accident building opposite the Julian Hodge 'skyscraper' on Newport Road, while the newsroom was located in an old chapel on Stacey Road, and the TV studios in another old chapel around the corner on Broadway. Even when the new Llandaff HQ was first inhabited, premises still had to be rented in Gabalfa and in Llandaff village to house everybody. Fortunately the 'Cooks' College' of the then University of Wales's Institute of Science and Technology, opposite the main building in Llandaff, came on the market in 1987. I alerted Director-General Michael Checkland who knew where every broom cupboard in BBC Wales was located, and he readily agreed to fund a sensible solution. I bought what became known as 'Tŷ Oldfield' for £3.1 million but which also included two student hostels we didn't need. They were sold on to the new Principal of University College, Cardiff, Professor Aubrey Trotman-Dickenson, whose Hungarian wife had once lectured me at Aberystwyth. He bought both hostels for £750,000 and reduced the net cost of Tŷ Oldfield to the Director-General to £2.35 million. At last those who had to visit us from other parts of town were integrated into the BBC Wales village on both sides of Llantrisant Road in Llandaff.

I was also pleased that the Swansea studios had been refurbished to cater for the growth of both radio services, and was firing on all cylinders again. It had been closed twice, first when bombed in the Blitz of 1941 which destroyed so much of the city; the second time by the Broadcasting Council for Wales in a misguided financial cutback in the 1960s. Having started my BBC career there, I felt quite sentimental when accompanying BBC Chairman Marmaduke Hussey to reopen Dylan Thomas's iconic studio. As we drove down the M4, he said: 'Tell me about this Welsh language nonsense.'

I laughed, not quite knowing whether to take him seriously or not.

'I'll tell you as long as you don't repeat that in front of the troops, Chairman.'

The old war hero behaved impeccably in front of his 'troops' – as one would expect of the husband of a lady-in-waiting to the Queen, but we lived on different planets.

BBC Bangor was in a totally different situation from Swansea. It had been promised a totally new broadcasting centre which included a TV studio, Plas-y-Coed, which had been delayed and then cancelled while the BBC's resources in Wales were re-evaluated following a bad licence fee settlement and the financial impact of the failed referendum of 1979. Instead, a small TV news and contribution studio was built into the new site in Bryn Meirion. R. Alun Evans, now Head of BBC Bangor, fought tirelessly but in vain for a greater TV presence in Bangor, despite being supported by the representatives from north Wales on the Broadcasting Council for Wales. Eventually, it was left to an independent resource company to build a TV studio in Caernarfon, but it closed down too when S4C switched its emphasis in north Wales to new lightweight video work.

However, BBC Wales had a long tradition in covering north Wales on outside broadcasts and on film, aside from the expanded newsroom staff required by the development of the three new services. Bangor was working to full capacity, with a staff of over 80 people committed to news from north Wales and a high proportion of Radio Cymru programmes. In truth, when Geraint Stanley Jones was Controller he had always been more concerned at the lack of facilities for the larger population of Clwyd than Gwynedd, a situation which has only been addressed in recent years.

There was one town whose poor facilities bugged me – my old stamping ground of Aberystwyth. Luckily, the Lifeboat House in the town was in a bad location for the urgent calls of the sea, set one block back from the Promenade. There it was in the late 1980s – an abandoned self-contained single storey brick building. I bought it for £30,000 and had it converted into a radio studio which served the town, gown and BBC Wales for over a decade before the university's new media building offered more modern accommodation.

Throughout my decade as Head of Programmes and Controller, I had inherited Geraint Stanley Jones's former TV PA as my personal assistant. Elizabeth Cameron had joined BBC Wales when Nan Davies launched *Heddiw* in the early 1960s, and had recruited Liz from their native Tregaron area in Cardiganshire. Liz was a highly experienced PA whom I was fortunate to have alongside me for ten years. She was the height of discretion and had an old-fashioned sense of propriety as well as perfect linguistic skills. I relied on her to correct my written Welsh since I had never taken it as a subject at school. Liz also understood the weird and wonderful ways the BBC rehearsed VIP funerals. Whenever a rehearsal for national events of this kind was staged, Liz would take the differently colour-coded volumes from the office safe and take full responsibility while I suddenly declared myself 'Not in Cardiff' – a clear dereliction of duty on my part. Having signed the Official Secrets Act, I dare not detail the BBC Wales Controller's responsibility in the event of a nuclear war. Suffice to say that the preparations for Armageddon throughout Britain were a total farce. Senior BBC executives who joined me from the other UK nations and regions for a briefing on the issue, to which we were all dragged kicking and screaming, found the occasion more akin to *Dad's Army* than Bletchley Park.

I was also fortunate in inheriting from Geraint Stanley an experienced general management group which I chaired every Monday morning. Teleri was the senior member, since programmes were always paramount, but regular input was also required from the three heads of finance, personnel and technical resources.

No management could be without a qualified accountant as Head of Finance. The quiet and trusted 'Phil the Till' Davies ensured we were never overspent by more than £99,000 in any year. I believed that an overspend of over six figures would prompt somebody in London to ask questions or even impose a cutback the following year. Phil's monthly and quarterly reports guided us smoothly through each financial year. The responsibility for controlling £40 million a year was not as stressful as dealing with the growing staff numbers.

We laid great stress on the importance of personnel management. The football-loving Scot, Andrew McCabe, ran his unit firmly, efficiently and with a laudable sense of perspective given the task of looking after the welfare of some 1,500 people by 1990. People have always been the BBC's greatest asset, the source of all the varied programme ideas, whether drawn from the creative minds of those involved in our internal fiction factory, the curiosity of the journalists, or the resourcefulness of the massive support staff. Everybody not actually making programmes, including top management, only exist to support the production staff. There were disciplinary problems, but no more than one would expect from any other industry.

Except for alcohol. The BBC as a whole seemed to be sustained on a cocktail of coffee and the demon drink. It was no different in BBC Cardiff, or perhaps more surprisingly in BBC Bangor at one point in the 1970s. Many of us drank too much for our own good, myself included. It had always been so, although that was no excuse. I recall seeing an ageing newsreader sinking a large 'Gin & It' before reading the sports results for a teetotal producer in the early 1960s. The only difference in general was that the most creative people seemed to suffer more than others. They included departmental heads, journalists, writers, former rugby internationals and chaired bards, actors, cameramen, riggers, secretaries – all were in the category of 'functioning alcoholics'. Some suffered from the stress of being in the public eye; others, such as journalists and creative writers, because it was part of their lifestyle in an institution where BBC Clubs were always near at hand. A few died tragically before their retirement age, some were disciplined, sacked or retired on medical grounds, but the majority continued to work normally. There was so little one could do unless their work suffered. The local doctor, the famous former rugby international Jack Matthews, had no answers and, although the BBC medical unit in London offered excellent back-up on general health matters, by the nature of the problem few were ever referred. It was the culture of the time and place as the reformed alcoholic and campaigner, actor Wynford Ellis Owen, has reminded me.

Given the growing financial constraints, I froze all vacant posts and requested a management discussion before any vacancy could be filled. This tactic in holding over 60 posts vacant succeeded in the first round of cuts. These were the days before a 25 per cent quota for independent producers was introduced. At the time I liked the idea of having the flexibility to commission more work from outstanding independent producers, such as my old friend William Aaron, or from Colin Thomas who worked for many years with the charismatic historian Gwyn 'Alf' Williams. We had to live with in-house productions unless we landed co-productions. The new age of the independent producer had already been introduced by Channel 4 and S4C, but I noticed that the cost per hour of S4C's productions from the 'third sector' was much higher than for BBC in-house productions.

The BBC, however, did not always offer value for money. The numbers of technical support staff demanded by some senior engineering executives every time we added hours of output, particularly in radio, seemed excessive. They had always demanded 'Rolls-Royce' technical standards which had delayed the introduction of phone-ins on radio or caused rows over lighting levels on TV epics such as John Hefin's series on Lloyd George. Money had been wasted on three London-designed master control radio studios in Cardiff, each of which had features better suited to full-blown symphony orchestras than to the simple continuity needs of talk and recorded music. On the other hand, senior engineers running the shop floor were awesome in their knowledge of the skills of both their men and machines. The most knowledgeable doyen of them all was Peter Adams who understood the workings of every wire, every machine and every studio in Wales, let alone the layout of the nuclear bunker in south Wales. Peter was a big man, a somewhat shy personality who could well have been mistaken for a university professor. We worried when he took a holiday, and insisted he nominate and brief a capable substitute during his absence. We also benefited from the wisdom of successive English heads of technical resources – Geoff Salter, John Corbett and John Elfed – both for their varied expertise and as dispassionate observers in a foreign field.

Finally, there was the BBC Wales Secretary, Northern Irishman Michael Brooke, whose role it was to oil the wheels between our management team and the Broadcasting Council for Wales. 'Never surprise the Chairman' was the management motto, since Alwyn Roberts, and subsequently John Parry, had to be informed before news of BBC Wales went into the public domain. Minutes of executive and Broadcasting Council for Wales meetings were kept short, and long-winded divisive debates curtailed with the words, 'a frank exchange of views followed'. Additional papers were expected to be no more than two pages long, otherwise busy people would not have the time to read them. The Broadcasting Council for Wales was regarded by many of its members as a great 'club' in which those selected to serve, from all walks of Welsh life, took part with genuine concern for and constructive criticism of programme quality. Great characters emerged from time to time. Eddie Thomas from Merthyr, the famous boxer turned trainer of world title fighters such as Howard Winstone, found a lifelong friend in shopworkers' trade unionist John Jones and Huw Lewis from Gwasg Gomer. Betty Campbell, a widely respected headmistress in Butetown, campaigned vigorously for more black presenters, and when I triumphantly announced the appearance of two black Welsh performers in the same month – Iris Williams and Linda Mitchell – she retorted, 'not enough!'

There was no pleasing Betty or industrialist John Elfed Jones, a constant critic of the newsroom. Then there were at least two other erudite women – the well-known Liberal candidate and medical doctor Jennifer Lloyd and Professor Elan Closs Stephens. Elan went on to become the Chair of S4C Authority and then Chair of the BBC Wales Trust, giving her a seat on the BBC Trust in London. Elan was the greatest networker I ever befriended. She eventually got to know everybody in the industry in Wales, as well as the top echelons of the BBC in London. She arrived at her first meeting of the Broadcasting Council for Wales as a young intellectual, the Head of Theatre, Film and Television at the University College of Wales, Aberystwyth. Following her first couple of interventions, Eddie Thomas told her in his forthright manner, 'You'll do well girl!' She certainly did.

Elan's first involvement in controversy during her long reign as the most senior lay member in Welsh broadcasting governance was a brush with the Welsh Language Society. It started in 1988 when Radio Cymru came in for criticism for its so-called failure to provide adequate programmes for young people in the evening. Meirion Edwards and I saw no good broadcasting reason for such a request, since radio listening in the evenings was negligible and the budgets were spent on the more important daytime and weekend hours. Meirion explained his position in a lecture at the National Eisteddfod, but the campaign continued with a break-in at BBC Bangor which caused hundreds of pounds worth of damage. The Broadcasting Council for Wales decided to form a sub-committee in order to meet with the Welsh Language Society. Elan and I joined trade unionist and Broadcasting Council for Wales member John Jones in what turned out to be three meetings stretching well into 1989. We could not understand why Radio Cymru was being targeted rather than S4C, but all was revealed when Ffred Ffransis, who was happier with a megaphone in your earhole and not given to rational argument, said, 'we have to start somewhere'. He was obviously looking forward to a long campaign beyond Radio Cymru, causing considerable damage on the way. Ffransis was a demagogue who dominated his younger members. He was totally different in character and attitude from the earlier leaders of the Welsh Language Society in the 1960s and 1970s with whom I had considerable sympathy. It was obvious he was expecting the BBC to provide youth programmes for S4C as well. The heat was deflected from S4C by introducing the subject of co-operation between S4C, Urdd Gobaith Cymru, the Welsh Language Board and comparisons with Scotland and Northern Ireland. It eventually involved a scheme which included non-broadcasting activities which required special funding, all of which diffused a difficult situation. I never found out how many youth programmes were produced in the end because Radio Cymru's editor, Lyn T. Jones, was gradually scheduling night-time hours under the original plan as I was leaving the BBC, pleased not to have to face Mr Ffransis ever again.

Slowly but surely the financial squeeze had its impact on staff jobs. When challenged to make efficiency savings there was always the temptation to enforce cuts through 'salami-slicing' the support departments in order to safeguard programme budgets. Over the years technology became more flexible, which allowed for savings in radio with the introduction of self-operating studios and fewer studio manager posts. High labour costs on TV outside broadcasts were cut with the introduction of lighter cameras and cables. By the late 1980s it was possible to protect production staff jobs through taking advantage of natural wastage in technical areas. The dominance of the engineers was on the wane, but it was replaced by the rise of the accountants. I lost 153 posts, many of which had been left unfilled while anticipating the worst. Voluntary redundancy catered for the rest, which avoided industrial action specific to BBC Wales.

On 11 May 1989 however, a one-day BBC general strike over

pay coincided with the biennial meeting of the BBC Board of Governors in Cardiff. The formal opening of Tŷ Oldfield was also expected to take place. In the circumstances there was no point in celebrating a mere increase in office space. Much worse was Chairman Marmaduke Hussey's insistence on a gung-ho charge through two lines of strikers outside the Llandaff main entrance on our way to a civic reception. It marked the saddest day of my professional life following 25 fulfilling years. I had been a member of a management team which had built a new broadcasting structure in Wales. I could not face the prospect of spending the rest of my career overseeing annual 'efficiency' savings when I had distributed the monies between the various departments so sparingly since 1974.

There was one other reason at the back of my mind. Some months earlier I had crossed swords with the highly controversial Deputy Director-General John Birt. The issue was the measly time given to opt-out bulletins for all the nations and regions after the main BBC1 news at 9.25 p.m. Even the Board of Governors seemed to be sympathetic to an increase in the bulletins to three minutes. John Birt called for an audit of the existing opt-outs from all the BBC's eight regions and nations, played each one back to us in a specially convened meeting, and then condemned all the bulletins collectively. He was obviously fighting the proposed extension. I could not contain my anger, telling him that all eight of us had been called to London only to be insulted purely because he had a political agenda. When I received supportive noises from my colleagues, Birt got up, muttered 'totally unprofessional' and walked out. The increase in the times of the bulletins was given a green light at the next meeting of the BBC Governors.

Following that episode I did not fancy my chances of surviving the probability of Birt succeeding Michael Checkland as Director-General. It was time to leave before he could get his revenge. It took him over 25 years to do so. In 2015, *Pinkoes and Traitors: The BBC and the nation*

1974–1987 was published in which Wales is only mentioned once. It consists of one quote from John Birt: 'BBC Wales was run like a small navy and the head of it thought of himself as the admiral. BBC Wales wanted outside broadcast vans parked outside the office, not because it was using them but as a status right, an outward sign of dignity.'

Geraint Stanley Jones was apoplectic about the whole book which referred to Scotland twice, not even once to the five English regions, while the story of Alasdair Milne's sacking was seriously biased. As to admirals in BBC Wales, Birt's attitude merely reinforced all the prejudices held against Welsh broadcasting by so many BBC senior executives ever since the founder of the BBC, Lord Reith, wrote that infamous condescending note in his diary: 'I settled Wales last Thursday.'

In 1990, aged 51, I left BBC Wales after 26 wonderful years, privileged to have been a member of a management team which revolutionised the broadcasting landscape of Wales. Listening figures for Radio Wales and Radio Cymru were excellent. *Pobol y Cwm* dominated the S4C viewing charts in May of that year and BBC programmes took seven of the top eight spots. The English-language TV output drew the largest audiences but was very much unfinished business, an unsatisfactory situation for a truly bilingual nation in which the English-speaking majority required a constant reminder and renewal of their national identity through programmes other than news and sport. It was an ongoing challenge for the next management.

I became Director of the small but wealthy Thomson Foundation in 37 Park Place, Cardiff, next door to the very radio studios of 38–40 Park Place where I began my BBC career in 1964. It involved advising broadcasters in the countries of post-Communist Eastern Europe and post-apartheid South Africa on their role in emerging democratic societies. Without exception, they were all envious of both the BBC and the minority channel S4C.

Meanwhile, Owen Edwards had retired from S4C and Geraint Stanley Jones returned from London to replace him as the channel's second Chief Executive. Teleri was due for retirement but acted as Controller for three months before leaving to write her autobiography. Meirion eventually joined me at the Thomson Foundation as did Head of Finance 'Phil the Till' Davies, and Head of Personnel Andrew McCabe. John Stuart Roberts left to write an acclaimed biography of Siegfried Sassoon.

The programme management team I had first joined in 1974 was no more. John Birt became the next Director-General. Geraint Talfan Davies, the son of my old boss Aneirin Talfan, was appointed Controller. It was the job his father had failed to get. BBC Wales was under new management – again.

Worship in Wartime

THE DATE IS 31 October 1939, nearly two months after Britain declared war on Germany. The place is Thames House, an office in the Houses of Parliament. The committee in session is being chaired by David Lloyd George, the former Prime Minister who saw Britain through to victory in the First World War and had recently refused to join Churchill's War Cabinet. Lloyd George is chairing the first meeting of the re-established BBC Welsh Religious Advisory Committee. Sitting next to him, the BBC's Welsh Regional Director Rhys Hopkin Morris explains that the BBC was offering a weekly Welsh prayer meeting and a monthly service during the war. Nothing, however, was advisory to Lloyd George. The Minutes are clear enough: 'Half-an-hour is totally inadequate for a Welsh service,' he stated. 'Time must be allowed for a reasonable number of hymns. Welsh preachers habitually adopt a style which begins in a low key and takes some time to climb up to its heights. For a successful service, a full hour is required.'

It was agreed to refer his demand to the BBC which resulted in a compromise – 40 minutes.

Lloyd George went further: 'The best men in each denomination should be picked as preachers and there should be no "log-rolling", no pushing of less competent preachers for reasons of sentiment or personal friendship.'

The Committee then agreed on the first five preachers best loved by the great orator. Hellfire from the pulpit was still the order of those distant days. Lloyd George felt strongly enough about the Advisory Committee to chair it throughout most of the war in his London office until he was too ill to attend.

Suffice to say that whatever they are called now, *Oedfa'r Bore* and *Morning Service* in English continue to anchor BBC schedules on Sunday morning to this day, as do a variety of 'Morning Thoughts' on radio.

The BBC Religious Advisory Committee was the very first standing committee to be set up by the BBC, such was the importance laid on religion by Lord Reith. In the 1970s and 1980s the Committee in Wales no longer chose the preachers. Theological differences were never even mentioned. Civilised discussion embraced the problem common to all denominational representatives, namely the dramatic fall-off in chapel and church attendances, particularly on Sunday evenings. The growing counter-attraction of TV was admitted to be only one factor in the trend towards a post-Christian society.

It was already a far cry from the time when young and old people were expected to attend services three times a day in Nonconformist Welsh-speaking Wales, as well as a couple of other prayer meetings during the week. Nobody expects 'hwyl' in sermons any more and ever fewer are turning up to listen to a homily in any form. The BBC, however, embraced Christianity by statute. It is committed to broadcast religious worship as a public broadcaster.

On TV the story is slightly different. *Songs of Praise* and its Welsh-language equivalent *Dechrau Canu, Dechrau Canmol* continue to hold a firm place in the schedules of BBC1 and S4C ever since they were created and launched from Cardiff by BBC Wales in the early 1960s. *Dechrau Canu, Dechrau Canmol* has regularly appeared in the top ten of S4C's viewing figures. In earlier days one could always fill the chapels and churches for a TV recording. Different communities welcomed being seen on TV. As time passed it became evermore difficult to fill the chapels for long recording sessions. Hymn-singing programmes continue to be unashamedly populist, but the element of worship in BBC religion on TV has taken a back seat.

Selected Bibliography

ALTHOUGH THE MEMOIR depends heavily on oral history and selected documents of my own, the following publications were helpful for quotations, background reading and the checking of facts.

Berry, David, *Wales and Cinema: The First Hundred Years* (Cardiff, 1996).

Bevan, Teleri, *Years on Air: Living with the BBC* (Talybont, 2004).

Davies, John, *Broadcasting and the BBC in Wales* (Cardiff, 1994).

Ebenezer, Lyn, *Clecs Cwmderi* (Wrexham, 1986).

Ebenezer, Lyn, *Radio Cymru 21: Pigion o Ddarllediadau* (BBC Books, 1998).

Eirug, Aled, *Can You Hear Me, Auntie? Defining A Nation – Wales And The BBC* (BBC Cymru\Wales 2009).

Gibbard, Alun, *Into the Wind: The Life of Carwyn James* (Talybont, 2107).

Gwynfryn, Hywel, *Ryan a Ronnie* (Llandysul, 2013).

Hannan, Patrick, *When Arthur Met Maggie* (Bridgend, 2006).

Jenkins, Gwyn (ed.), *Llyfr y Ganrif* (Talybont, 1999).

Jenkins, John (ed.), *Carwyn: Un o 'Fois y Pentre'* (Llandysul, 1983).

Jones, Lyn, *Grav* (Llandysul, 1986).

Jones, Lyn, 'SSX Yn Galw', Darlith Gymdeithas Deledu Brydeinig – RTS, Eisteddfod Genedlaethol Abertawe, 2006.

Jones, Rhydderch T., *Cofiant Ryan* (Llandysul, 1979).

Jones, Tegwyn and Huw Walters (eds), *Cawr i'w Genedl: Cyfrol i Gyfarch Yr Athro Hywel Teifi Edwards* (Llandysul, 2008).

Lucas, Rowland, *The Voice of a Nation? A Concise Account of the BBC in Wales 1923–73* (Llandysul, 1981).

Morgan, Dyfnallt (ed.), *Babi Sam yn dathlu hanner can mlynedd o ddarlledu o Fangor, 1935–1985* (Caernarfon, 1985).

Reynolds, Peter, *The BBC National Orchestra of Wales: A Celebration* (BBC Cymru\Wales, 2009).

Richards, Alun, *A Touch of Glory: 100 Years of Welsh Rugby* (London, 1980).

Seaton, Jean, *Pinkoes And Traitors: The BBC and the nation 1974–1987* (London, 2015).

Smith, Dai, *Wales! Wales?* (London, 1984).

Stephens, Meic, *The Oxford Companion to the Literature of Wales*, (Oxford, 1986).

Walker, Peter, *It's Not Just Cricket* (Bath, 2006).

Also from Y Lolfa:

TELERI BEVAN

Years on Air
LIVING WITH THE BBC

£9.95

The Broadcasters of BBC Wales, 1964–1990
is just one of a whole range of publications
from Y Lolfa. For a full list of books currently
in print, send now for your free copy of our
new full-colour catalogue. Or simply surf
into our website

www.ylolfa.com

for secure on-line ordering.

TALYBONT CEREDIGION CYMRU SY24 5HE
e-mail ylolfa@ylolfa.com
website www.ylolfa.com
phone (01970) 832 304
fax 832 782